SWEET DISORDER

AND THE

CAREFULLY CARELESS

SWEET DISORDER

AND THE

CAREFULLY CARELESS

THEORY AND CRITICISM IN ARCHITECTURE

ROBERT MAXWELL

PRINCETON PAPERS ON ARCHITECTURE

Sweet Disorder and the Carefully Careless
is the second volume in the series
Princeton Papers on Architecture
Princeton University School of Architecture
Princeton, New Jersey 08544-5264

Princeton Papers on Architecture
Ralph Lerner, Dean
Alastair Gordon, General Editor
Ken Botnick, Series Designer

Cover: Design Writing Research, New York
Cover Photograph: James Stirling's Staatsgalerie: Stuttgart, Germany
(Photograph by Rosemarie Haag-Bletter)

Published by
Princeton Architectural Press
37 East 7th Street
New York, New York 10003
212.995.9620

Library of Congress Cataloging-in-Publication Data
Maxwell, Robert, 1922–
      Sweet disorder and the carefully careless : theory and criticism
   in architecture / Robert Maxwell.
         p.   cm. - - (Princeton papers on architecture ; 2)
      Includes bibliographical references.
      ISBN 1-56898-005-1 : $17.95
      1. Architecture, Modern- -20th century.   I. Title.   II. Title:
Sweet disorder.   III. Series.
      NA680.M37   1993
      720 - - dc20   93-32943
                                                          CIP

1   ROBERT MAXWELL WITH JAMES STIRLING AT MESULGEN, 1992.

This book is dedicated
to the memory of
James Stirling,
a good friend
and a true architect.

CONTENTS

PREFACE

I first met Robert Maxwell at a design thesis review at Harvard in 1982. I was teaching there at the time, and he had been recently appointed Dean of the School of Architecture at Princeton. Princeton has always been known for fostering an intense debate regarding problems in contemporary design, and my colleagues and I were curious to know what kind of impact the new dean would have on the School and the other members of the faculty. As soon as he began to speak about the student work before us, I was reminded why so many of Princeton's faculty were invited to such affairs. His insights and erudition were to be counted among those architects from places in which design and its theories are understood to be inseparable.

I had no way to foresee that a decade later I would be in the enviable position of offering him a place in the School's series of publications, the *Princeton Papers on Architecture*. This, the second volume in the PPA series, is being published in honor of the contributions made by Professor Maxwell to the School of Architecture at Princeton over a quarter of a century, including seven years as its dean (1982–1989). The influence of his writing upon the various forms of architectural practice has been significant, and the importance of this first collection of essays, written over the course of his career, is rooted in his having been a pioneer in bringing contemporary discourses from intellectual domains outside of architecture into writing about architecture.

Sweet Disorder and the Carefully Careless is foremost the work of an insider—an architect, not simply a critic. Through his years in practice he has struggled with the revisions to modernist architectural practice in building as it has been influenced by the historical development of modern architecture. As a critic he is an important member of the post-war generation of architects, including his fellow students Colin Rowe and James Stirling, who established a renewed critical stance towards the pre-war European modernist tradition.

Robert Maxwell's own journey is illustrative of the severe dislocations and cultural shifts which catapulted architecture after World War II into the diverse forms it takes today. His education was interrupted by the war when he served in India as an Acting Captain in the Royal Bengal Sappers and Miners, the same regiment in which Professor Alan Colquhoun, another central figure in that generation, also served. Returning to Great Britain after the war, he took up practice with various firms in London, finally joining the firm of Douglas Stephen and Partners from 1962 through 1990. He began teaching at the Architectural Association in 1958, and four years later joined the faculty at the Bartlett School of Architecture and Planning at University College, London, where he continued to teach for the next twenty years. He was a Professor of Architecture there from 1979 to 1982. Parallel with his dual interests, he taught both architectural design and theory. He first came to Princeton in 1966 as a Visiting Professor of Architecture, having already achieved substantial distinction as an architect, teacher, and critic by that date. He returned three more times, ultimately being appointed Dean of the School of Architecture in 1982, and held that position for the next seven years. Under his discerning leadership the School maintained its prominent position in architectural scholarship, and continued to be a national center for teaching and research in design.

It is his work at Princeton, and his prior work as an architect and educator, that makes this book a fitting addition to the *Princeton Papers on Architecture*. This collection of essays will make his wide ranging insights available to a much larger audience than has been the case previously, and it fulfills the intention of the series: to grapple with the elusive limits of architectural discourse, and to uncover hidden possibilities for better understanding architects and architecture. As with all of the titles in this series, the sponsorship of the Jean Labatut Memorial Fund and the Hobart Betts Publication Fund has made this publication possible.

Ralph Lerner
Dean, School of Architecture

INTRODUCTION

Criticism is a genre of writing that requires a sensibility—some kind of sensibility—to register the qualities of the object of scrutiny. I cannot claim to have a unique sensibility, I know I am no Adrian Stokes; but I equally cannot pretend that I am an objective eye. To admit one's bias, then, is the first duty required of a critic. The problem is, however, to know what one's bias is, even to know one's ideological position. Like the quest for identity (who am I?) the quest for definition (what am I?) is not susceptible to any final answer. These elucidations are probably better left to others, but in case others are not that interested, it may be as well to make an attempt oneself. This is the task I have set myself with this collection of essays.

Most of these texts were written over the last ten years, while I have had the good fortune to be teaching at Princeton University. As many others have found, the pressures of teaching are so immediate that they tend to push longer-term projects to the back burner, and so it is only at the end of my Princeton period that I have summoned up the energy to place these writings into the record. Most of them first appeared in various architectural magazines, and I have indicated the date of first publication where applicable. Some of these are virtually unchanged in form, some are revised in places, but none of them have been re-written completely, except to the extent that they have all been amended by substituting *that* for *which* in about half the cases, a revision that testifies to my former vagueness about the use of the relative pronoun. This is a point on which American writers are generally more discriminating.

I wish to acknowledge in the first place the encouragement and help that I have received from Ralph Lerner, Dean of Architecture at

Princeton. It was he who insisted on this undertaking, and it was he who worked out how to use the advanced technology that will turn the hard text of ancient publications, dating from before the era of word processing, into the electronic pulses that are the raw material of our times.

I have also had tremendous help and encouragement from my wife, Celia, who knows how to vary praise and blame in a way that really tells, and that I could not accept from any other. Important also for the undertaking have been the sympathy and encouragement of my publisher, Kevin Lippert; and some crucial responses, from Alastair Gordon, who helped me to envisage the difference between a collection of texts and a book.

I also have to acknowledge the myriad conversations with friends—part of the on-going pleasures of life—conversations that often turned out to have helped nurture ideas and develop a point of view. First and foremost, Colin Rowe, who, while I was still a student, taught me to mind form, and thus helped to form my mind; then, Alan Colquhoun, who in countless friendly arguments helped me to sharpen it; Reyner Banham, now alas dead, for his role as the Irremediably Other, with whom one had to contend.

Countless other useful insights have resulted from contact with a wider range of friends, some of whom have probably forgotten my existence, some whose existence I have probably forgotten. The ones that come to mind are Peter Carl, Charles Jencks, Peter Cooke, Martin Pawley, David Dunster, Martin Goalen, Claude Schnaidt, Tomas Maldonado, Pierre Saddy, Giorgio Ciucci, Demetrios Porphyrios, Leon Krier, Yolanda Sonnabend, Rita Wolff, Joseph Rykwert and Barnaby Milburn, in Europe; and, in America, Mary McLeod, Odile Hénault, Diana Agrest, John Shearman, George Baird, Anthony Vidler, Kenneth Frampton, Peter Eisenman, Michael Graves, Detlef Mertins, David Mohney and Rodolpe El Khoury. All, in some way, at some time, helped me to nudge an idea along and so to clarify my thoughts.

My thanks are also due to IBM and their servant Word Perfect, without whose promptness and assiduity this document would never have reached the light of day.

LEBENSPHILOSOPHIE OF THE CRITIC

These essays cannot claim to be considered as belonging to either history or scholarship, and this is hardly surprising, as I did not receive the training of either a historian or a scholar. I was trained to be an architect, and as a result found myself practicing and teaching architecture over many years. In the course of these years it became obvious that as an architect I had to depend on a more or less innate capacity to pass a judgement on the issues that are encountered in the design of buildings, and hence on the qualities to be sought, as well as found, in individual buildings. It is this judgement, exercised over something approaching a lifetime, that has led me to believe that what I have been doing, for most of this time, falls under the rubric of architectural criticism. Retrospectively, it's apparent that this criticism must have been formed through personal taste, but the effort to justify its results leads one inevitably into the realm of architectural theory, and that is why I conclude that these essays as a whole stand for the exercise of critical judgement and make necessary the attempt to define a theoretical position that will justify this judgement.

So this book is to be taken as a critic's meditation on some central issues in architecture today. The tone that results is, I am told, somewhat ruminative. But isn't rumination—the chewing over of the raw material—a pretty fair description of the critic's job? Whereas the historian has to try to remain as much as he can a scientist in his respect for the facts, seeking only to place them into a broad framework, the critic can not do his job without taking these facts into his own system, without embarking on a process of diges-

tion and interpretation. A degree of interpretation may be inseparable from all story-telling, of course. But there is an evident difference
of emphasis between the historian, whose judgement of events
should be as objective as possible, and ideally be shared by other historians, and the critic, whose judgement should be based on a clear
critical position, for which he may be brought to book. In compensation for this relative license, we may note that the "raw" facts of
history are sometimes difficult to establish, outside of the historian's
own position and prejudices; whereas the "raw" facts for the critic
are simply those works—in this case buildings—that he undertakes
to explain or criticize or justify. These buildings exist outside of his
judgement on them, and their continued existence, in spite of his
criticism, may be seen as a kind of reproach, a sort of control, a nearly objective limitation on the range and scope of his interpretations.

The buildings that I shall refer to are sometimes part of the
established history of architecture, and sometimes new claimants to
be part of that history. No critic worth his salt can refuse to engage
with the building that is freshly minted, about which no established
opinions are as yet available. Here the architectural critic must
approach, with an appropriate degree of temerity, the job of theater
critic, a job so fearsome in its reverberations that some critics have
become known for their power to determine how long a show will
run on Broadway. The architectural critic who moves in with the
opening of a new facility that is not about to be removed at his
behest, can hardly affect how long a building will be left standing;
but he may, by the aspersions he casts, affect the professional standing of the architect whose work he pans. Indeed, circumspection
may be so advisable in an age of lawsuits, that the criticism must be
muted and even tactful. It is also true that the critic who is in some
sense a failed architect is so aware of the pitfalls that lie along the
design process that he automatically assumes the best in every case.
This excess of tact, so widespread in professional journals of architecture, has somewhat vitiated the art of criticism within architecture—a recognized fact that once led Reyner Banham, in a memorable speech at the Architectural Association, to claim that the whole
race of architectural critics was mealy-mouthed and impotent.

I have also practiced the precaution—with one exception among
the examples that follow—of visiting the buildings that I criticize,
unless they are published as projects which may or may not get
built. Sometimes visiting the building only confirms prior impres-

sions, but it can also affect the sense of scale. When I finally got to see the Unité at Marseilles it seemed a lot smaller than I had expected, whereas Villa Savoie was exactly right, incredible for being precisely what I had imagined, probably because I had studied it so intensively. Since every building of necessity occupies a unique spot on the globe, the visit in itself helps to clarify what is the same and what is different in each particular case. But this is not specific to architecture—every production, every performance of *The Magic Flute*, is also a distinct event and therefore unique. The opera critic will similarly be on the look-out for what is the same and what is different in every case.

I have long pondered the meaning of Reyner Banham's description of a unique chance meeting on a New York sidewalk of himself, Joan Littlewood and Cedric Price, at which the idea of The Fun Palace was first mooted. History, he claimed, was made in an ordinary moment of time. The critic has to learn to live through ordinary moments of time that are also part of history because the buildings he deals with are parts of history. Every contemporary moment recedes at once into historical time, and is part of history by the time we get round to assess it, to write it up. Only our own spontaneous moments, as in eating new potatoes, or making love, escape this framing, mainly because we don't have to write them up. But what if we have to relate them to our shrink? Nothing completely escapes from our delayed assessment, from our awareness of the act of making a judgement, of having made a judgement. Nothing can be shaped and made visible to others while it is still hot and fluid. The critic, in distancing himself from what has just happened, joins with the journalist, who must put sometimes incredible events into a framework that will give them some credibility. Banham, again, gave one material for thought, with his preference for recent events about which one might hope to seize some intimate aspect, lost to the observer arriving by a later plane. Yet the speed and closeness of the event as it happens may prevent us from seizing its essence, just as the relatively static view of the remote event, like distant mountains seen from the train, changes only imperceptibly, and remains cloaked in a haze of distance. Either way, there must remain a degree of uncertainty.

The critic cannot work without first impressions, but my own experience has taught me to be wary of them. So in the importance that I allow to the act of distancing, to the process by which the criticism only gains precision through the labor of constructing the text, I reveal a temperamental bias as well as a professional caution. If so, it is the bias of privileging reserve over commitment, of preferring memory over sensation, of separating life from art. The distinction that must be made between life and art is the subject of the first essay in this collection, and I place it first because it reveals an approach which I must accept as part of my own innate prejudices. For me there is an interesting nuance between allowing a sweet disorder to take over, in the case where one is emotionally at ease, and the cultivation of the carefully careless, which is the only sane policy in cases of uncertainty and ambiguity.

This temperamental bias is probably the result of being nearsighted and be-spectacled from the age of six: unable to hit a cricket ball or even see a rugby ball except from the position of hooker and then only momentarily. Those who are endowed with kinaesthetic skills probably cannot imagine the limitations of someone who never learned to ski. The judgement there is so internalized and immediate as to be inseparable from the act. And what fills the space that separates the critic from his exposure to experience? Clearly, words fill that gap. So the critic must accept his limited status, in which the webs he spins with words are his primary material, but secondary to the objects that he describes, indeed, parasitic on them. Without the work of the artist, of the original architect, the critic would have nothing to work with. While the theater critic may exercise a social power that prevents a play from being viewed as successful, that judgement will only be a temporary one from the point of view of posterity. Yet it must be obvious, and even just, that the artist will hate the critic, the whole race of critics, and will be right to see the profession of criticism as lower than the that of the artist. At the same time, the critic exercises an indispensable role in assessing original work, in helping to explain it, to give it meaning, and hence to aid the assimilation of that work into society, and into culture. This I regard as the potentially constructive role of the critic, and I believe it is wrong to see the critic as one who only sees what is wrong, who carps rather than cares. The critic thus takes upon himself a role as intermediary between the individual architect or artist and society in a wider sense.

These essays bear the imprint of a particular temperament: they all have the sound of one voice. Consistency is something else. We know that a person is recognizable by his handwriting, and, from

De Buffon ("Le style est l'homme même"), a man by his style, but we also know that no one's character is without contradictions, least of all one's own, to which one has privileged access and in which there is no denying the existence of doubt. Judgements accumulated over years also betray a certain changeability, a development along certain lines, a hardening here, a softening there. In sum, it becomes a matter of decipherment, even for the critic, to gain a clear idea of the position from which these judgements have been made, or even if there is one. No doubt a career in public life would have done more to systematize prejudices and allow construction of such a position. The question here is, rather: what, if any, position do these writings represent?

During the sixties one became aware of the fact that not having a clear political position simply meant that one was committed to the status quo. Never having joined a political party, or owned shares, one was still identified as being a member of the bourgeoisie, a fully participating late Capitalist, because one went along with things as they were. As the Bible had made clear, he who is not for me is against me. On the other hand, there was also a certain appeal in the doctrine of the dominance of the *zeitgeist*, the pervasive mentality that went with the times, from which there was no escape, whatever one's political bias. Some combination of these opposite forces, perhaps, may account for the fact that some liberals were seduced, in 1937, by the Nazi promise to get things done quickly, and that many other liberals supported the Spanish Republican cause; or for the fact that to be received as an intellectual in France in the fifties, one had virtually to be a member of the P.C.F. Clear goals seemed to promise faster progress, and confer on life the excitement of taking sides, the appeal of a narrative.

Perhaps it will be as well then for me to state my political sympathies before anything else. I could never accept either Socialism or Capitalism. For me both of these positions were clearly partisan, aiming to advance the conditions of one social class against another, and society seemed historically to have depended on a variety of social classes, providing a richness that a single class society would apparently lack. The more utopian idea of a classless society did not appeal, or even seem possible. More seriously, these available political alternatives were doctrines, positions affirming belief along with dogma, and therefore corresponding to the idea of an hypothesis in science, but without the benefit from which science draws so much advantage, of being able to be put to the test. To choose one would be to lose the other, and therefore the whole in which they fitted, the whole out of which they had come. Insofar as Capitalism was conservative and Socialism was progressive, they seemed rather to be complementary, much as brake and accelerator are both useful for controlled progress in a car. Since each was directed to a fixed goal, they both seemed to remove entirely the possibility of steering, so essential for good driving. No doubt this attitude was the result of having been saturated from birth in an empirical environment, but it may have stemmed equally from having been brought up in a divided society—Northern Ireland before the war—where none of the people I knew seemed to be properly accounted for by the opposing beliefs in which they had to be situated. Still less could I accept the virulent form of Christianity to which I was subjected through a strict Presbyterian upbringing, which seemed to curtail all enjoyment and situate it after death. Resistance to over-determination went with hunger for life. Out of this desire to be inclusive followed a preference for a philosophy that avoided either-or choices, that saw a benefit from continuing somehow to transcend oppositions that could only be viewed as too particular and as anyhow transient, oppositions that placed the critic between false alternatives. So I adopted the role of mediation. This preference for "both-and" was present long before Venturi made it an adage, or Structuralism a method.

The assumptions that underlie my approach as a dedicated intermediary are derived from a certain formulation made by the German sociologist Georg Simmel, and first experienced by me in the work of the philosopher Ernst Cassirer, who adopted it, I believe, from Simmel. (It was Colin Rowe who put me on to Cassirer). In this formulation, life is seen as a sort of phenomenological force, a spirit that exists at the level of the cultural horizon, and that is in a constant state of development and evolution. It is composed on the one hand of traditions, rituals, settled ways of doing things; everything that falls under the heading: it worked before, why not now? On the other hand there are all the forces of change, from the impact of science and technology through to the work of innovative people, thinkers, inventors, artists, and philosophers. The forces of tradition and the forces of change are in constant opposition, but also in a state of rough balance, allowing some picture of the future to be projected at any time. Yet, retrospectively, it will have been seen that everything is actually changing all the time. Everyone places himself, herself in relation to this incipient change, some welcoming it and identifying with the new, others resisting the new and identifying with some aspect of tradition. All belong to the same moment in time. In Simmel's view this process is continuous and inexorable, and every moment in the evolution of cultural consciousness is a sort of treaty, or temporary compromise, between the new and the old. Life is a constant struggle between new contents and old ones, but change is only visible because of the changes in the forms that accompany it. Forms, then, are the means by which contents are made visible. They are both unavoidable, and indispensable, yet must be struggled with if change is to be manifest. This is the life philosophy to which I subscribe, and which informs the essays that follow.

To speak in these general terms about criticism and the role of the critic may be seen as pretentious, and the justification for it can only lie in the extent to which it affords an explanation for the stance taken and the bias exercised in the course of the work. Beyond this, the critic must also labor to make his prejudices reasonable, to construct an ideal system around them, and thus to define his ideology. This is what I attempt in the concluding chapter of this book.

SWEET DISORDER AND THE CAREFULLY CARELESS

A sweet disorder in the dresse
Kindles in cloathes a wantonnesse:
A lawne about the shoulders thrown
Into a fine distraction:
An erring Lace, which here and there
Enthralls the Crimson Stomacher:
A Cuffe neglectful and thereby
Ribbands to flow confusedly:
A winning wave (deserving Note)
In the tempestuous petticote
A careless shooe-string, in whose tye
I see a wilde civility:
Doe more bewitch me, than when Art
Is too precise in every part.

Robert Herrick

When is disorder sweet and when sour?

We have all retained from childhood both sweet and sour memories of our own disorderly experience, or of the disorderly behavior of others. I suppose we generally react to disorder as a disagreeable experience when it is thrust upon us, but sometimes take pleasure in imposing our disorderly conduct on others. It would appear that disorder is agreeable to the extent that we are choosing it, and not subject to it.

But disorder may have a more positive appeal, as well as a more fundamental one. Order is also something we count on, so long as we can choose it, and not be too subject to it. An excess of order can be just as disagreeable as subjection to disorder. We are rather finely balanced between the two.

Law and order are hardly in themselves the fruits of civilization, although they appear to be necessary for it. We do not call for law and order until they appear to be in doubt. Their function is merely to bring sufficient security to life, so that tomorrow may be anticipated and enjoyed.

It is no doubt only from a basis of this security that we could characterize a "wild civility" as attractive: Herrick's poem is written from the stance of a civilized man who can afford to relax the rules. He contrasts a measure of pleasing disorder with an art too precise to be bewitching. His "sweet disorder" may be interpreted as an indication of sexual interest and perhaps accessibility, behind the formality of convention.

In the comedy of manners we accept the rule of law, but merely as a convention—a useful guarantee of social cohesion and the reliability of social contracts. As convention we know it to be arbitrary, overlaying a more dangerous and satisfying level of behavior. In sexual adventure a limited contract *à deux* replaces the social contract, permitting a shared descent to the springs of danger and power.[1] Herrick, writing as he did some 250 years before Freud, could not approach these depths, but his elegant verse resonates with fresh tones when read aloud in our rather hollow situation.

The baroque exuberance of Herrick's verse expresses an almost touching confidence in the sweetness of mild disorder, with its suggestion of intimacy and personal release. In its more heroic manifestation as the vehicle of the Counter Reformation, the baroque could of course achieve the expression of sexual ecstasy not directly, but as a manifestation of religious art. Despite the evident self-confidence of the baroque as a style, we may note that erotic content could only be approached by way of a religious program legitimated by the forces of law and order. This ambivalence may be explained in the first place through a psychological analysis, and this has been attempted.[2] We may need, however, to reappraise our cultural history with more regard for the social and anthropological implications of changes in the symbol system. A critical view of art from this point of view would surely reveal the delicacy of the balance between assent and refusal of the status quo, explaining how an individual innovator or a sudden stylistic impulse may be felt as genuinely subversive. Insofar as innovation is not merely the adding of a new term to the series, but involves a re-statement of the rules, it implies an attack on the rule-system of the established order, and the painful reassignment of existing values prevalent at any one time.[3]

English society, with its peculiar admixture of pragmatism and puritan ethic, has provided many examples of a fluctuating or ambivalent response to innovation. Our national sense of good form, of the advantages of the status quo, has reinforced the fear of disproportion and excess, particularly in the field of morals. Since, on the whole, English social history has a libertarian flavor, this Anglo-Saxon attitude has provided continentals with something of a puzzle.

In particular, the English attitude towards the French Revolution revealed the existence of a finely balanced dichotomy between the desire for order and liberty, still alive and struggling today. Voltaire and Diderot were enthusiastic about England as the home of liberty, but Chateaubriand, who actually lived and worked in London, (once as refugee, once as ambassador) learned to temper his enthusiasm with skepticism. No one has responded to the English puzzle with more enthusiasm than Stendhal (perhaps because he chose to live in Italy).

According to Stendhal, whereas in France fashion is a pleasure, in England it is a duty. The English fear bad form and vulgarity, exalt good taste:

> De là la mode bien plus absurde et bien plus déspotique dans la raisonnable Angleterre qu'au sein de la France légère; c'est dans Bond-Street qu'a été inventé le *carefully careless*.[4]

Stendhal views this as an absurdity; an absurdity which arises from a denial of nature. English husbands, he says, are so proud of their wives' modesty that they are forced to spend their evenings getting drunk together instead of dallying with their mistresses, as any decent Frenchman does. And the English wives are forced to spend long hours in going for walks, using up their nervous energy in a healthy way in order to be too tired for sex. However absurd, in Stendhal's view, we may hope that all this walking contributed towards an improvement in the English scene. The English invention of the landscape garden, intended to be enjoyed through perambulation, is perhaps a masterpiece of sublimation, but surely the most complete expression of the carefully careless.

In the English landscape, nature is first tamed, and then allowed to go wild in a very civil way. The lake, seen from the house, is placid. The grotto, seen from the edge of the lake, is disturbing. Seen again from the house, the lake is placid, but slightly disturbing. In the English country-house system, as epitomized in Jane Austen, a young man may be guilty of impropriety, but never in the grotto, where the combined disturbance would be too marked. Elements of different character are juxtaposed in a free relationship, approachable or avoidable to the degree that their suggestiveness is welcome to the conversation. The conversational nature of the arrangement is nicely displayed and satirized in the novels of Thomas Love Peacock.

The romantic movement proceeds from the carefully careless to the sublime. We can either ride wild horses or we can't: wild horses must be ridden, if at all, in a desperate rather than a carefully careless state of mind. The moment of the carefully careless is a transitory one, in the historical sequence. The forces in fact unleashed by the French revolution, and by the Romantic Movement, have turned out to be both powerful and dangerous. It is not until we get to the end of the century, with the Art Nouveau, that it again becomes possible, with Oscar Wilde, to exercise care recklessly. Stendhal's discovery of the carefully careless could perhaps only have been made at a time when classical and romantic values were, historically speaking, still in balance. Jacques Barzun has suggested, however, that the terms classical and romantic are misunderstood through becoming identified with particular historical periods. He claims that they define, rather, two perpetual poles of a human dilemma, corresponding to the hellenistic categories of apollonian and dionysiac.[5] In one, control is paramount, in the other, inspiration. Both control and inspiration may be constant demands of the human psyche, corresponding in cybernetic language to reductive and generative processes.

It is possible, in this light, to see all cultural manifestations as a mechanism whose aim is to ensure a balance between control and inspiration, between order and disorder, in a dynamic situation of constant change. Different as these attributes may seem to be, and in spite of the fact that at any one time they may be in opposition, they are both concerned positively with the same issue—the degree of control needed to assure and to structure an ever surprising future. An individual response to and generation of these qualities will exist at a multitude of different levels ranging from the subconscious through controlled behavior (self-image) into relationships with group alliances. Temperament plays an important role: the pessimist (Keats or Colin Rowe) expects the worst from the human animal, and bewails a lost order; the pessimist is only very carefully careless. The optimist (like Shelley or Reyner Banham) expects the best from the human animal, and foretells an era of freedom and sweet disorder.

At the level of individual perception, the categories of order and disorder become binary poles of a somewhat thermodynamic kind of psychological system, in which we recognize systems of order and in which we constantly work to extend the range of the systems of order we recognize, so reducing the disorder with which we are initially faced. Our perceptual mechanism is balanced so that we are never faced with too much disorder at any one time. Our tolerance of disorder is related to the amount and constraint of the order we think we can see as well as to our confidence in dealing with disorder. Security in our orderly life can at any time develop into boredom, with the need to generate variety. The categories of order and variety have been suggested by Eysenck as variables in a model of aesthetic response.[6] In this model, derived from an idea of Birkhoff, aesthetic satisfaction in a work of art will be the product of the order and the variety contained in it. This, however, is a crude model that takes no account of the variation in perception of these qualities as between the artist and the viewer, to say nothing of the difficulty of measuring such imponderables on any common scale.

An interesting attempt has been made, however, to supply a measure of aesthetic perception by applying to it some concepts of information theory.[7] Abraham Moles has given some very interesting indications of the way in which qualities of variety and richness in a work of art are perceived by means of an order which is perceptible only in part. He suggests that in listening, say, to a Beethoven symphony, we are presented with a totality of information which we structure and assimilate in syntactical groupings, using our knowledge of Beethoven's "vocabulary" to recognize the form of the music, and hence through the form glimpsing a varying content. In terms of information theory, the syntactical groupings generate a variable presentation of information rather like an electroencephalograph; Moles suggests that this clumping of information relates to our perceptual threshold and ensures that we can only register a part of what is presented: enough to enjoy it, never enough to dominate it—hence our willingness to listen to the Ninth Symphony for the nth time! It is an ingenious theory, which takes a gestaltist view of the integration of information into pre-existent wholes; yet tries to explain the effect of the perception of both the banal and the original in relation to the degree of familiarity and complexity of the information presented, and therefore in a purely mechanistic way.

Recent developments in art, however, have outpaced the theorists. The invention of abstract art has enabled us to examine in an entirely new way the problem of minimal content.[8] In the art of minimal content, the viewer or auditor enters into the transaction, using the work partly for its intrinsic qualities and partly as a vehicle onto which he projects additional qualities from his own repertoire. Minimal art forms do not present an interesting complexity, but rather a puzzling simplicity. A whole level of understatement is offered for the consumer to fill out at his own pleasure. This system works both with comparatively generous outlay (De Staël, Pollock) or with highly reduced outlay (Rothko, Reilly).

A corollary of minimal art is the proliferation of art-in-life, the capacity to recognize an aesthetic statement in a life sequence by a technique of minimal prompting. If the participant structures the content which he perceives in art, he can also "aestheticize" the content which he perceives in life. This theme, which is consonant with a search for new levels of art in everyday life (remember Wordsworth?) has been particularly adopted by the architects, whose art is by definition an attempt to structure living activities. Hence the interest for our generation of "Parallel of Life and Art" (the Smithsons' first major exhibition at the Institute of Contemporary Art), a theme which was taken up again in "This is Tomorrow" and again in the Archigram exhibition, "Living City." I shall always remember, with gratitude, the inclusion in this latter of two views of moving people, interpolated via periscopes, into the formalized static material of the exhibition.

Whereas for the artist, the interesting problem lies in testing our tolerance of very simple yet ambiguous situations which can be interpreted in a variety of ways, for the architect or city planner, the problem is rather how to generate a satisfying complexity from a simple and essentially controllable system. Whether modeling art on life, or life on art, however, the key concepts are those of information theory and of cybernetics.

In information theory, a distinction is made between the code, or pre-analyzed program, and the message, or data, actually transmitted. This distinction applies also to computer programming. In architecture, the same distinction comes through in terms of an attempted differentiation of structure and infill. Le Corbusier sketched this distinction in the Unité d'Habitation, and other attempts at a two-level installation have been made by Louis Kahn, Habraken, Yona Friedmann, Archigram; of these Kahn's was the most concrete and Friedmann's the most abstract. Denis Crompton has suggested the idea of the city as a computer, electronically modeling itself simultaneously with the actual life movements taking place within it, and allowing electronic generation in turn of further life movements. The speed of electric circuitry would enable the model of the city to interact continuously with the actual city. Similarly, in the city-grid of Yona Friedmann, the generation of journeys and of functions is in a state of constant and controlled flux.

In such concepts, an attempt is made to dissolve the dichotomy between life and art. The art of city management becomes so sensitive and so powerful that it can respond to the individual's whim. At the same time, the city takes on a systemic character, for it can accept and represent only those richnesses that are generated from its own basic program.

In the excitement of electronic circuitry and its registration of the whole of life (not a sparrow will fall to the ground, perhaps, without the computer taking account), a way has been imagined of creating whole environmental systems which are extensions to the individual and his immediate cohort. Inevitably, these projections are most easily made in the area of imaginative play which makes least demands on the integration of many contradictory activities. Peter Cook's Plug-in City is a fun city, implying a reduction of the constraints operating on life. It is a wish-fulfillment dream, not a projection of probabilities. By presenting a city in which everything that is fun is possible, it makes a gesture which dissolves life into art. At the other end of the scale we have the movement which aims to dissolve art into life—the happenings, participation, doing-your-own-thing however odd, the rejection of institutions, the rejection of finite artifacts and of the art order in things.

It may be that a sense of the dissolution of the boundaries between life and art has always attended any period of decisive change; new styles which appear artificial and highly contrived at their first appearance become in due course part of the "natural" background of life. The English landscape is one of the best examples of the carefully careless achieving in due course a state of sweet disorder. From the point of view of the innovator, whether he homes in by dionysiac jet or apollonian helicopter, he struggles in a paradoxical situation. To create the new order he must dissolve the old, extending the boundaries of art to take in more of life. But this process, viewed historically, is only the substitution of one order for another. This may be too cool a point of view for the artist, who needs to feel committed and to believe in his vision as the ultimate weapon. Such an apocalyptical view was certainly adopted by the Futurists, and, as Colin Rowe has demonstrated,[9] is a major element in the ideology of the modern movement.

As critics, at any rate, I believe we need to become more aware of the anthropological implications of our progressive perception of new orders through artistic activity.[10] We operate in a cultural continuum in which ritual and taboo towards established values are in a constant tension with the natural appetite for variety and a fresh future. To review the Archigram city of the future in the light of W.H. Auden's lecture on ends and means may be a salutary experience.

> To set in order—that's the task
> Both Eros and Apollo ask;
> For Art and Life agree in this
> That each intends a synthesis,
> That order which must be the end
> That all self-loving things intend
> Who struggle for their liberty,
> Who use, that is, their will to be.
> Though Order never can be willed
> But is the state of the fulfilled,
> For Will but wills its opposite
> and not the whole in which they fit,
> The symmetry disorders reach
> When both are equal, each to each.
> Yet in intention all are one,
> Intending that their wills be done,
> Within a peace where all desires
> Find each in each what each requires
> A true gestalt where indiscrete

Perceptions and extensions meet.
Art in intention is mimesis
But realized, the resemblance ceases;
Art is not life, and cannot be
A midwife to society.
For Art is a fait accompli:
What they should do, or how, or when
Life order comes to living men,
It cannot say, for it presents
Already lived experience,
Through a convention that creates
Autonomous completed states;
Though their particulars are those
That each particular artist knows,
Unique events that once took place
Within a unique time and place,
In the new field they occupy
The unique serves to typify,
Becomes, though still particular
An algebraic formula
An abstract model of events
Derived from dead experience,
And each life must itself decide
To what and how it be applied.

From W.H. Auden: New Year Letter

Originally published in *Architectural Design*, April 1971.

NOTES

1 Mary Douglas: *Purity and Danger*, 1966, for an anthropologist's account of the fine balance between order and disorder in both "primitive" and "developed" culture.
2 See particularly Rudolf Arnheim: *Towards a Psychology of Art, The Hidden Order of Art*, and other titles.
3 For a somewhat obvious example see the case of Neizvestney versus Kruschev in John Berger's *Art and Revolution*, 1969.
4 There is no more appealing example of the desire of the rationalizing mind to explain the world of feeling than Stendhal's *De l'Amour*. His recognition of the role of convention in defining feelings is contrary to the normal direction of Romantic thinking and places him squarely among the moderns. Stendhal: *De l'Amour*, 1822; Editions de Cluny, 1938; (Flammarion, 1965, p. 164).

5   Jacques Barzun: *Classic, Romantic and Modern*, 1943; Anchor, 1961.

6   H.J. Eysenck: *Sense and Nonsense in Psychology*, 1957.

7   Abraham Moles: *Information Theory and Aesthetic Perception*, 1958; University of Illinois, 1968.

8   Gregory Battock (editor): *Minimal Art*, 1968. Compare Panofsky: *Meaning in the Visual Arts*, 1955: "A spinning machine is perhaps the most impressive manifestation of a functional idea, and an 'abstract' painting is perhaps the most expressive manifestation of pure forms but both have a minimum of content."

9   See particularly C.F. Rowe: "Mannerism and Modern Architecture" in *Architectural Review*, May 1950.

10   Malinowski: *A Scientific Theory of Culture*, 1960, is the merest outline of such an approach.

CRITICISM

2   HILLINGDON CIVIC CENTER (VIEW FROM THE SOUTH): UXBRIDGE, ENGLAND
Andrew Derbyshire of Robert Matthew, Johnson-Marshall Partners, 1979.

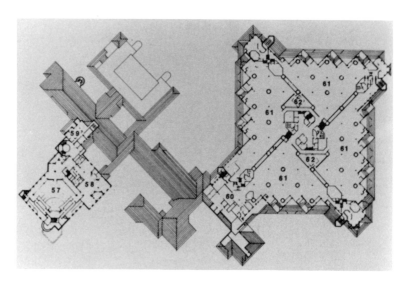

3   HILLINGDON CIVIC CENTER (4TH FLOOR PLAN)

HILLINGDON CIVIC CENTER, UXBRIDGE

ARCHITECTS: ROBERT MATTHEW, JOHNSON-MARSHALL PARTNERS

The Civic Center at Hillingdon, one of the new London boroughs formed during the reorganization of local government in the early 1970s, has generated a good deal of controversy among English architects. The controversy arises entirely from its appearance. The organizational form is not at all exceptional, based as it is on the usual separation of civic and administrative offices. This basic organization no doubt could have been translated into a mainstream modern notation, with the pyramidal office block contrasting with a separate group of facilities focusing on the council chamber. This functional distinction may form the basis of the plan, but not in this case, the expression of a genre that is unmistakably picturesque.

There have been precedents for civic buildings that remain modern in detail through the use of such normative features as strip windows and cantilevers, but that produce a more or less picturesque mass, reminiscent of vernacular architecture. Hillingdon is not only picturesque in its massing and grouping, but is plainly stylistic in its detailing. The rich red brick and the massive tiled roof are supplemented by a whole apparatus of projections, angles, setbacks—plus a general proliferation of local features. Finally, when we get to look at a straight bit of facade, it turns out to have windows set in brick recesses enriched by dental courses, reminiscent of the corbelled string courses of the twelfth-century Worms Cathedral. This German connection produced some facetious comment but has clearly contributed to the acceptance of the scheme by council members and community alike. The center in fact is already a popular success. Everyone can see that Hillingdon has character, it looks like the "real" buildings we come across on vacation: it is touristically valid.

Its success seems to depend on the reactivation of popular notions of European architecture, low-key suburban buildings and a familiar English tradition of brick and tile. It seems to be characteristic of our epoch that the evidence for an architecture of our times is confusing. Atavistic (Hillingdon) and futuristic (Pompidou Center) images compete for attention: each is as avidly consumed. The use of imagery that Robert Venturi sees as essential for the production of meaning in the visual arts has become foot-loose and fancy-free; and Charles Jencks can feel justified in accepting an unbridled eclecticism of images as the necessary price of pluralism, itself the natural corollary of a "free society."

Until recently, architects have been unwilling to admit the presence of images in their buildings, preferring to present these as having derived from a strict system, whether a rationale of conceptualization or a technique of production. There are still architects who would prefer to close their minds to the varied associations that all forms evoke, and try to insist on a determination of forms if not by function, at least by a reductive typology of form-function combinations. Such a standpoint increasingly appears to be not so much a rational system of production as a closed code of reproduction, the characteristic of a professional elite whose judgments are not open to popular appraisal.

On the other hand, once we admit that the user's perception of architectural character, based on his own nonprofessional modes of association, constitutes a potential response to be manipulated, what discipline can hold the mistress art together? Kitsch enters the field of judgment. Images can jostle for attention as they do in advertising, their aim being only to further consumption.

In Britain, architects have for the most part responded to this problem by adopting a sub-modern, loosely functional, and vaguely picturesque style, homogeneous but full of variation. Aptly called "institutionalized nook-and-cranny," (see fig. 2) it clings to function and a psychology of place while attempting to avoid image and meaning. It hopes to make modern building acceptable without the need to embark on the dangerous path of stylistic self-consciousness. From this viewpoint, the use of decorative brickwork, which reminds even laymen of German castles, would be seen as a provocation, a breaking of the bonds of technology and function that have held for the last fifty years. This exploration raises the specter of artifice and makes architecture a dangerous profession. Many see Hillingdon this way.

Andrew Derbyshire, the partner in the architectural firm of Robert Matthew, Johnson-Marshall Partners, who was chiefly responsible for the design, is disarming on this count: "In 1970, the Borough asked us to design their new offices, and we discovered to our mutual pleasure that we were both in the middle of a reappraisal of the state of modern architecture in Britain . . . Our experience over the last twenty-five years of building in this country . . . had led both of us to dissatisfaction with the state of the art, and a wish to do better."

For Derbyshire, what had been lost in the post-war period of modern architecture was the native English tradition that had found its chief expression in the Arts and Crafts movement of William Morris and the Garden City Movement of Ebeneezer Howard and Raymond Unwin. In architects like Webb, Shaw, Voysey and Mackintosh, Britain had a developing tradition of sensitive design that had already achieved a radical adjustment of architecture to daily life well before the Modern Movement came into being. After World War I, this tradition faded, and an eclectic neoclassicism took over, a fact Derbyshire blames for the vacuum in the native tradition that allowed the new ideas of Le Corbusier and Walter Gropius to take hold.

Furthermore, Derbyshire places a special emphasis on the role of the locality in influencing his thought as he began to prepare his plans. The area was combed for examples of traditional building: churches, schools, and the forms of suburban housing were given a new appraisal. The preponderance of a brick-and-tile vernacular suggested that these materials should be used in the Civic Center so that it would appear as a native and not a foreign element in the environment.

One does not have to doubt the importance of these factors nor the popular success of the building, nor Andrew Derbyshire's sincerity, however, to feel that the result is architecturally unconvincing.

The adoption of a tradition is certainly some kind of a hedge against inflation in the world market in images. A tradition limits severely the models that can be used as a framework for design as well as providing a coherent set of ideas that cannot be arbitrarily extended or ignored without a struggle. To work within a tradition would seem to involve a close study and an understanding of the modes and techniques of that tradition, as well as a general sympathy with its aims and character. Derbyshire is clearly in sympathy with the picturesque tradition and has identified with many of the aims and methods of Parker and Unwin in their creation of the garden suburbs (his practice offices are in Welwyn Garden City). He also has a strong commitment to finding a true social architecture. All these intentions without question entitle him to adopt a tradition, but do not guarantee that he can immediately perform as an architect within that tradition. His architecture would have to place itself within the tradition, not joining it, but extending it from within. Can we accept Hillingdon on this level?

In Britain today there are few practitioners who could be confidently placed within a tradition opposed to the narrow functionalism of the Modern Movement. Perhaps we have to go back to Lutyens to find our last great traditionalist. He was steeped not only in French Classicism, but in the local English vernacular. He could and did make surprising new combinations in which we can see rather grand classical concepts brought down to a vernacular scale of operations, a transformation that corresponded to the new class of clients whom he served.

By comparison, Derbyshire has come to this tradition from a background of successful practice within the mainstream of modern design. His first large undertaking—the layout and construction of York University—was an exercise in the application of the CLASP constructional system. This vanguard effort attempted to demonstrate that building by system was equal to any civilized task in architecture. Most of the work with which he has been involved to date falls within the kind of design most people would tend to categorize as managerial, efficient, anonymous.

Derbyshire's professional background is clearly evidenced in the organizational character of the Hillingdon Civic Center. The complex's size and bulk is broken down into two separate entities representing a division of function, and expressed, curiously, by a division in character.

The Borough offices are strictly segregated and treated with a systematic exactitude. They build up into a large square mass with a square structural grid, subdivided, however, on the diagonal into four triangular quadrants at half-levels. These are defined by narrow, open wells that allow a glimpse of the adjoining spaces. Organizationally this formation results simultaneously from the wish to break down the scale of the office requirement (the biggest single category in the program) while still maintaining the cooperative ends of the organization as a whole. The proliferation of dormers, eaves, nooks, and crannies around the elevation of this square block establishes a set of references to the diagonal axes—the subdivision—as against the orthogonal structure—the whole.

The opposition of orthogonal and diagonal axes becomes a formal game whose aim is to produce visual variety out of a gross functional homogeneity. It results in some strong-arm tactics, like the porches in the southeast and southwest corners where the right-hand bay in each case is a blind alley.

To different degrees, exposed functional elements, such as staircase towers, vent openings in the roof, and vents to the basement car-parking areas, have been adjusted to fit in with the prevalent system of projecting angles, in order to successfully convey what can be regarded only as an ingenious fiction. But it would be fair to say that the difference in treatment of those elements that are functionally produced and those that result from the formal game alone reveals the fictional. Because of a surface treatment that appears to be generated by important divisions of the spaces behind it, modern bureaucracy has been given an acceptable face. The architect believes he is serving a tradition—but he is really serving the demands of management. From the point of view of the domestic tradition of brick-and-tile architecture, we end up with the feeling that this tradition has been used for limited ends, not consolidated and restated from within.

In the other half of the scheme, some half-hearted references by comparison to the diagonal/orthogonal play are made, but the logic of the system is relaxed (see fig. 3). It is in these conditions that the more deliberately decorative aspects of the style are apparent. In the absence of the geometrical tour de force, a more conservative character emerges, and this allows an appreciation of the more traditional modes of linking forms and combining them. Here again, though, there is a certain ungainly obtrusiveness of functional elements, such as the well for the large circular staircase. These accents introduce a note of austerity reminiscent of industrial installations and destroy the geniality of the whole. We have an impression of awkwardness rather than grace, toughness rather than trust. The general effect of the two groupings denies both the loose-fit conventions of management and the loose-lap tradition of the picturesque.

The building emerges as a hybrid with all the disturbing aspects of a multi-headed monster.

The dilemma of postmodernism (which is simply the dilemma of an architecture awakened to its own sentient qualities) will not be resolved by the free application of images, but by the growth of imagination. Derbyshire is right in believing that the only safe course for the sentient architect is to adopt a tradition and hope to be accepted within it. That will depend entirely on his imagination in working for that tradition. To grow into a tradition, to be capable eventually of extending it, is the only worthwhile task. Apprenticeship and a certain humility are perhaps the first step. We don't see that yet at Hillingdon.

Originally published in *Progressive Architecture*, August 1979.

4   ALEXANDRA ROAD HOUSING: CAMDEN, ENGLAND
Neave Brown for the London Borough of Camden, 1979.

5   ALEXANDRA ROAD HOUSING
At left: Reception Home, Evans & Shalev Architects, 1979, at right: public housing.

ALEXANDRA ROAD, CAMDEN

ARCHITECT: NEAVE BROWN FOR THE BOROUGH OF CAMDEN

Revisiting Alexandra Road, the feeling which came to the top was quite simply envy of the standards of finish and construction achieved here by architects in the public service. They do, after all, have the power of a big machine behind them! Any private architect who has had to struggle to produce decent housing from a yardstick budget will know what I mean. They will probably recognize that moment of quiet desperation on noting that the last minuscule tree has been uprooted and the brick sandpit partially demolished to provide missiles. It is a realization that the design of housing is not just a matter of good intentions, that there are social problems that cannot be solved by design alone; a suspicion that the design of housing raises problems of imposing a degree of uniformity on what must rather want to be a proliferation of individual preferences and aspirations. Yet traditional house architecture in streets and terraces is on the whole uniform in character. How can the design of modern schemes equal it in its coherence without descending into a whimsical search for visual variety?

Here at Alexandra Road one can still believe in the power of design. Everything is still brave and new. The concrete is still white, the warm brick paving unbroken, the burgeoning plants well protected by reams of intact chestnut paling. Every aspect of the exterior, from access guard-rails through to the communal flower boxes has a well designed, robust feel to it: nothing skimped, nothing cheap. There is nothing makeshift to invite casual disrespect or violence. Only the litter of new coke cans in amongst the sprouting ground cover below the community center gives any indication that the denizens of this model settlement are not anything but beautiful people.

What is offered here is certainly a brave new world. The project seems to be the very epitome of social democracy at work. It adheres to the innovative tradition of modern architecture where rational design is the agent of liberation from defunct social hierarchies; from the days of masters and servants. Here there is a place for everybody, and in the sun. It was a tradition, of course, which at its inception did not recognize itself as a tradition, since tradition was precisely what it was against. Outside the defunct social hierarchies there could only be an ideal world, irradiated by justice.

It was not only architects who had this dream: it was a deeply held tenet of the socialism that came to power in Britain in 1945. Architects shared it, and took as their job the invention of a pattern of order to express and implement this sense of equality of opportunity in all things, and particularly in the conditions of the everyday world. Alexandra Road is in a very definite sense the achievement of that spirit, in a way that the little Unités of Roehampton were not, still less the outsize Unités of Southwark.

It was remarkable that when Le Corbusier died, it was a non-architect critic, John Berger, who mourned for the socialist aspirations embodied in the idea of the original Unité, where other critics thought only of its monumentality, and of the stones which could be thrown on that account. The prevailing mood of critics and architects today is to renounce all forms of monumentality while discounting at the same time anything savoring of social utopia. Both are seen as artificial and, therefore, insincere. 'Architects' dreams' are execrated as if they were mere attempts at personal aggrandizement. Ideology, instead of being something that requires clarification—an effort of thought—is seen as something which can be avoided altogether.

But ideology is not perhaps so easily avoided. It seems to permeate the production of an epoch, whether it is actively thought about or not. The conditions of production of housing design inevitably result at a certain moment in a judgment as to what is to be changed and what retained in existing models. The choice is not one of avoiding ideology or of giving way to it—but of striking a certain ideological balance between existing norms and modifications of them. Ideology is reflected in both the passive and active elements of this choice. The current interest in rehabilitation of old houses for instance, whatever the good reasons for it, still represents an ideological stance. In the same way, attempts to solve the problem of mass housing will always be limited by the concept of 'mass housing.' Yet the examination of that concept—as a problem to be solved—does offer the opportunity to revalue all the issues involved, and to advance our understanding about what can be done. Alexandra Road seems to me a positive and courageous attempt to solve the problem of mass housing, and for this reason it is a valuable experiment which deserves our serious attention.

The problem of mass housing is not so much a part of housing, traditionally conceived, as of problem-solving: it arises, that is, from the attempt to stand outside traditional norms and analyze them by rational standards. Whatever the general advantages of simply repeating the traditional forms of street and terrace, for instance, there must remain detail problems of adaptation to the requirements and expectations of our times. Neave Brown has recognized these problems as problems of relationship and sequence and of interference and amenity: "the sequences which require immediacy of contact, house and private open space, house to communal open space, house to the pedestrian system, to car parking, to the attendant functions . . . Problems of overlooking, privacy, light penetration, space about buildings, daylight and orientation . . ."[1] It is the insistence on detailed satisfaction of all these aspects, together with the general intelligibility of the overall layout, which characterizes 'modern' design.

The satisfaction of all these aspects was pretty straightforward in the early days of the Modern Movement when the value of traditional forms was not only not appreciated, but rejected as part of the old order. Subsequently we have seen, over the last fifty years, a step-by-step recognition that rationality alone does not make a viable environment, and that abstraction may clarify relationships to the point where they are squeezed dry of human sentiment and meaning. Neave Brown has no doubt shared in this process of disillusion. He has certainly come to recognize the virtues of the traditional forms of street and terrace, the numerous points of social contact it encouraged, the "cohesive street society"[2] it generated.

The key to Alexandra Road lies in appreciating what the architect has attempted to do to reconcile the demands of rationality with the expectations of ordinary people. In doing this he has followed up a line of inquiry belonging specifically to his generation: how to combine the advantages of rationality and analysis of needs with a respect for the already functioning facts of social life. This program of a generation was succinctly expressed as one of the chief aims of Team 10, the generational successor to CIAM: "This new beginning . . . has been concerned with inducing, as it were, into the bloodstream of the architect an understanding and feeling for the patterns, the aspirations, the artifacts, the tools, the modes of transportation and communications of present day society: so that he can as a natural thing build towards that society's realization of itself. In this sense Team 10 is Utopian, but Utopian about the present."[3]

The belief underlying this statement of aims is that there is a crucial stance towards existing patterns which understands them, yet stays outside them to achieve their transformation by analysis and design. It is this sense of closely observed lanes which permeates the work of the Smithsons in the early 60s: their pamphlet on 'Urban Structuring' begins with pictures of children at play in a street. How to capture that vitality, displayed in often hostile surroundings, and free it within a new architecture? The somewhat architectural concept of 'street,' which is not just a street but a source of life, appears subsequently in various transformations, from the 'street decks' of the Smithsons' Golden Lane project, through to the mat of 'streets' which constitutes the grid of Candilis, Josic and Woods's Free University of Berlin. The source of it must be found in Le Corbusier's description of the central access corridor in the Unité at Marseilles as a '*rue intérieur.*' It reappears, greatly transformed, as the main experience of space in Alexandra Road (fig. 4). Here it is a genuine pedestrian way, open to the sky, fronted by dwellings on both sides, only rationalized in the sense that it is a strictly pedestrian space, completely segregated from vehicles by being constructed on the roof deck of the parking basement, and forming part of an 'access system' which extends into stairs and a single elevated walkway at the fifth floor level. This upper level walkway follows the street in its gentle curve like a kind of *doppelgänger*, a remnant of the street deck from which so much was hoped, but now clearly an adjunct of the main walkway which it overlooks and from which it is visible. It is this primacy of the main pedestrian space, together with the principle that all dwellings, including the highest, relate to its datum at ground level by the use of a walk-up organization, which is the chief characteristic of the scheme. It concentrates on the idea of a prime social space used by all, not fragmented into merely repetitive layers of access: a space clearly regarded as potentially capable of generating a 'cohesive society.'

The other source of form in this scheme also involves the idea of a more intimate relation to ground and site. I am not speaking merely of the evolution of 'low rise, high density' as a convention of housing policy, but of that original turning over of the slab block on to the ground which Le Corbusier himself put forward, as early as 1948, for a development at Sainte Baume, and a year later for a sea-side development at Cap Martin.

In this second design, standard repeating cells of a slab block are separated into horizontal layers projected back on to the diagonal slope of a hillside. At each layer, a real ground level intervenes, separating the rows of cells. All the cells have this ground contact, along with views out over the roofs of the next layer below, while remaining parts of a closely knit unity. This happy idea has since been widely imitated, with Atelier 5's Siedlung Halen at Berne probably the best known example. At Alexandra Road, on a fairly flat site, the idea is transposed so that the building itself recreates the idea of a hillside site, with slopes too steep for cars but not for people.

In this way the building form becomes part of the shape of external space. Building mass and spatial volume are designed together as part of the same hierarchy of private and communal sequences. Entirely vanished is the total abstraction of functions and their reformulation within an idealized Cartesian space, as in the regular parallel rows of Hilberseimer: entirely absent is the neutral etherized space in which Unités were meant to float like so many liners in a tidal basin. Alexandra Road takes much of its shape from its context —the 'acoustic wall' against the railway to the north, pedestrian links to shopping and bus routes towards east and west, a sense of space and sun to the south. Yet it still observes all the detail requirements of the architect's self-imposed functional sequence (the segregated parking level, the distribution of private terraces and gardens, access walkways, communal space and facilities). There is no arbitrary visual variety, as in the romantic housing of Ralph Erskine, no deliberate accidentals to confuse or conceal the real sub-divisions. Every dwelling has a clear identity, not by diversification, but by its typical location in the cross-section.

The importance of the section is primary. It is this which controls the mixture of dwelling types, the apportioning of the sun, view and access. Although the context produces differences along the length of the development, these variations of placement are accentuated by the discipline of the section and the regular rhythm of the raking party walls along the length over which it is extruded.

These cross walls and the staircase balustrades, whose profiles they follow, create a series of screens around each individual dwelling or its pair. They give privacy while at the same time intensifying the defensive qualities of the space immediately in front of each. They make visible and articulate the shift from the domain of the small group of dwellings to the domain of the scheme as a whole. The effect is not unlike that achieved in Netherfields (the "Grunt Group" scheme at Milton Keynes) by the use of projecting panels between houses, but it benefits here from being an integral part of the structural form. It is also reminiscent of the way in which at the Royal Crescent in Bath, the giant order of columns clarifies the general form of the terrace, while individualizing the house fronts behind it on the nearer view.

What gives Alexandra Road its integrity is precisely the way in which it balances concern for the architectural object and the unity of the whole, and a social sensitivity which stresses the sequence of private and public, individual and group. The mechanism of this transition is the physical organization of the building, thus the 'structure' is at the same time physical and social. The material fact is given a social meaning. There is no superfluous material in between. This is what I mean when I say that it embodies a clear ideology, and this is how one can characterize it as a project in social democracy.

So rational design has triumphed at last? If mass housing can be approached as a problem of design, I believe Alexandra Road comes as near as it can to a solution. If we have any doubts, these doubts are not about the details of the scheme, what might have been done better, but rather about the limits of design as such in relation to the contextual structure in which it is inserted. Here Alexandra Road performs a positive service by enabling us to see more clearly what are the issues involved.

The site as a whole incorporates two major east-west spaces: the hard street, and the soft garden space to the south. The parallel continuity of these spaces is varied where the lower house terraces end, giving room for insertion of the community center, boiler house and central services, the special school, the home for the physically handicapped and the children's reception home. How accurately this grouping of social services reflects the character of the Welfare State! Who could be against the physically handicapped, especially when they are served so superbly by their architects Evans and Shalev? Yet the result of this grouping of housing and social buildings results in a ghetto-like character—at the moment idyllic, but potentially vulnerable. It constitutes an enclave I think, in the sense that Kenneth Frampton has defined it[4]—that is, an area where the negative tendencies of society at large are countered by a positive quality of environment. Perhaps that is simply to say that it is a zone of ideological clarification.

I believe that it is this sense of highly selected qualities which raises doubts: we are not sure if this is the real world or a simulacrum of it. Dismantling the play pits is one response: it reasserts the ordinariness of the new, reduces its implied demand for ideal behavior, makes it part of the daily struggle. This hasn't happened yet at Alexandra Road, and perhaps it never will. The crucial psychology of forms is not, after all, based on a one-to-one relationship with feelings, whereby each form can arouse an appropriate response; but rather, on their ability as a structure to correspond to alternative feelings that are already there. For example, the gentle curve of the main spine produces at the same time a softening of perspective and an intensification of convergence. It has qualities both of an amphitheater and of a bend in the road. It can articulate both a feeling of individual freedom and of dominance of the group. According to one's predisposition, the shape of the scheme can be both a solace and a provocation.

My own first reaction to Alexandra Road was that it was too big and appeared to be another megastructure providing an overall framework for all the possible functions of life. On examination this impression diminishes: it is rationality, not megalomania, that puts the wall against the railway for the whole length of the site, which piles the dwellings as high as possible on this boundary without breaking contact with the ground. As we have seen, there are very specific qualities of shape that relate the scheme to its environmental context, so that it can form continuities via the pedestrian links, the spread of soft space through the adjoining Answorth Estate to the south, the forecourt which relates parking, school, community center and shop. The scheme as a whole is well integrated into its context and in the end constitutes a unique and specific place. Yet it has been designed as an entity, and an entity it is.

It is so thoroughly designed that its bigness reappears as a kind of benevolent despotism, a sense of definition of the very terms of life.

Where rational design once had an abstracted quality, it has now acquired an ingrained quality. We feel the architect's intention to penetrate the social milieu: "To make a perceptible order requires more than an assembly of parts, more than the recognition of meaningful relationships by the tactical arranging of the pieces. It requires the integration of all the pieces into a single gesture in which unity and interdependence can be recognized at whatever level they are perceived."[5]

This attitude, in the face of a political situation that opposes the Welfare State to free enterprise, is an understandable one. To achieve good results, nothing can be left to chance. Yet the operation of chance (real chance, not a designer's imitation of it) is what gives cities their open-ended character. So long as housing is conceived as a compound of many functions, it can be thought of as analogous to the planning of any good building with a complex program.[6] This approach inevitably leads to a totally composed and closed form.

Alexandra Road is a superb piece of design, but by its very achievement it raises the question of how such designs can merge into the fabric of a city. I could have wished that at Alexandra Road the classification of parts which is so strong a discipline in the design of the residential buildings, could have loosened up when it came to the disposition of other distinct elements on the site. The street, still a pedestrian spine, could have been more of a street if the various institutional buildings had been inserted along it, somewhat in the manner of Shepheard, Epstein and Hunter's plan for Lancaster University. As a perspective of houses alone, it lacks that vital quality of intervention, the fundamental premise of Colin Rowe's 'Collage City.'

As it is, one of the most enjoyable moments which the scheme provides is that jump in character which occurs where Evans and Shalev's children's reception home takes over the duties of the acoustic wall (fig. 5). There we have an actual demonstration of the next step by which genuinely different characters of adjoining buildings will recreate the loose continuity of the living city.

Originally published in *The Architectural Review*, Vol. CLXVI, No. 990, August 1979.

NOTES

1 Neave Brown: "The Form of Housing," *Architectural Digest* Vol. XXXVII September 1967.
2 Neave Brown's phrase, "The Form of Housing."
3 The Aim of Team 10: *Team 10 Primer*, ed. Alison Smithson, Studio Vista, 1968.
4 In his lecture at Art Net Rally 2, 1978.
5 Neave Brown, "The Form of Housing."
6 Ibid.

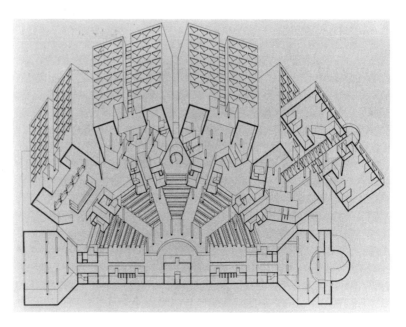

6   RESIDENTIAL CLINIC FOR THE TICINO: SWITZERLAND
Unrealized project by Mario Botta, 1981.

FUNCTION AND SYMBOL
A DESIGN BY MARIO BOTTA

In the Ticino where Mario Botta lives and builds, controversy about the death of architecture or the advent of postmodernism seems curiously remote. Modern development has come late to this most southern corner of Switzerland and it does not seem to bear the stigma it carries in so much of the West, where its utopianism appears to have contributed too much to social alienation, and its opportunism appears now to be no more than the passive agent of late capitalism. Here modernism partakes more of the inevitability of the movement towards material improvement, which it is difficult for the developed industrial countries to deny to countries like India or even Greece, or for Switzerland as a whole to deny to one of its poorer regions.

It is not that Switzerland is immune from ideological criticism—one would be hard put to find a more capitalistically committed city than Zurich; nor is it that Switzerland's provinciality assures the relative harmlessness of all that it does for its own welfare, a country that produced Le Corbusier and Hannes Meyer has to be at the center of the myth of modernity. And perhaps that is an explanation, to some extent, of the way an architect like Botta can succeed, within a framework which is at one and the same time indubitably local (he is a local boy made good and all his buildings to date are within a few kilometers of his birthplace), and also at the level of a world-wide horizon and potential. Modernity as such is no sin in Switzerland and modern architecture in Switzerland rarely seems alien, as it so often does in Britain. The idea of an efficient Swiss clinic, for instance, conveys modernity rather as a Swiss bank account conveys anonymity. Modern buildings in Switzerland are well-built to a good standard of workmanship, age gracefully and are seen as a good investment.

Moreover, with so many mountains, buildable land is valued and not squandered. There is a care taken about the act of building itself which underlines its value as an investment; and the insertion of fresh buildings into the landscape is filtered as much by a stiff mesh of social acceptability as it is by the need to adapt to difficult or crowded sites.

It is not that Mario Botta accepts the nature of that piecemeal development from which his own career has benefitted: his houses, inserted into more or less chaotic scenes, but never out of sight of a mountain, have blank walls and recessed, carefully screened openings which avoid looking out upon the worst adjacent horrors; and which ensure that the external volume stands out as simple and massive in scale, tuned to the mountain profile and the distant view, looking beyond the social setting to a natural one. In this insistence on a relationship with the permanence and immanence of nature lies the principal dimension of Botta's modernity, and his determination to evade the more reactionary modes of social demand and consumption.

In the early years of the Modern Movement the engagement with nature was mediated through abstraction, which somehow linked the new visual language of simplified forms to an idea of fundamental relations as in mathematics. Somehow the measurable would reconcile truth and necessity, showing them to be one and the same. It was with this confidence that the moderns could reject social conventions in order to uncover a new perspicacity in dealing with social affairs. It was with a similar confidence that Hannes Meyer could reject symbolism and composition in favor of an invisible pattern of efficacity. But Botta's masters were none of them confined to a purely physical and materialistic view of design. Le Corbusier, Carlo Scarpa, and Louis Kahn all valued, in their various ways, a metaphysical dimension in the physical object. Botta appears now as the heir to a modern tradition that can deal even-handedly with function and with symbol, with physical fact and psychological act. His objects are not the result of a functional analysis produced by searching short-sightedly through matrices and charts: they approach function as something malleable which can be classified and generalized, so that it can be adapted to broad formal generalizations. And these formal generalizations, in turn, arise from a few basic insights at the level of a metaphoric language of enclosure and release. Botta's approach is dialectical rather than reductive, putting form and function into a mutually productive relationship; these qualities can be clearly seen in the project under discussion (fig. 6).

If Botta's design for a residential clinic for Ticino (1981) had been built (and it is eminently buildable), it would surely have demonstrated again, as with his school at Morbio Inferior, his magic touch in relating building mass to land form. With him there is no organicist nonsense about melting into nature, or issuing forth from natural forces. What we find, rather, is a forceful grasping of the terrain, making the land form into a major element of the architectural conception, which is then expressed in forms of the starkest lucidity. Yet in return, the architectural forms, by their clear contrast with nature, demonstrate their provisional status, their dependence on purely human ideas of association and convention (as with the uniform cornice line). As a result, forms of a platonic exactitude are experienced as fragile creations of the mind. With the project unbuilt, it may seem rash to impute such qualities, except that similar effects can be discerned, and experienced, in the case of the school at Morbio. There, for example, the external amphitheater between the two main volumes acts as a focus by which landscape flows into and around the building, endowing its peremptory and apparently abstract forms with a forgiving sensuality. Again we find a dialectical relationship between the man-made artifice and its natural setting, in which the building form assimilates the landscape and is in turn assimilated by it.

In the case of the complex of sheltered housing that we are looking at here, there are complications not present at Morbio. These arise mainly from the fact that the main space, which relates all the segments of building, is internal rather than external. Its organization with wheel, hub, and spokes is concentric, making it a socially introspective space, focussed by the bridges—its spokes—and withdrawn from the landscape by the great depth of the splays formed by the six residential units. Instead of the free lateral access for individual classrooms which, at Morbio, is offset by the long central axis, we find here a relationship between the social space, as a control mechanism, and the individual cells which, at the extreme of each radial unit, press themselves up against the horizon as if trying to escape. The degree of concentration and control is not quite the inexorable control of Bentham's panopticon, however. The diameter sliced through at the intersection with the hillside maintains the outward directionality of the space, and the slots between the splayed units put it in touch with the horizon across the 180° sweep. Yet it does make visible the central purpose and organization of the institution: this is not sheltered housing as we conceive it in Britain, but something much more regulated, with a typically Swiss regard for propriety and security. It partakes as much of the character of a nursing home, a sanatorium, or a geriatric hospital.

The dialectic between the natural and the artificial still rules, however, and is particularly manifest in this continuum which has as one pole the social stimulus (and control) of the card room at the gallery hub, and the relative isolation, and perhaps consolation, afforded the cells, with their close views of the horizon. The great central hall, with its pattern of radiating roof lights, would have some of the underground qualities of the library in the Capuchin Convent at Lugarno; half buried in the mountain, it acts as a kind of railway concourse, sending out and receiving packages of various kinds, and acting as a passive absorber of many movements. It is in this mixture of abstract, psychological and practical organization that Botta shows his firm grasp of a modern tradition.

In the crisp organizational concept by which the six residential units are tied together both socially and centripetally, the project betrays its rationalism. Function is still honored as a source of form—yet not as the sole source. There is an even balance between the articulation of the brief into elements, and the treatment of each element (the group defined by the residential units) as having its own axis, its own symmetry and its own dignity. The analogy is again with the classroom units at Morbio, each one of which is a little house (and a classical one at that). In the Corbusian model, which now lies a little way back in the past, the communal areas would have been revealed as a single, dynamic, free-flowing space, showing *pilotis* on the outer faces, dissolving the identity of the individual elements. The force of this model is still present in the overall systemization; but the parts are given much more independence, so that the whole is not imposed on, but is made up of the array of, the parts. Each residential unit impinges on the central space somewhat as a house on a public square; and this respect for the unit is also the decisive aspect of the external volume, where the units are ranged like comparable towers, again conveying an urban idea of the assembly of similar parts. Instead of the main social level revealing itself through *pilotis*, we find a complex and subtle game with the central slots which further break up the residential groups, at this level widening into terraces. Instead of flowing between neutral cylindrical *pilotis*, space is organized by separate structures, each residential unit coming down to ground, below the main social level, emphasizing the residential and masking the institutional aspect, and contributing to an idea of the building complex as a kind of city of towers.

This respect for the separate units of construction clearly comes out of Kahn, as does the expression of the individual cells by means of triangular openings. Instead of Corbusian rationality, we have a Kahnian fundamentalism. At one side functional elements are matched to a set of pre-ordained spaces in a way that would have been seen as contrived only a few years ago. On the other hand, each separate group, and each separate cell, is conceived as a fundamental unit of space, its frontality (marked by a central slot) placing it into a metaphysical context where it relates the individual to the horizon. Botta justifies his raked balcony fronts by a psychological idea of protection, in this case maximized at the corners, minimalized at the center of exposure. But this, while acceptable, is only a part of the story. The main effect of the way space is marked is to cancel out the homogeneous uniformity of the Corbusian frame and institute a more heterogeneous composition, with more respect for the individual unit.

And this respect for the unit, we may surmise, has a further dimension: it conveys also a respect for the individual. Space is measured out in units which converge, or blend, but which are always discernible and which always place themselves in face of the individual, like an altar in a chapel. There is a chapel, at one end of the main axis, nicely balanced by the lunch room at the other end. In a way all the main spaces convey a certain devotional character. They are all imbued with a reverence for direction, for extension, for limits—the fundamentals of enclosing space and making it intelligible. This humanism is only won at the price of a certain austerity, it is true, and we could not claim for Botta that he has rediscovered an architecture of humanism. But by showing that function and form can be dialectically related, in a way that is both sensuously powerful, and intellectually indeterminate, Botta has opened up a further chapter for the history of modern architecture.

Originally published in *International Architect*, Vol. 1, Issue 5, 1981.

7   THE HIGH MUSEUM (INTERIOR VIEW): ATLANTA, GEORGIA
Richard Meier & Partners, 1984.

8   THE HIGH MUSEUM (EXTERIOR VIEW AT NIGHT)

THE HIGH MUSEUM, ATLANTA

ARCHITECT: RICHARD MEIER

The new High Museum at Atlanta is clearly a positive focus of local patriotism: when it opened in October 1983 the museum already had more than 15,000 charter members paying by subscription—and it has since been busy with a stream of local people. The contractor's agent noted that public interest was excited by the spectacle of construction, and it has continued unabated. Undoubtedly the main atrium space and its ramps are a great novelty, inviting participation like an attraction in a funfair. Parties of school children negotiate the ramps at speed, while older people take to them more cautiously, proceed with a stately self-consciousness, and arrive triumphantly at higher levels as if they had acquired new skills. All appear to enjoy the spatial geometry, the sensation of a gradual ascent which somehow effects the transformation of a low viewpoint into a high one. This mechanism, powered by just a slight effort— no more than we are happy to expend in the course of an afternoon walk in the country—sets us on a rigorous course within guide-rails. It amounts to a didactic exercise whose object, evidently, is to lead us to the discovery of geometrical space.

What persuades us to this methodical perambulation? Once launched, we are in the grip of a compulsion. Each change of floor level requires at least two, usually three, traverses of the quadrant. Even to move from one floor to another to continue our perusal of the works of art, sets us in motion like the pendulum of a clock— the repetition reinforcing the abstract nature of the experience. Is this some kind of reenactment of the abstract poetics of pure motion, the step-by-step evolution of a figure in space, suggesting Boccioni's *Bottle Evolving* or Duchamp's *Nude Descending a*

Staircase? Or is it something more metaphysical, the white noise of a silent machine, like Duchamp's image of two planes harboring a ball of twine?

The regular unfolding of the narrow ramp around its curved wall is in any event an unexpected substitution for the convention of the grand staircase (fig. 7). While it delineates—and causes the observer to delineate—a geometrical figure, it enables him also to occupy a notional center from the periphery—a center which leads into the recesses of the museum galleries. It is altogether a strange notion, and it exercises an unusual appeal, tinged with danger, like the space of a dream. The regular grid of square openings perforating the spinal wall adds to this sense of transgression by the suggestion of an incomplete or ruined building, offering escape at the same time as reinforcing the sense of control, as if we were in some kind of rationalist penitentiary dedicated to perpetual movement.

The sense of control is emphasized by the monochrome landscape. Everything is white, except for the gray carpet on the ramp. A diffused, glowing white under cloud, a brilliant ski-slope white under sun—the atrium is sensitive to every change in the quality of the natural light that enters it. The uniform whiteness, against which people and works of art are clearly distinguished as being interruptions, reinforces the sense of dedication to an ideal. Yet, by an unexpected paradox, it results in making the environment not harder, but softer. Reflections from one surface to the next bind the intersecting planes into a complex entity: the building becomes a system of mutually adapted parts working together—the very definition of a mechanism. Thus the geometric clarity of the spatial continuum is constantly offset against a kaleidoscope of impressions as the white substance coagulates on our retinas to register, in every successive viewpoint, as a graphic richness of texture. One is reminded of Moholy-Nagy's *Light-Space Modulator* (of 1923 to 1930) in which a dynamic construction of entirely verifiable planes and meshes is arranged to cast cinematic shadows onto a screen, transmuting its own finite geometry into the indefinite aspects of a graphic mystery.

The combination of an incontrovertibly finite space and the endless variations of silhouetted pattern projected onto the retina creates a mystery which entertains as it bemuses. It is impossible for an architect who has practiced ascents on the ramp at the Villa Savoie, intellectually irresistible but sensuously unrewarding, not to respond to this sweetness and light. It amounts to a demonstration *pro bono publico* of the Corbusian dictum on the play of light as the source of architecture: here, the play of light falling upon the candid boundaries of elementary space produces by itself a sense of fullness and sufficiency. It transmits at the same time an intellectual satisfaction and a beauty that floats freely in the eye of the beholder. It exercises a popular appeal without resorting to the pathos of vestigial images of popular sentiment.

The sensuousness of Richard Meier's architecture has to be stressed. It is an integral result of his method. In order that the white substance of the building shall be both intellectually and emotionally charged, it has to be imbued with an entirely abstract life. Externally, the building has to be freed from the wear and tear of the weather. The white buildings of the International Style, it has been noted, do not grow old gracefully, nor do they accept patina or staining without loss of authority. The High Museum is even more strenuously committed to purity and danger, but through a thorough attention to building technology, it has a better chance of retaining it. The enameled steel panels which clothe it are self-cleansing and do not age: like tooth enamel they are committed in principle to being white. If rust should appear (which could only be the result of hidden damage during construction) the offending panel can be replaced. The building must remain pristine, abstract, outside of temporal diminution, undying. Even the base course of off-white granite plays its part in this system of values, producing an effect of graphic nuance, as in a perspective rendering, rather than insisting on the traditional transition to earth and dirt.

Thinking again of the Villa Savoie—its intellectual ramp, its corporal vulnerability—it is clear that white-walled architecture has benefitted from technological advances. It seems that it has taken modern architecture some fifty years to learn the secrets of bodily health. Like the earlier examples, the High Museum is constructed of concrete and steel, but this is not the material that meets the eye. Through an evolutionary process, still susceptible to organic metaphor, the equivalents in building of flesh and skin have achieved their special destinies, each assigned to its role—one of providing physical stability, the other of establishing a precise surface geometry.

This specialization has exacted a cost however, in the elaboration of the modular, and not always modular, panels and their all-embracing system of joints. The joints speak of an assembly process, and of a complex organization of parts. Gone is the simple claim of modernism that some principle of bare necessity—the structural material itself—could fulfill all roles. Modern architecture today is no longer naive; like its counterpart, postmodernism, it is knowing and it is embroiled in artifice. The distinction, if it is valid at all (which I doubt), is certainly not between sincerity and shallowness. The High Museum is athletic in the care with which it has exercised in secret so that it can meet the eye without flinching, without blemish.

What we seem to be dealing with here, however, is still modern architecture: that is, an architecture founded on the idea that only abstract space is free to follow the exigencies of function. This central precept emerged in the early twenties, when current techniques of building were not adequate to achieve fully the weightlessness of pure abstraction. Put slightly differently, it has taken half a century for modern architecture to come to terms with the actual, as opposed to potential, conditions of production of industrialized society. Gropius and Le Corbusier spoke of the potential of industrialization, and emphasized standardization as the key to serial production. They evidently had in mind a system that was already, in its elements, the raw material of architecture, made visible in grids and cells. Universal forms, however, are not the reality of today's industrial society under capitalism. The successful industrial product does not exhibit its structure, or its mechanism, but conceals it behind a glossy surface. The High Museum appears to conform to this description, but also to adhere to a machine aesthetic in the precision of its geometry. It utilizes serial production both through its use of standard steel joists, for the most part buried in concrete, and the modular steel panels which define its visibility. There can be no question that it achieves a controlled aesthetic through understanding and exploiting the real conditions of industrial production.

On the evidence of Richard Meier's work, a style of building which fulfills the pragmatic, as distinct from the ideological, premises of the Modern Movement has finally become possible, only by a process of evolution rather than by intellectual fiat. Such an evolution can be found in other products which first appeared, in principle, in this century: the safety razor, the telephone, the automobile. It has taken some fifty years, since the Model-T Ford, to transform the automobile into a universal object of mass production and consumption. The hidden machinery performs ever better, and the steel and glass exterior, no longer determined only by physical considerations, speaks directly to the eye through an evolved language of expression which we may call the connotative semiotic of the automotive system. Every 'new' model is but a variant of the old: as with clothes, each new product is but a step in a space within cultural history, suspended between an ever varying 'aptness' and a continuing utility.

The car is a typical product of today's society. It may bring or make worse certain problems: death-toll on the roads, congestion in the streets, high energy consumption, privatization of public man. Its future is in no way guaranteed—rather its fate is tied up with that of society itself. It has become essential in that society, as architecture hoped to be. If the building industry is not to the same degree tied into the conditions of daily life, that may be an advantage as much as a disadvantage for architects. It is at least worth asking why the question of style is so much less agonizing in the car market than it is in the market for buildings.

In terms of the relatively slow and evolutionary progress of engineering design, the case of the automobile forces us to confront the comparative time-scales of innovative practice, and to recognize the very different speeds of development of technological and artistic endeavor. The High Museum also forces upon us fundamental questions on the status of the Modern Movement in architecture and the gap between ideological aspiration and pragmatic success. Currently, the Modern Movement is being treated simply as a style, and a style whose authority has been spent. The High Museum may then be praised for its nostalgia, or dismissed for it. But the rational premises of the Modern Movement were concerned not only with style, but also with the objective possibilities of abstract form, seeking a new balance between appearance and reality. Viewed from these premises, the High Museum is an improved model, offering better functionality along with more seductive body-work.

Moreover, it seems to me that the High Museum does this without renouncing certain long-accepted social tasks of architecture: filling a civic role with dignity but without subservience, responding to local patriotism but without sacrificing cultural ties, boldly setting out to make its popular appeal through the pleasures of geometric space. In these terms, it retains a basic integrity which should give us pause.

This social acceptance may be the result of the same time-lag we have noted in the evolution of products. Since the task of architecture is more social than physical, it is hardly surprising that the evolutionary process should be complex. The kind of white-walled architecture that was adumbrated in only a few pre-war masterpieces never became the norm. The term "International Style" came to be applied to glazed boxes, business architecture, often with no trace of whiteness. The post-war architecture of the sixties and seventies fluctuated between the severity of glazed surfaces and the hysteria of brutalist protrusions. But a few buildings—in the United States perhaps the Carpenter Center and I.M. Pei's National Gallery in Washington—gave themselves a didactic mission: to lead the public into architectural space. In both of these cases it is the ramp that lays down the preferred route, substituting for the abruptness of the staircase the experience of gradual assimilation. It is worth noting that the Pompidou Center in Paris makes use of the same kind of forced routing of the public as the prime experience and the principle way of explaining itself. Clearly there is an ideological difference between the Pompidou's power-driven escalators and the High's self-powered quadrantal ramp; but both are unexpected experiences that the public survives, and enjoys.

I have concentrated, in these remarks, on the basic features of the High Museum—its geometric space, its sensuous whiteness—as they seem to embody the essentials of its reiterated modernity and its situation within a strictly modern pursuit of purity and danger. It is impossible to know whether the public's ready acceptance of the building is owing to its novelty, or to its familiarity. In context, the whiteness alone is startling enough. But the building also exhibits many more conservative features. In places it has quite conventional square windows. There is a complete absence of stilts—the building meets the ground and adapts itself to the existing levels. The platform to which the approach ramp leads is a "townscape" space that permits separate access to the auditorium, and on through to the old museum. Within the gallery layout, it is noticeable that the absolute division of space within the *plan libre* has been modified by the introduction of internal window openings to create something much more like a series of rooms, as gallery curators prefer. The succession of smaller spaces has been tailored skillfully, perhaps too completely, to the specific objects of display and their appropriate grouping. All these more conservative features, and the attention the architect has paid to detailed requirements of the brief, result in an environment which is compliant and accommodating. They no doubt do a great deal to soften the impact of a building which in its main features might appear doctrinaire.

Again, there is a crucial difference with respect to the white-walled prototypes of the twenties. Modern architecture was then a reaction to the eclecticism of the nineteenth century but in itself it appeared to have no history, and to be somehow outside of history. This has changed, and the High Museum is full of references to the recent history of architecture. The general system of opposing large blank wall areas to areas of concentrated glazing is a convention of the modern building. It allows us to read major volumes like foyer or staircase tower. Against this, the pattern of regular square windows appears retroactive, a gesture towards the neoclassicism of Libera or Loos. The indirect entrance sequence, turning us away from an impossible door in the exact center of the quadrant, and leading us into the slot of space that separates the four quarters of the plan via a double-curved lobby, is entirely reminiscent of Le Corbusier's Salvation Army sequence, including the initial portico. The stepped-back exterior of the atrium has a Russian Constructivist look: certainly the motif of aiming the entrance sequence straight at the center of rotundity is pure Melnikov (fig. 8) and Melnikov's strange circular house, with its pattern of floating wall openings, produces an effect very like the perforations in the curved inner wall. The general disposition of the atrium, rising in the angle between rectangular masses, is clearly derived from Stirling's History Faculty at Cambridge; the slim elevator tower, detached from the adjoining mass, speaks to me of Louis Kahn's Richards Building in Philadelphia. Others will find, no doubt, many more such references, in whole or in part.

But these reflections of modern architecture's short history do not give us the key to interpret the total form of the ensemble. This is no longer a demonstration of the *plan libre* but rather a meditation on the ambiguities of dividing and articulating volumes. Instead of seeing an L-shaped mass embracing a quadrant, we are asked to consider a group of four loosely attached cubes, one of which has been changed into a quadrantal volume. A value is given to the narrow space between the four entities, into which the entrance leads, and towards the crossing on which the ramp bases its arc. Such a plan has more to do with Kahn than with Le Corbusier. However, the whole process of leading us first directly towards the center of convexity, then off to the side in order to penetrate along the interstices, is derived from Le Corbusier, as is the general method of the composition whereby the horizontally curved lobby and vertically curved auditorium are made to act together to contain and soften the brutality of the initial gesture. The knowledge that the perforated wall behind the glass skin is the locus of a thin and repetitive transverse movement by means of the ramp is hidden from us until we are standing within the atrium. In that displacement of the entrance, and its substitution by the narrow tutelary path which defines the space, lies the tension and the power of the design.

Originally published in *A. A. Files*, Summer 1984.

9   NATIONAL GALLERY OF CANADA: OTTAWA, CANADA
Moshe Safdie Architect, 1984.

THE NATIONAL GALLERY OF CANADA

ARCHITECT: MOSHE SAFDIE

Moshe Safdie, best known for his Habitat residential complex on the St. Lawrence River, was once the standard-bearer for a futurist architecture that would assemble itself out of technological necessity. Large units manufactured and finished in the controlled environment of a factory were to be brought ready-made to a heroic infrastructure and slotted into place according to an aleatory scheme of permutations and combinations.

If the resulting impression of biological crystallization is successful at Habitat, it is because of the patient hidden work of the engineers who tracked the diverse loadings of this complex structure downward to their footings and distributed millions of steel bars accordingly. The building stands frozen in an initial gesture that is also its final one: the processal system that is celebrated in it is symbolized rather than exhibited.

Whatever the arguments in favor of an instrumental modernism, Habitat can now be seen from the beginning to have resorted to an arbitrary aesthetic. The kind of pattern that might result from a biological determinism has to be simulated, like any other form of expression, within culture. We can find the seed of an arbitrary aesthetic of rectangular volumes in the decorative door panels of Hoffmann (1902) or in Malevich's Suprematist architecture (1922). That kind of proliferative pattern probably reaches its apogee in Fritz Wotruba's Church of the Holy Trinity in Georgenburg, Austria (1965), where it stands forth as purely sculptural enrichment for a holy shrine.

The partly random play of cubic volumes in the contemporaneous design for Habitat follows a very similar aesthetic, although it now supposes a quasi-biological teleology in place of individual artistic intention. Its artistic intention is, as it were, subsumed and masked under an ideological commitment to the process of becoming and changing. The references are, broadly, Peter Cook's Plug-in City, on the one hand, and adobe villages in Mexico on the other. I always found it unbecoming that Safdie should refer to his architecture as "the vernacular of our times," thereby attempting to give social prestige to an arbitrary aesthetic of process, and place himself to one side as the mere agent of its self-revelation, rather than the originator of its idiosyncrasies.

Why rake over these old coals? Who now believes in the biological determinism of chance encounters, except, perhaps, at the level of biology? Today, in interrogating our own history, we are in increasing difficulty as to what is cause and what effect. Actors simulating strong emotions are found to undergo the same changes in body chemistry that the emotions themselves naturally engender. The fake determinism of Habitat can be seen in retrospect to be perfectly situated in the cultural stream of its time. The interest for us lies in the contrast of two points of view—that of 1965 and that of 1985. What has happened to us in the gap of twenty years? What has happened to Safdie?

To the extent that his National Gallery exhibits a series of crystalline structures we have a superficial suggestion of continuity. The degree of repetition of elements, both in the tiered atria of the Great Hall and the Entrance Pavilion, and in the south face towards Majors Hill Park, is reminiscent of a proliferative aesthetic, even a procreative one (in the sense of showing larger and smaller entities of the same kind). However the accidental juxtaposition (of Habitat) is replaced by a geometry of octagonal relations producing square and triangular facets. In spite of some resemblance to the glass architecture of Bruno Taut, the result is a-historical, decorative and populist.

The entrance sequence, if we include the colonnades facing the vehicle set-down in Sussex Drive, consists then of a decorative screen drawn around the building (fig. 9), creating points of access at the south-east and south-west corners and continuing in subdued form across the west face to the final octagon which gives access to the triangular restaurant. The concept thus emerges of a wrap-round system of public access which on three sides surrounds the body of the galleries. These, by contrast, are fairly solidly lumped together into a rectangular mass, articulated by two internal courts, whose only crystalline connections are made through conventional glazed rooflights. A last, rather forlorn, crystal octagon is found at the remaining (north-east) corner. Its presence adjacent to the car set-down is clearly a presage of the impending excitement of the Great Hall at the opposite corner: but it is also a witness to the architect's intention of attempting to animate the single bulk of the galleries by a string of glass facades wrapping the package four-square like Christmas ribbon. At the four corners stand Mother, Father, Junior and Baby, the components of the nuclear family. What has happened to Safdie is what has happened to us all: the return to figuration.

In thus laying the basis of a strong popular appeal, Safdie has shown his customary cleverness. The four episodes signify the moments of joy in the family outing: Baby stands for anticipation, Mother for welcoming embrace, Father for domination of the internal and external landscapes, Junior for cream cakes and tea.

I would rather not talk of the way the octagonal personages are tied in to the rectangular mass behind. Basically, that mass is lodged in their backs. It looks and feels uncomfortable. The building will do more for people than it will do for architecture.

The popular enjoyment of the entrance sequence will probably ensure a positive response to the building as a whole, somewhat in the same way that the external escalators at the Pompidou Center in Paris draw crowds close by the art works, while at the same time enabling these to be completely by-passed. More elaboration, more study, of the central block of galleries, more differentiation, more mystery of their architecture, might have enabled these spaces to enhance the enjoyment of the art works and at the same time foster a sense of architecture in the souls of the non-committed. An ideal example of such a possibility is Frank Furness's Gallery in Philadelphia.

There is something weird and wonderful about the present predominance of the art gallery as a social form. It now accounts for an impressive proportion of the up-market sector of architectural production. It is a need of our time.

We can see in this phenomenon the embodiment, for our age, of an essentially didactic function, a necessary representation of history and tradition, of standards of excellence and individual heroism, which may be tritely labeled as "cultural heritage;" however this effort may be compromised by the standards of mass society, we probably feel that it must be undertaken and re-presented, if our society is to survive. At the same time there is the need, in doing this, to appeal to a non-intellectual level, to make an approach to the needs of mass men, to popularize. It is no easy choice: on the one hand, the specter of sterile intellectualism; on the other hand, the risk of the parallel shadow of superficiality, of having art reduced to merchandise, of seeing art consciousness measured in terms of numbers of visitors per year.

By concentrating as he has done on the superficial movement system, Moshe Safdie has courted an easy popularity. He has captured art for the masses, run a ring round it, but not opened it up to the sense of surprise and wonder. Indeed, the somewhat systemic character of the central gallery mass echoes the systematic cells at the Tate Gallery rear extension (not Stirling's front addition) and the systematic shed spaces at the Pompidou Center. It is as if the modern functional paradigm could deal only with specific routes, but not with destinations. Thus the systemic approach, so evident in Safdie's work in 1968, is still present here, in a muted form.

In a world of simulation and of popular imagery, could one begin to feel that architecture, in order to express the greatness of a culture, demands respect as a field of expression? To recover its full potential it will have to be given more than the wrap-around treatment, especially if that treatment is to accentuate the superficial aspects of the family outing.

Originally published in *SECTION a*, Vol. 2 No. 2, Montréal, April/May 1984.

10   SEATTLE ART MUSEUM: SEATTLE, WASHINGTON
Venturi, Scott Brown and Associates, 1991.

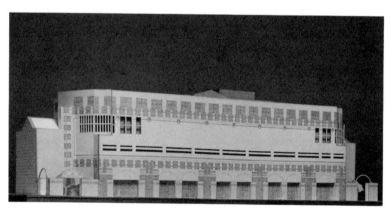

11   LAGUNA GLORIA ART MUSEUM: AUSTIN, TEXAS
Venturi, Scott Brown and Associates, 1988.

TWO ART GALLERIES
ARCHITECT: VENTURI, SCOTT BROWN AND ASSOCIATES

Venturi, Scott Brown and Associates have recently designed two art museums that make a positive use of decoration: the Seattle Art Museum and the Laguna Gloria Art Museum in Austin. These two art galleries share a number of characteristics. Both are intended for relatively small downtown sites with a single extensive street frontage on the longer side; both adopt the stratagem of situating the main foyer space just inside this frontage, so that it acts in parallel with the sidewalk at ground level. At Seattle the street drops with a dramatic gradient towards the waterfront, giving this parallel gallery the character of a grand staircase. At Austin the stair takes on a similar directional flow, but is contained narrowly between walls in the central zone of the building. Further, both buildings make a virtue of one apparently unavoidable property of today's art museum—its propensity towards blankness: the largely blank and windowless walls of the gallery areas are treated frankly as sites for decoration. Our first impression of both buildings is that they are decorated.

Venturi, who invented "the decorated shed," surely has a right to decorate an art gallery. To be sure, the phrase originally seemed to take its meaning from makeshift or tawdry examples, where one supposedly honorific facade is picked out for treatment while the rest of the building betrays its utilitarian or threadbare status. We are familiar with this idea from countless wild west film sets, as well as from the incomplete appearance of nineteenth-century street architecture in America, where the street frontage is heavily ornamented, leaving the sides unadorned. Nor is the idea foreign to Europe, as many city churches throughout Italy attest. But there seems little doubt that in these two museums, Venturi has carried the idea to its end: the decoration is not restricted to a small portion of the building, but is extended to all its visible parts, becoming the main point of the architectural statement. He appears to have set out to prove the validity of a decorated style.

In both cases, too, the aim of using decoration has been at least in part to achieve a large scale, as a way of enabling these buildings, small as they are, to compete against the surrounding high-rise buildings of a modern city. At Laguna Gloria, the entire wall above ground floor is treated as a single enormous panel of limestone, decorated around all four edges, "like a flag." At Seattle, the wall is ribbed in vertical lines that juxtapose the incised name of the gallery, along the top, with the irregular play of stone arches and openings along the base. Both buildings make a positive use of color, not just as an applied mask, but through the integral use of colored building materials. The result in both cases is distinctive; very American, very Venturi, a little defiant, perhaps, like a man coming out in earrings for the first time.

In using decoration at this scale Venturi is comfortably situated within his own theory. From the beginning, he has argued for applied decoration, as we saw with the applied timber moldings on his mother's house, or with the bands and panels of white marble at Guild House, not to speak of the "applied" television aerial. Those touches were understated by comparison with these new buildings. The transformation of a house facade by the addition of a cheap timber molding might seem to be an improvisation, the sketch of a gesture rather than a genuine commitment to an architecture of applied surfaces. To sketch the gestures in stone seems altogether more explicit; some might feel, more blatant, but that is already a loaded term, implying a moral judgement, and one should try to avoid that kind of over-simplification. If these buildings are designed as essays in decorated architecture, that cannot of itself be condemned. If this critic is nevertheless uneasy with the results, a more substantial reason has to be found.

Criticism of decoration certainly cannot be levelled from a stylistic point of view, as was contained within the ideology of the Modern Movement in architecture. A moral condemnation of capitalist architecture applies to the entire social and economic basis of that architecture, and does not allow for any purely stylistic discrimination. Even within the modern style, with its apparent absence of decoration, we have learned to expose the existence of a decorative aesthetic: in Mies's use of applied steel mullions, or in Le Corbusier's use of apparently randomized concrete mullions, as at La Tourette. Today's method of construction, in the United States at least, and probably world-wide, consists of a structural frame which is faced with separate skins outside and inside. A "modernist" building such as Richard Meier's High Museum in Atlanta follows this imperative as inexorably as does the latest neoclassicist business tower by Kevin Roche. Everywhere, the modernist assumption that the basic structure of a building can be left exposed as an architectural statement *de profundus* has been abandoned in favor of a sleeker and weather-resistant outer skin. A surface, then, on which any message can be written. Even stone, real stone, which used to be the guarantee of a building's integrity, is now available only as a facing.

As I have long argued, semiological investigations have clarified the human tendency to add expressive elements to every artifact. The idea of a truly functional artifact, which is shorn of all expedient or incidental or pre-conceived impurities, is now the most difficult of all artifacts to reconstruct. This is not to say that another development in naked architecture might come about, perhaps as a reaction to over-decorated buildings. But such a development will not be able to rely on our pre-semiological innocence, it will, on the contrary, be a hard-won aesthetic. Moreover, even when a puritan rule has been imposed from above, the human tendency towards expression breaks through. In the years of Chairman Mao, all official Chinese wore the same semi-military suit; but it was noticed that the Chinese delegates to international conferences, on closer examination, sported an array of cut, color and cloth, with a view to making possible discriminations within the rule of regimentation. It seems that the wish to express qualities through aesthetic choices is entirely understandable, and clothes are a functionally efficient way of allowing this. Why then should we not expect that buildings, in order to fulfill their social purpose, should not be appropriately clothed?

Robert Venturi has yet another justification, for he has followed precedent. His present mastery of architectural forms has been to a very large extent guided by his admiration for one hero of the Modern Movement—Alvar Aalto. Traces of Aalto's influence abound in Venturi's work, and are particularly evident here in the Seattle Art Museum, with its use of facetted walls and plan configurations, and complex combinations of short segmental curves and counter-curves. He can always point to the fact that Aalto, for all his canonization within modernist dogma, made no bones about including decoration in his design service. This was not restricted to light fixtures and door handles, but included applied column casings, applied decorative surfaces in bent plywood, and the use of contrasting facing materials such as the two-tone stripes in the marble facing on the Wolfson Cultural Center, or the application of marble around the entrance of the otherwise completely brick facades of the library at the Otaniemi Institute of Technology. So there is ample precedent for the use of decoration from within the work of one of the most widely respected masters of modernity.

These art museums strike us as being also very American, and there is plenty of precedent in the American Arts and Crafts movement for applying decorative patterns to the outside of a building. One has to look no further than Frank Furness, whose National Academy of Art (in Venturi's native Philadelphia) displays an array of variegated colors and textures on its principal facade—rusticated stone, decorated spandrels in the pointed arches, sculpted panels high in the walls, brickwork in plain and patterned panels, and a variety of noisy rhythms in brackets and dentals at all levels. Venturi's book *Complexity and Contradiction* contains very specific praise for Furness, who was expert in creating an architecture of complexity by the play of opposing elements. His building for the National Bank of the Republic, said Venturi, evidenced a play of "violent pressures within a rigid frame." In the Seattle Art Museum, by comparison, the juxtapositions of free-standing and applied arches, and the deliberate dislocation between the applied figures and the actual openings, seem restrained, even tasteful.

Perhaps this is simply because we have become used to the collage system of composition which Venturi favors. While collage permits the accumulation of riches, it does so only at the cost of a loss of credibility with respect to the individual figures that are pressed into service. Any figure that bears too strongly its origins outside of the composition inevitably becomes an implicit criticism of the integrity of the composition itself. As Massimo Scolari has noticed with his experiments in collage à la Max Ernst, the predominant emotion engendered by collage is a species of irony that immediately collapses into melancholy.

The lightness with which Venturi composes may provide a clue as to why his results, striking as they are, appear to fall short of the invention of a decorated style. Of course, he might deny any such intention, yet one feels that there has to be a *raison d'etre* for all the individual elements that are to be combined in a building, outside of contingency, personal taste, empirical restraints or improvisation. The decorative elements in Aalto do not set up doubts about the underlying tectonic approach. With Venturi, these elements *are* the underlying approach, and the very fact that they are so exquisitely tailored to the individual performance raises doubts about what remains if they are dissolved.

If we compare these buildings with another case of a decorated building in the Arts and Crafts tradition, we may begin to form an impression as to what is disquieting about them. I am thinking of Louis Sullivan's National Farmers' Building in Chicago. There we find colored terracotta tiles used to decorate a whole facade, and the principal motif is a large-scale framed panel, not unlike Venturi's panel at Laguna Gloria. Sullivan's system of composition is fundamentally classical (a classical that includes "gothic"), so it is combined in a straightforward way with large thermal windows, one to each facade. The effect is weighty rather than lightweight, and very American also. Since the decoration and the architectural figures complement each other, they presuppose a whole that is harmonious and not difficult. Venturi, by contrast, is committed to the idea of the difficult whole, and this seems to follow from his feeling about the Zeitgeist. Today, in an eclectic age, there is no certainty outside of contingency, personal taste, empirical restraints and improvisation. Of the decorative panel above the entrance at Wu Hall, in Princeton University, he said (I paraphrase): It is reminiscent of an Italianate Tudor entrance, but it is flat, not a reincarnation, a reminder, an emblem. With Venturi, the acceptance of this loss of authority, which makes him truly a modern architect, sets limits on his own potential.

Venturi has enjoyed the fragmentation of architecture, as part of the fragmentation of our times. Fragments can be composed with lightness and freedom, they do not protest overmuch. It is the contingent nature of his compositional method, not the extensive use of applied decoration, that limits the potency of his forms.

Originally published in *Casabella* 540, Milan, November 1987.

12   MISSISSAUGA TOWN HALL: ONTARIO, CANADA
Jones & Kirkland Architects, 1982–1985.

MISSISSAUGA TOWN HALL, CANADA

ARCHITECTS: JONES AND KIRKLAND

Mississauga is said to be a suburb of Toronto, but this description is misleading. It is an adjacent center of growth. Heading west out of Toronto in the direction of Mississauga is very much like heading west out of Dallas in the direction of the 'twin' city of Fort Worth: there, it's far from obvious at what point you've finally reached your destination, because of the erratic impact of development along the way. Here also, in an urban landscape dominated by spreading factory sheds along with the urban paraphernalia of drive-in banks, motels and gas stations, the eye searches for a landmark, for something of significance to latch on to. Indeed, the horizon is interrupted at irregular intervals by large lumps of building, all vaguely impressive, even sacramental—like gaunt cathedrals of the twentieth century—until, on closer approach, they identify themselves all too clearly as industrial installations, or more mundanely, as hotels or office blocks. Eventually, a closer grouping of office blocks on adjacent sites takes on the semblance of a miniature downtown—a downtown that is coming rather than going. Then, soon after, another problematic mass, a tightly-knit group that has something industrial, or agricultural, about it; but also a touch of Bavarian monastery or Italian hill town. This time, closer approach does not dissipate the mystery. This time, we are dealing with architecture, and we have reached the improbable hub of the future city of Mississauga (fig. 12).

As we approach, the massing of Mississauga's Town Hall resolves itself into two aspects: a fore-court flanked by colonnades that extend in front of a large pedimental mass, and a close encounter of varied building forms that cluster behind it, on its north side. The fore-court is unmistakably formal, with its central pool and double rows of copper beeches: there is no doubt that the building 'faces' south; and in this it follows what is indubitably a local tradition, for to face south in Toronto means addressing not only the sun but the great lake, and a world of business opportunities and cultural engagements that exists indefinitely on the far side of it. To the north lies the tundra.

If you work here and use the underground parking lot which lies beneath the plaza podium, you will ascend to ground level via one of the two terminal pavilions, one to each colonnade, and will then follow the colonnade to entrances which lead through lobbies to the Great Hall—the central space of the building. The central opening on the south facade, however, which gives directly onto the winter-garden, is reserved for rare and important ceremonial occasions. The winter-garden, with its mossy columns and fluttering birds, speaks of a warmer clime and imparts a touch of fantasy, which impinges on the Great Hall as well. If you arrive by taxi or bus you'll be dropped off at a central point on the north front, entering the Great Hall towards the winter-garden, towards the light. The juxtaposition of these two central spaces is important in creating a sense of place, for the winter-garden, by screening the view out to the ceremonial plaza, prevents the building from emptying itself prematurely. It produces a density in the direction of the main axis to match the density of the cross-axis. The cross-axis could be said to balance the council chamber on the east with the office block on the west, although with some shifts of geometry, and with the introduction of other elements like the grand staircase and (higher up) the clocktower.

These complications are useful in modifying the symbolic meaning of the principal oppositions employed by the architects, which all the same work orthogonally around the bi-axial focus in the Great Hall. The Great Hall mediates the building: it opposes the empty plaza with its ceremonial entrance, screened by the fantastical garden, to the humdrum sidewalk entrance on the other side, with its constant stream of arrivals and departures; it opposes the council chamber—an enclave of privilege and responsibility—to the office block, with its daily comings and goings. It thus takes on something of the quality of a city square, absorbing and neutralizing the presences of the Commonwealth, of the City Government, of the Union of Workers, of the People. It reconstitutes a city within the city, compensating for the suburban sprawl outside by an architectural compaction within. But although the oppositions are more or less bi-axial, they are not so obvious as to allow meaning to drain away at a glance. The Great Hall is cool, not hot. There is no exaggerated use of emblems, for instance, or of emblematic 'figures' on each face of the square. Yet there is no doubt that in adapting the ancient idea of axes, the architects have been thinking not just about the ordering of the spaces, but about their meaning, and about the representational nature of the vertical surfaces that define them. In a very definite way, this building is 'about' the representation of function. It is a serious attempt to make public architecture, to return architecture to a theater of public life.

The Great Hall is a four-square, four-story high space, surmounted by a pyramidal glazed roof. At ground level, the space expands behind colonnades on all four sides, but at the higher levels, wall surfaces, punctured by small square windows, define the volume the way a town square is defined by surrounding buildings. The columns and the upper wall surfaces are picked out in *verde alpe* marble from Carrara, with narrow bands in black Uruguayian granite. The floors are also covered with polished marble, pink squares of *rosso verona*, also banded in black granite. The effect is both lush and austere, certainly grand. It suggests something of the prompting towards largesse which might be appropriate to a good hotel, or the indulgence of a shopping mall, until one remembers that this is the seat of government, the theater of politics, not of consumption. At the same time it represents the varied functions of a community center that provides a great many services: advice on business development, an art gallery, a public fitness center equipped with the latest muscle machines, a sauna, squash courts, a public restaurant, a center for daycare services, a wedding chapel, a scenic garden, an outdoor amphitheater, a sculpture court, and a variety of venues for private and public functions. Tours of the Civic Center are featured, including views from the clocktower of the current state of the Mississauga townscape; and, since this is Canada, the water feature in the ceremonial court converts to an ice-rink in winter. The presence of all these activities is somehow spoken for in the interior facades of the Great Hall: looked at as a kind of department store or shopping mall, it is on the austere side, but looked at as the seat of government, it is positively encouraging to citizen participation; it amounts to an assertion of community and urban identity in the face of a formless and unfinished environment. A float bearing the picturesque silhouette of the building was featured in a recent civic parade: one could say that promptings to consumption have been replaced for the time being by promptings to civic order, and that the building by evoking a theater of action poses in succinct form the question of democratic renewal which has been claimed for architecture in the postmodern era.

Strictly, it is the Council Chamber that is the theater of government, and this impression is confirmed within it. In the circular space, the diameter divides the benches of the councilors from the seating reserved for the general public, and while the councilors are certainly treated as actors, and have a very good behind-the-scenes support system, they are not only on show, but accountable to their audience. The sense of theater is reinforced by the paired Tuscan columns that define the edge and support the banded wall that supports the dome. At the time of my visit, a test had just been run on the acoustic performance of an opera singer in this space, with apparently promising results. It has indeed something of the intimacy and voluptuousness of a small opera house, complete with an artistic decoration of the dome itself—skyblue and studded with stars that depict an evening sky over Mississauga, the stars twinkling by means of a miracle of fiber-optics, together with a portrayal of a Native American legend of the Great Bear and the Seven Hunters, which in Native American folklore, explained the changing of the seasons through the progression of a hunt. Remote as this legend may be from the realities of developmental politics, it has something of the calming effect of all mythical art: violence and death have been transformed into unearthly beauty, an encouragement to councilors and partisans alike that, one day, their dogfights may be ennobled.

Each principal space has been decorated by the architects so as to express its function, in social terms that all can understand. The councilors' caucus room is a particularly good example: it repeats motifs similar to those found in the council chamber, but with wood rather than marble, so that the character turns towards club rather than theater. The foyers outside of the council chamber, where the members are lobbied, are comparatively undecorated, and become 'modern' looking by that very comparison, as if to express the informality appropriate to the activity of lobbying, and also to a space that is compositionally to be classed as *poché*. This is very skilful decoration, if that is what it is. By a similar token, the grand staircase, which gives access to the various public offices, is distinctly grander in conception and in finishes than the offices themselves, and these are everywhere decorated, though in simpler materials, using the same family of details that are used in the honorific parts of the building. The impression made by the staircase is due not only to its noble ancestry—*Scala Regia* genre—but to the calculated way that its matte walls are enlivened by narrow bands of polished marble that reflect the light on down from the high skylight above. Economy in the use of marble becomes in itself a means of sensual enticement, and at the same time repeats the themes of the building, with its stone bandings and stone podium, reiterating the sense of identity. The building becomes at every level, inside and out, a representation of a primal meaning, a sort of peoples' palace.

The architects have worked to ensure that all parts of the building fall under a consistent rule of decoration. This has involved the design of special fittings, such as the dished wall lights. It has also involved a judicious choice of materials, like lining the elevators with stainless steel panels that match the standard doors. Some of the door fittings are standard off-the-peg items that were first marketed in the thirties, and the prevailing atmosphere is indeed somewhat thirties, without being exactly imitation Art Deco. The rule of consistency means that even the potted plants, which are ubiquitous, are always large, and always contained in the same jumbo earthenware pots. This limitation prevents them appearing as tat, though presumably smaller and tattier house-plants will make their appearance within individual offices.

It is refreshing, and unusual, to have so much to engage with in the interior of the building. It has been more usual for architects to 'save' their concept on the outside, and abandon the inside to its occupants. Part of this attention to detail must be due to the climate, which in this part of the world is severe enough in winter to make indoor living essential; indeed, the Civic Center is billed in the official brochure under the architects' original competition title: "a building for two seasons." Again, the identity of the Center has been forcibly asserted against the suburban formlessness outside, as much as against threats of snow and ice, proclaiming an inner empire with every confidence that it will be taken up by the people. Those that I talked with took evident pleasure in being in possession of a stylish building.

While this may mean no more than that everyone has been glad to move into a posh new facility, it raises once again the question of popular appeal. This building shows every indication of becoming a popular success. It has been designed to be made sense of, and it does make sense. The decoration of the interior, which joins together in a single character the intentions behind the choice of door handles and light fixtures and architectural moldings seems to come over as something deserving respect. The architects clearly belong to a class of experts who know what they are about, like the special effects people of "The Empire Strikes Back," or the producers of Sade's music videos. Every part of the building has been taken into consideration, and has received its share (a 'proper' share) of the whole. The result is that no space seems left out, and no part seems unloved.

The outside of the building is equally explicit. The prominent cylindrical form of the council chamber clearly honors an institution, while carrying reminiscences of grain silo. The municipal offices are given the autonomy of an office-block, with the culminating silhouette familiar from well-known examples standing free on their own sites in Canadian cities. The clock tower is a clock tower, with suggestions of water-tower. The pedimental mass is a front, with overtones of barn. The parts of the building are not therefore enigmatic in themselves, but seem familiar, although somewhat unexpectedly associated together.

That they belong together, however, seems not in doubt, since the same meticulous attention to materials and detail binds them together into the same loving care as the inside spaces. The bricks were imported from Pennsylvania, chosen not only for their color, texture and large size, but for their freedom from problems of efflorescence. The 'stone' bandings are made of acid-etched pre-cast concrete, which looks exactly like limestone in context. The roofs are of copper, which will one day be a coppery shade of green, and the aluminum trim has been anodized this terminal shade in advance. This is a far cry from the too-easy simulation of fanciful images in plywood or stucco, which we have come to associate with the postmodern. The mode of building is substantial, intended to last, and it seems to be part of its acceptance by the community that the funds to build it were all raised in advance, so that the city is not in debt on account of this investment.

But if the building is perceived as amiable, and if it has succeeded in communicating some idealized sense of its purpose to its users, as it seems to have done, does this make it good architecture?

The critic must remain skeptical about this question. There have been many cases where a building has found acceptance in its time, and been rejected by a wider public. The sense of the satisfied user is part of a good situation that makes everybody concerned happy; responsibilities have been fulfilled, the architects are looking for another opportunity and another client. But the judgement of architecture seems to call for another kind of assessment. By this I do not mean the moral judgement that asks only one question: does this building serve society as it is? This judgement seems to collapse at once into a moral condemnation of the building along with the society that it manifestly serves: if the society is corrupt, how can the building be otherwise?

If the building finds a ready response in its public, this can mean only that it shares an ideological position with its public. In this case, the shared attitudes must certainly include the expectation that through the operation of capitalist economics and the opportunities for profit that real estate development offers town and business alike, the hinterland will grow as rapidly as possible so that the Civic Center really will find itself the center of a dense urban scene, at which point the wide expanse of its ceremonial plaza will take on a quite different value, just as will the cheek-by-jowl placement of the office block, reception wing and council chamber. Clearly the building was designed in that expectation, and can only reach its fulfillment when those conditions have been realized. These conditions were not imposed by the architects, they were explicit in the competition brief, prepared with the advice of George Baird. Any number of the competition entries were designed to this brief, and several might have gained as much success as did the winners in achieving its goals. To be able to decide if this is a case of good architecture, we need to turn to something outside of development policies, social acclaim, professional competence, ideological convenience. We need to refer to the condition of architecture, and ask how this building affects that.

There seems no doubt that the building has communicated a character, and that it has succeeded in this by means of a skilful rhetoric, making allusions not only to the familiar silhouettes of agricultural elements, or city elements, but to a generation of buildings that were loved and accepted for their details, like thirties cinemas and town halls. It is the density of allusions thrown off that enables people to place it into their conceptual maps, and so to place themselves in it. But this play of allusions extends also into a less popular realm, where it engages with architectural theory. The division into separate elements, for instance, is a reaction against the packaging of buildings into a single bland box. Not only does this disaggregation reduce the scale, but it allows the architect to re-enter the field of composition, as has been ably demonstrated on many occasions by Leon Krier and his followers. It has been pointed out that the pedimental 'barn' at Mississauga could be derived from the pedimental gateway at the entry to Krier's school, in the project for a school at St. Quentin-en-Yvelines. It also has a relation to the narrow *barre* building which has figured in many constructivist and neoconstructivist compositions, the fundamental type which has cells strung on a single corridor because they are all entitled, in a rational and egalitarian world, to the same orientation. More exactly, since such a form establishes a decisive front, it brings us back to Le Corbusier's exploration of frontage zones as if they were canvases against which cubist volumes could be placed in play, in front, as in the case of the Salvation Army Hostel in Paris, or above, as in the Unité at Marseilles. The play of office tower, clock tower, and cylindrical tower, above the barn-like silhouette of the pedimental block makes a clear reference to this idea of composition, and this is something different from simple character reference, in that it brings into consideration the means of assemblage, the very basis of abstract art.

Equally, one can concede that the cylindrical mass of the Council Chamber has more to do with Asplund, and Nordic classicism, than with grain silos, however convenient that association may be in this case. In a wider sense that interest is strong today, as architects test their hold on classical antecedents by comparison with other societies for whom it was exotic. But the form also has a fascination because it is such a strong plan figure that it raises immediately the age-old question of *poché*, the means by which, outside of it, the architect can modulate back to the dominant orthogonal system of spaces. Here, as we have noticed, the *poché* space is given the positive value of lobby—a place for lobbying—which makes it functionally useful, not just a lost zone for closets and service stairs. This is a highly significant trait, for it shows that the architects are in the business of trying to restore *poché* as a useful principle of planning, allowing them to employ a hierarchical set of spaces without returning all the way to traditional plan making. A further instance of this occurs in the various uses made of the volumes immediately behind the pedimental wall: these are sometimes significant spaces, such as the Chief Planner's office, and sometimes not, suggesting an ambiguity as to whether this is a *barre* block or a frontage wall, that is, whether it acts as a separate spatial element or as a screen which relates to the composition as a whole. This ambiguity may be found throughout as a mode of questioning the space of decision which lies between abstraction and concretion, and which lies also between the use of forms that are known and bear meaning, and the syntactical mode of setting these forms together to generate new meanings.

It is not enough to characterize this architecture as contextualism, or regionalism, because to be contextual and regional is part of the duty that is laid on every architect who wants to do a good job. Clearly, an architecture limited only to making associational allusions ends up in Disney's empire. To be anything more, architecture has to place itself inside its own tradition, which is to question the value to architecture of the discoveries of the day, such as abstraction (we should perhaps refer to it as "abstraction"). And, in particular, to test the traditional modes of operation, to see if they are still valid; composition being the most important of these.

It is the nature of these concerns which makes this building of particular interest to critical theory. It projects a point of view which is as antipathetic to postmodern kitsch as it is to negative dialectic, and other forms of protest. The one reduces architecture to consumption, the other rejects architecture in order to reject consumption. Such judgements are satisfactory only to those who wish to remove architecture from its position as discourse.

Originally published in *Architectural Design*, Vol. 58 No. 1/2, London 1988.

13   PERFORMING ARTS CENTER, CORNELL UNIVERSITY: ITHACA, NEW YORK
James Stirling Michael Wilford & Associates, 1989.

PERFORMING ARTS CENTER, CORNELL UNIVERSITY

ARCHITECTS: STIRLING AND WILFORD

On the Opening Day, the Architect related how he had overheard a family group in the café across the street: after a prolonged inspection of the new building from this vantage point, the man finally said "Well, I guess it's some sort of Florentine rip-off"—which the Architect took to be some sort of compliment. It certainly was a more than reasonable response from a member of the lay public.

At this point College Avenue is the main thoroughfare leading towards the University. The Center is the last building on your left as you move out across the bridge over Cayuga Gorge, leaving behind the College Town area of Ithaca. The site thus has two frontages: to the street, and to the gorge. They are carefully separated by a free-standing octagonal pavilion, which masks their junction, and marks the end of Town. The other two faces of the Center are close to the sides or backs of existing buildings—the Architect refers to them as, simply, "backsides," and they indicate that the building is contextually sewn into its surroundings.

Because of the prominence of the octagon, and the building being otherwise set back from the street, we have the effect of a little piazza (fig. 13), to the character of which the adjoining building on the left— a nineteenth century brick warehouse, now an apartment building, makes a significant contribution, so there is altogether a townscape feeling about the way the Center impacts on the street— and the Architect made no bones about referring to it himself as "this Italianate hill village."

The Center does indeed look Italianate, even Florentine, from its aspect to the piazza. From the depth of the building, but tall enough to be visible from the street, appears a slim tower—clearly a campanile rather than a spire. The octagonal pavilion has a distinctly Pisan feel to it, and the main gable facing the street seems to have all the characteristics of a fifteenth-century Florentine church, except the doors. Where the doors might be expected, we have instead a pergola, similar to the one at the Tate Gallery, offering relaxation rather than redemption, and turning us off gently to the right, where the porch beckons.

On closer examination, nothing turns out to be quite what it seems. There is no tall nave behind that there ecclesiastical facade, but a tightly stacked section consisting of a four-square experimental theater surmounted by a dance studio—two substantial working spaces of a very demanding program; the octagonal pavilion is neither chapel nor baptistery, but harbors a bus shelter, surmounted by a pair of easy-access agency offices; and the campanile contains no bells, but houses the elevator shaft. So, the picturesque Italian hill village which we see is not at all a fact of life, but a mental image. It is projected from elements whose reality is not historical, but contemporary; not diachronic, but synchronic; not the result of purely scenographic cunning, still less of the whimsical simulation of a fictional history, but of a precise organizational structure. Not a semantic dream, but a syntactic coup.

To understand how this combination of fact and fiction has come about is to appreciate the Stirling cunning in action.

There is one element that does more to clinch the scheme than any other: the loggia. The loggia is supremely important both as townscape and as composition. It reconciles the fiction of appearance and the facts of organization. The loggia leads a double life. At the physical level, it acts as the primary means of circulation, funnelling movement from both ends to the center. But it also acts at the fictional level as a representational facade, conjoining the classical, the romantic and the modern in a single architectural entity of great power and grace.

From the far side of the gorge, where you are on the edge of the campus, the loggia spreads out with civic majesty, embracing the natural scene (which is stupendous), asserting its allegiance to the University and its ideal of rational discourse. Although its extension is strictly linear, its terminations turn their roofs as if to adumbrate an act of enclosure, as if to suggest the possibility of a courtyard. But a courtyard would be out of place above the raging waters of the

Cayuga River. Nevertheless the gesture is there. Its existence is made explicit for us if we recognize its kinship with the loggia projected for the Library at Latina, where a very similar structure returns at either end for a full two bays. At Cornell, the curtailment of this return, which shows only through the exposed section of the roof structure, is both reticent and incisive, and demonstrates not only a sensitivity to the particularity of place but a more unusual capability of generating form by means of playful mutilation. One is aware also of a lurking histrionics, the opposite of tasteful modesty, reminiscent of the downright cheeky way in which the Florey building opens its courtyard in the direction of Queens College and engages the dreaming spires of Oxford in a somewhat more muscular embrace. The Center, by the spread of its principal facade, turns its face towards the campus of which it is a part. The campanile underlines this allegiance not only by resembling other towers on campus, but by nailing the Center bang on center, emphasizing the formality of the axis it marks and the unity of its composition.

The river facade has other interesting properties. It is not just a row of Tuscan columns. There are naked cruciform steel columns, emerging from, or superimposed upon, robust square masonry bases. The facade as a whole is thus divided into two horizontal bands, corresponding to the two stories of the accommodation behind, and also to the sectional disposition, where the lower half of the loggia is partly enclosed by an all-weather glazed passage, and the upper half is punctuated by occasional windows of the mezzanine offices. This complexity of the loggia gives it a role of representing the building it fronts, rather than being a mere application of a standard columnar form. It speaks for the inhabitation of the building, giving it something of the substance of a cellular structure rather than the emptiness of a portico. And this elaboration of the form allows the simpler cylindrical columns which mark the terminal bays to take on a smoother and more dynamic aspect: they suggest the ideal condition to which the loggia presumably aspires, and thus constitute porches to the portico. Where the loggia impinges on the entrance piazza, the contingent slope of the roof is concealed, and the porch takes on the significance of a formal gateway, attracting the motion of entrance from the wider space of the piazza. The role of the detached octagonal pavilion is both to contain the space of the piazza, and mark the end of town, and to separate the two principal facades, so that an element of surprise can attach to the porch perceived as a fragment.

The double role of the loggia may be seen as displaying the fundamental dialectic at work in Stirling's method. It reconciles the needs of civic fiction and functional fact. The two are not merely added to each other, but intimately bound together, each absorbing part of the other. The all-weather lobby occupies just under half the width of the loggia, but only about a sixth by volume: its intrusion into the primary space of the loggia represents a diminishment of its civic aura, but not the loss of the space. We may construe the dialectic from either side with impunity: the practicality of the all-weather lobby is ennobled by its share in the civic symbol; the symbol is not vacuous, but energized by its acceptance of the circulation system. One thinks here of the ready way in which Stirling accepted the need for a public footpath through the Staatsgalerie at Stuttgart: it shares in the central courtyard without destroying its formal significance: the empty center, with its echoes of Schinkel, is re-invigorated by the passage of many feet. One senses something else: the need to identify a public presence through the traces of its movement. This was a need of heroic modernism in the days when function was the only acceptable source of form, as exemplified for all time by the ramp at the Villa Savoie, and there is a sense in which this remains an essential premise for Stirling, whatever subtleties may follow.

At Cornell, the ramps and stairs are not only necessary, but are made to be formally significant. Pedestrians arriving from the car park at rear are inducted into the loggia by way of the helical staircase at the far end, arriving bemused and slightly surprised by their sudden ennoblement. The pedestrians arriving at the piazza are sucked in by the open bay of the porch and set on route by a straight stair pointed at the open loggia, along which they must proceed to the center before finding the entrance doors. There is a more immediate single door, suitable for wheel-chair users, which leads directly into the air-conditioned zone of the lobby, where the drop in level is accommodated by a series of ramps, conducting again to the two central bays that form the foyer. Each route is appropriate to its users, but without realizing it they are made to dance to the music of time, embodied in the precise formulation of the functionality involved. There is a formal symmetry of the two terminal bays of the loggia, tempered by the exact differentiation of the functional needs as they occur. It must be admitted too that in all three cases the visitor is ushered into the central space of the building in a sidelong manner, without being able to appreciate its full formal splendor. It is only at the interval when the central doors to the loggia can act like French doors to a terrace, that we come fully into possession of the grander space of the loggia. So there is a functional compression of the plan within the formal *parti*.

It is tempting to see the source of this dialectic in the work of Le Corbusier, above all. His loggia to the Parliament building at Chandigarh is similarly detached from the bulk behind it, thus imposing a civic unity upon a functionally varied interior. The form of that loggia is also complex, in order to embody within itself the conflict between the ideal and the contingent. The regular bays of the loggia represent the Cartesian space of the free plan grid behind it; but the heavy piers and organicist canopy speak for the empirically displaced and moonstruck auditorium. Le Corbusier's rendering of this dialectic is essentially given to us in terms of human predispositions and conflicts: "A man is a brain and a heart, reason and passion . . ."

I believe this drive to pressure function and form reciprocally is the primary source of Stirling's power. Compared to this the fictions projected in hi-tech and the facts ignored in revivalism are deprived of substance, and the result in those cases is one-sided and lacking in credibility.

The presence of this drive in Stirling's approach to architecture may be gauged at every level, including that of the details. Thus, the masonry of the exterior surfaces is clipped to the facades without mortar, allowing rain water to drain away out of sight. This indicates an acceptance of the realities of modern construction methods and economics, where walls are no longer 'stood,' but 'hung.' Yet we are still allowed the satisfaction of a stone building, of horizontal stripes, of Italian reminiscence, to shore up the necessary fragments against our ruin. (There is an additional satisfaction that the stone here is of local provision, from Vermont). The dialectic allows the two aspects of dream and reality to be held in balance, and by a profound rhetorical interplay, to reinforce each other.

The disposition of the interior also bears the marks of this conflict, and again shows an extreme compression of form and function. The accommodation consists for the most part of large performance spaces, and they are compacted together in order to fulfill the demands of the program on a difficult site. Not only is there a full proscenium theater, but two experimental theaters, a dance performance space, other studios, a small cinema, rehearsal halls, class-rooms, offices and a foyer. Getting all of this together is an achievement, not only within a tight site, but also within a tight budget. ($168 million works out at $148 per square foot). The spaces had to be stacked vertically, and the placement of the single elevator at the formal center is crucial, giving a dumbbell configuration to the circulation. In this respect the elevator shaft's prominence externally is proper, though the strict symmetry and the Italianate character are added ingredients. It is then a matter of expedience that the proscenium theater does not fit into this scheme. The heavy bulk of the fly tower could only be handled at the rear of the site (where the architect had hoped at one time to enliven it with a mural of the view of the campus which it blocks). So the theater is frontalized to the loggia and to the gorge, and the enclosed lobby is pressed into service as a set of ramps, distributing half the audience to the farther side of it, balancing the ramps in the direct access from the piazza on the other side. Thus, again, the contingencies of the planning are forced up against the formal *parti* in a surprisingly intimate way. Stirling has been characterized as a neoclassical architect, but he takes liberties with axis and symmetry the way a rock musician takes liberties with the demands of tonal progression.

Let it be said, however, that the enforced intimacy is perfectly acceptable in this context. The foyer, which looks too small on plan, accommodated a full audience on Opening Day in spite of being encumbered with half a dozen dining tables. As we have so frequently found in any number of old London theaters, compression helps conversation.

The compression is a success of the syntax, not a fault in it. And there are individual moments of great generosity. For instance, the dance studio is transformed by the jutting bay window, with its invitation for drama to spill over into public view. Formally this window is also a compensation for the lack of church doors in the gable fronting the piazza. Again, the foyer-*cum*-entrance lobby has a distinct physiognomic character, due to the way the space rises up against the inner wall above the mezzanine foyer: it seems to speak for the mystery of the performers. Finally, the proscenium theater is a veritable miniature opera house, beautifully proportioned and intimate in feeling. One would like to hear Mozart performed there. The swelling mushroom capitals are graceful, but sufficiently industrial in derivation to combine with the lighting gantries which run between them. There is compaction of form and function, but done with such confidence that one receives it not as conflict, but as balance.

By this balance, we may find both irony and solace. The work is indubitably of our times, yet what it does to retrieve our cultural heritage is not timid, but bold and audacious, putting the symbols at our service. That is why we may be grateful, and be willing to suspend disbelief.

At Cornell, irony and solace are held in a wonderful balance. The jokes are not at anyone's expense. The perception of an Italianate village is not inappropriate in a university town. The result is a building that is both accommodating and edifying. It seems comfortably scaled to the community that will use it, and the interaction of Town and Gown in that community echoes the mixed ideality and reality of its dialectic. Of all Stirling and Wilford's post-Stuttgart work, it seems to be the most lyrically suspended between gaiety and grandeur, between the demands of form and function. If it is postmodern, that is because it recognizes the play of rhetoric in the revelation of truth: but in architecture, there can be no truth that betrays function. There is no betrayal here.

Originally published in *The Architectural Review*, September 1989.

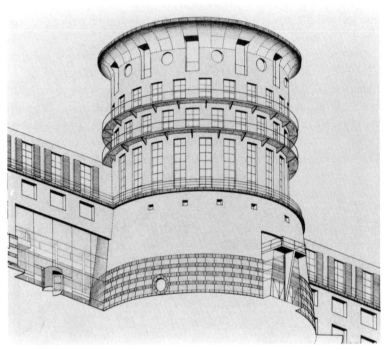

14   MUSIC ACADEMY (AXONOMETRIC DRAWING OF TOWER): STUTTGART, GERMANY
James Stirling Michael Wilford & Associates, 1990.

MUSIC ACADEMY AND DANCE THEATER, STUTTGART

ARCHITECTS: STIRLING AND WILFORD

Stirling and Wilford are to build another slice of Stuttgart, close to their renowned Staatsgalerie. The new phase of construction comprises a music academy and dance theater. It is sited beyond Eugenstrasse, the road which runs at right angles to the Staatsgalerie to the front of the Staatstheater (opera house) and which thus divides and unites the two schemes. Eugenstrasse will be blocked off and up-graded to a pedestrian zone with trees and paving, making a green sequence extending from the Galathea fountain on the hill behind the Staatsgalerie to a new civic square in front of the opera house.

As befits its function, the treatment of this square will be broadly neutral and civic. In contrast, the courtyard at the heart of the next phase will see a resumption of the tense formal dialectic that marks the external spaces of the Staatsgalerie. The two projects are intentionally connected both formally, in terms of the integration of volumes, and informally, through the civic meanings associated with them.

The Staatsgalerie has been an enormously popular building—with the public (especially young people) and with architectural critics. As one of those who had not seen the building when it opened I had maintained some reservations. The plan with its central open rotunda presented a powerful figure, and the reference to Schinkel's Altes Museum, albeit in terms of a roofless void, seemed both apposite and witty. By allowing the general public to traverse this space on its way to somewhere else, the architect defused any incipient academicism—indeed cocked a democratic snook at the ponderousness of institutions. But in strict architectural terms wasn't this a bit of a throwaway, like a rock band including a passage from *Eine Kleine Nachtmusik*? And weren't those steel joist porches frankly appliqué?

All these doubts fade away on inspection. Rather than a collection of episodes amiably connected to an ambulatory narrative, it was the unity of the whole that made sense. What impressed was the totality of the main figure—not the rotunda as a 'mere' quotation, but the strict and necessary combination of circular rotunda and rectangular sculpture court. This tight relationship dispels any sense of episodic denouement and focuses attention on the main axis. The open-sided sculpture court allows the galleries to embrace the rotunda, but also to acknowledge the wider civic space that extends across the town park. The sculpture court is effectively split in two by the rotunda, but also drawn together by the pull of the views down into the drum. A kind of inner-city density results, as if the rotunda were part of an underground system (indeed the pedestrian way it contains is part of a city-wide network). The tight relation of the elements of the principal figure is given firm expression at the point where the coved cornice of the gallery block draws back to accommodate the bulge of the rotunda—a moment of exactitude that is both abstract and erotic in the sheer pleasure it gives.

This sculpture court is not a lost realm, as I had wrongly supposed, but a place of orientation and meditation well suited to its role as final destination for the gallery visitor. By returning us to the wider view it reminds us of the city and our place in it. It provides a sense of identity and a consolation. The coved cornice suggests intimacy, with the proportions of vertical to curved surface exactly calculated to produce this effect. With the generously spaced French doors allowing easy egress from the galleries, it is like the garden side of a princely house, a kind of winter palace of great charm and humanity. This effect is enhanced by the lushness of the creeper-covered surfaces: the greenery (flaming red in autumn) provides a sort of descant on the main theme through the play of vegetation, with the wall creeper nodding to the bushes growing on the rim of the rotunda. The reference to Piranesi and the power of ruins is delicate but definite. As with the 'joke' air vents to the parking podium, formed apparently casually by throwing out a few courses of masonry, we are in the realm not so much of witticism as premonitory warning.

In the music academy and dance theater we again find a game plan which involves the relations of circle and rectangle. There is a symmetry at work behind the apparent diversity of form. Corresponding to the spatial figure of the rotunda and sculpture court is the play between the cylindrical tower of the music academy and its forecourt. The entrance to the concert hall is in the base of the tower, on axis. Further forward, the entrance to the theater academy side-steps towards center to nudge the axis without occupying it. This imparts a diagonal bias to the space which is given meaning by the presence of another pedestrian way that emerges from a slot in Eugenstrasse, winding out between the curves of the amphitheater and the music tower to dissipate towards the general building podium and the pedestrian bridge into the park. As with the pedestrian ramp within the rotunda, the asymmetry which models the pedestrian movement through the site is set against the strict frontality of the buildings and their entrances. The entrance block of the dance theater obscures half the tower base (in elevation at least) and nudges the axis in just the way that the accordion window marking the main entrance to the Staatsgalerie nudges the central axis of the main rotunda. The positive volume of the music tower thus corresponds to the negative volume of the rotunda. According to Stirling the correspondence will be evident to a pedestrian ascending the rotunda ramp, for at a certain point the cylinder of the tower will exactly match the hollow cylinder of the rotunda. Thus both schemes are committed to the game of formality and informality, using the elements of axial stasis and diagonal movement to generate a dynamic balance.

The off-setting of a generally classical framework against a functionally justified intrusion or distortion amounts in Stirling's work to a settled approach to design. It compares with and, I believe, derives from a distinct dialectical tension in Le Corbusier, which he himself described as the balancing of logic and contingency, reason and impulse, brain and heart. In Le Corbusier there is often a similar contrast of formal and informal: for example in the Villa Savoie, where the central ramp, though affirming the axis, operates through asymmetry at the point where it emerges to open air, and is offset and subverted by the more efficient 'pedestrian way'—the dog-leg staircase placed at one side.

The urbanistic scale of the Stuttgart project gives this dialectical character in Stirling's work a new significance, for it suggests a route towards the renewal of public architecture. It offers an unusually relaxed architecture that is not straining to reopen basic questions, but that can play ball quietly with public convention and existing civic values without becoming subservient. As part of this settlement, we can attach significance to the contrast between the tense dialectic which animates the external spaces within each phase of the development and the relative calm that attaches to the central garden formed between the two phases, where civic values predominate.

This calm will be evident when a treasured public monument—the Schicksalsbrunnen, or Fountain of Destiny—is re-sited here on the axis of Eugenstrasse at the point where the pedestrian way emerges into a wider space. This fountain was designed in 1914 by Earl August Donndorf and was formerly located on the same axis, but behind the Grosse Haus. Destiny broods in typical art nouveau fashion over a basin terminating in two sculptural groups, each one a couple, although with this nice asymmetry, that in one the man is comforting the woman, while in the other the woman is comforting the man. A new moment defined by a new location will imbue this work with meaning for a new age.

No one would think of Stirling as anyone's tame architect: his image has always been tinged with cheekiness, a Lucky Jim from a redbrick university rather than an establishment figure. This independence of mind is clearly part of his creative stance. It seems that he has now found a way to combine his raw creativeness with a forbearance which can accept contingency that is not in itself the source of new form, but that can become so in a more limited way as accommodation with the status quo. So the theater garden at the bottom of Eugenstrasse, defined by Stirling elevations on three sides, its frontality sharpened by a typical pergola across the inner face, is clearly Stirling, but it is modified to accommodate the presence across the road of the Staatstheater as a valued part of Stuttgart's civic inheritance. Even more surprising perhaps is the readiness to accommodate the Landtag building at the southern extremity of the new development, which is admitted as the volume defining the 'other' side of the forecourt of the music tower.

This accommodation with the existing city was never ruled out at the Staatsgalerie. The elevational division into two zones—surfaces faced in stone and surfaces faced in stucco—was clearly a way to accommodate urbanistic convention as well as save money on finishes. The facades of the Staatsgalerie to Urbanstrasse, across the back of the site, are much lower in key and more accommodating to the scale of a narrow street than the heroic front—notwithstanding the massive and cheeky air extracts along the rear walls of the galleries.

The extension of this (back) street facade throughout the length of new construction presented a problem of urban design which Stirling has solved through a kind of forbearance. There will be quite a lot of new building, but the existing buildings close to the junction with Eugenstrasse will be retained to provide some genuine urban variety, and the long new facade will terminate in a pavilion intended to reflect the typology of these urban units. Urbanstrasse will be enhanced, not destroyed, by the impact of the new. More of the 'appliquéd' steel porches will come with the new facades, to mark entrances of varied degrees of importance. The architecture is no less playful than in the main elevations, but seems here more episodic, as befits a street architecture. Already this accommodation is evident in part of the Staatsgalerie that faces on Eugenstrasse: an existing bay window is reflected in a new high-level projection that affirms a certain representational duty while becoming part of a more abstract play with forms. There is a real fascination here in observing how Stirling can make such accommodations without engendering any sense of pastiche.

It is understandable how the president and council of the state of Baden-Wurttemberg could decide to commission their architect for this new development directly, without the architectural competition that is the more usual means of public patronage. They wanted some grandeur, but they also wanted a fair bit of street. The State clearly has confidence in the ability of the architect to deliver both fireworks and street lamps. Underlying this confidence is the recognition that Stirling is an architect who can deal even-handedly with creative upsurge and diurnal flow: to accept his work does not mean surrendering to either an unknown technological future or to a facsimile of the past.

And what of the music tower itself? Clearly it is the crux of the development, not only as the completion of the figure of the main formal theme of circle within rectangle, but also because of its own extraordinary character. For a long time Stirling has been looking for an opportunity to design a cylindrical tower. It is a form that occurs again and again in his projects, along with other elements of a repertoire that is practically a primer of basic architectural types: the loggia, the prism, the cube, the cylinder.

At the music academy the abstraction of the basic shape is clothed with an array of motifs that refer both to the development of Stirling's architectural language and to their present situation. The vertical windows and the coved cornice refer directly to the sculpture court of the Staatsgalerie, while the general proportions of the tower are carefully related to the landscape of urban Stuttgart, which is already marked by a number of 'stubby' towers. So the new tower will not only complete the counterpoint of the figures in the extended scheme, it will also send a message out to the city as a whole, a message of confidence and renewal. We may well come to see Stirling as the architect of Stuttgart.

As to the way in which the openings at the top of the tower meld into the curve of the cornice: that too is accommodation, but it is also a stroke of genius (fig. 14). It imbues the tower with a vague *terribilità*, closer to a turbine-generator housing than a medieval machicolation, but actually like neither. If anything, it suggests the papyrus decoration on ancient Egyptian capitals. As Karl Popper used to insist: whatever the probabilities, the future is, finally, surprising.

Originally published in *Architecture Today*, No. 13, November 1990.

15 VITRA DESIGN MUSEUM: WEIL AM RHEIN, GERMANY
Frank Gehry, 1989.

VITRA DESIGN MUSEUM, WEIL AM RHEIN, GERMANY

INTERNATIONAL FURNITURE MANUFACTURING FACILITY & DESIGN MUSEUM
ARCHITECT: FRANK GEHRY

A short distance out of Basel, on the German side of the frontier, there is to be found a small industrial park consisting, so far, of four factory units. They are simple industrial sheds: three of them neat and orderly, the fourth neat but disorderly. The first three were designed by the English architect Nick Grimshaw, with that straightforward, if somewhat constrained, sense of propriety to which the empiricist tradition has accustomed us. Everything is rationally disposed, clean and properly in place. The small volumes of the service spaces have been placed outside the main volumes, not so much to enliven the outsides as to satisfy an analytical predisposition, an ideological commitment. The fourth shed is just as valid empirically, but its effect is not of neatness but of exuberance. Certainly there has been an intention to enliven the outsides. When the client, Rolf Fehlbaum, came to his fourth unit, he thought of his small but representative collection of furniture, its provenance ranging from nineteenth-century to contemporary, and a library of trade catalogs and other documentation. These required housing, in a museum and small library. Why not combine the Design Museum with the factory, to the benefit of both? With this idea, he approached Frank Gehry. Gehry was interested, but the museum commission was too small in itself to be economically viable for him so far from his home base in Venice, California. The solution was obvious, eventually: Gehry would design the factory as well. So a way was opened for something unusual to happen.

Rolf Fehlbaum is clearly an unusual entrepreneur, a man with an interest in design history and a penchant for modern art. The choice of Gehry proved congenial, and Gehry approached the task with his usual enthusiasm. He visited the site with his friend Claes Oldenburg, who was to provide a central piece of sculpture as a frontispiece to the group. As long-time collaborators, these two respected each other, and were also in a sense rivals. Each regards the other's art—sculpture, architecture—as exclusive yet permeable domains, equally open to imaginative shaping, each essential to the play of scale in large objects. It is hardly surprising, then, that Gehry's proposals took on immediately the goal of providing buildings that work as sculpture, and can combine sculpturally with whatever Oldenburg comes up with in due course.

The fourth factory unit is a rectangle like the other three, of concrete framed structure with a stucco finish and large windows. The stucco finish is important, as providing a neutral backdrop to the museum out in front. The north facade, facing the road, is arranged on two floors, with trucking access below and offices on the mezzanine above, from where they gain a spectacular view of the Swiss alps. The architecture of this production unit, stucco aside, is basically as dumb and ordinary as the Grimshaw units, except that when we come to the front corners, something begins to happen. The service units and entrance canopies are pulled outside the volume, not so much from rational predisposition as to satisfy the curiosity of an inquisitive child. The effect is to prove an enrichment, a kind of ornamentation, of the plain mass of the shed.

Out in front, placed centrally, but approached from the west side access road, is the Design Museum (fig. 15). In itself, it is a not untypical Gehry building in which not only each functional volume, but each and every element, is separately articulated and expressed as part of a sculptural whole. The volumes of stairs, ramps, elevator, entrance canopy, clerestories, and *canons de lumière* are all set in motion to sway against each other in a dance both elephantine and light-footed.

Furthermore, the lateral elements attached to the factory unit, being of similar form, are drawn into the dance. A motion is imparted to the whole group that is all-embracing and all-powerful, pulling us into a new spatial experience. Entirely gone is the classical sense of embellishment, the way the sequence of entrance volumes function at Le Corbusier's Cité de Refuge against the neutral grid behind. Here the backdrop is drawn into the music, there is a resulting ambiguity about what is stage and what is play, and the users, or at least the visitors to the museum, are given a sense of participation. The whole effect is unexpected and playful. Approaching from the road, there is no immediate way of separating front and background elements, so the illusion is given of having a more extensive domain at one's disposal, as if it were a kind of campus. In fact the museum acts as a screen to the mundane arrivals and departures of the furniture vans. But through this *lèger-de-main* the whole complex is set into a swaying and grunting motion that puts the visitor on the alert as to his sobriety. It is remarkable that so much enjoyment is achieved with so little expenditure in building, or in alcohol.

Gehry is known for his economical approach to architecture, for his ability to get the most out of tight budgets, to transform cheap materials by some kind of material magic. He is an iconoclast, a modernist through and through, and he glories in improvisation. Yet what surprises us on looking closely at the drawings is the economy of the architectonic means he employs. Although the ensemble has a cumulative effect which is unexpected and even astonishing, each of the elements, taken separately, is perfectly sane and eminently constructable, in a functional sense. Although Gehry has associated and collaborated with artists, and has the right to consider himself one of them, he doesn't cease to think purely as an architect. If anything, his case proves that architecture based on a hands-on, empirical approach need not be sequestered from the other arts, but shares with them the quality of constituting a medium. It can be playful, and it can carry an emotional charge without insisting on its institutional *gravitas* at every moment. In the right hands, it can speak poetically out of its every-day competence, without falseness and without pretension. What is Gehry's secret?

As we have noted, he is iconoclastic towards the holy cows of architecture, while his approach to clients is provocative and inquisitive, looking out as much for their emotional wants as for their physical needs, on the lookout always for novel angles and fresh ideas. In this he repeats the time-honored formula of the modern architect, who always aspired to see through the trees to the wood, to uncover the soul of the project. Gehry does this however without too much pomp and circumstance, more like a child delving into the bran tub for a prize or a memento. In this respect he is level with the postmodernist who looks out for contextual or historical "references," although with Gehry this quest is more internally directed and psychologically oriented. There is a quality of immediacy, and a sense of play.

It's a quality not that frequently to be found among architects: a little in Le Corbusier, in Niemeyer perhaps, in Libera, in Plecnik, and latterly I suppose in Venturi, definitely in Graves. One does not feel it in architects like Scharoun or Aalto, and in general Mies and Gropius between them imparted to modern architecture such a sense of mission that it seemed irresponsible to think of play other than as a serious task of accommodation ('children's play'). If it's to be found anywhere in the high modern period I would look for it in Hugo Häring, whose buildings, ostensibly issued from functionalist dogma, are actually surprising and childlike. Gehry's secret may be not so much that he has a sense of humor, as that he does not erect barriers between his inner and outer life. Maybe he has a very good shrink.

There is something more. For all his iconoclasm where the sources of high architecture are at issue, Gehry remains nevertheless sensitive to its theory and history. This may be partly a matter of study, partly a matter of instinct, more likely the two interacting with each other. He does not peddle references in the now trite manner of the commercial postmodernists. But he is evidently fully aware of the associations of architectural forms, not just of the inherited repertoire but of the opportunities of applying that repertoire in local situations. Forms are part of a unified continuum of man and nature, where fish and snake are architectonically alive. Forms have evocative natures, they link everything together, they enclose a semiotic potential. They constitute a keyboard that can be played. His sensitivity to context is not a matter of external relations alone, but of an acute sense of drawing boundaries and varying intensity within the work. This amounts to a fluent capacity for framing the action. Sometimes the surroundings will justify idiosyncrasy, as in the suburban hinterland of his native Venice, California where everything is so varied that surprise becomes virtually impossible. Sometimes it's rather a matter of situating his building as a center of action against a backdrop of neutral or nondescript character. Sometimes the project itself must be divided so that one part of it acts as setting for the other, the more active part, as with the administration building in the Loyola Law School. Sometimes it's a matter of very carefully controlling the action so that it occurs in just the right spot, producing the maximum effect for the minimum outlay. Louis Kahn said that for some parts of a building to be really "good," other parts would have to be "bad." What we're talking about here is performance art, the art of achieving effect. Knowing what will "work," in a theatrical sense; the sense of timing (knowing when to pause), and the sense of occasion (knowing when to tell a joke). Gehry out of his understanding and love of theater has found a subtle and powerful way to put architecture into motion. In his awareness of the demands of the moment (the moment to speak, the moment to stay silent) he reveals himself as a master of rhetoric. In his press release for this commission, in his description of the way the corner pieces of the factory and the museum all work together, we find these words:

"A consistent, albeit differentiated, formal vocabulary ties the various pieces together as one moves through and around the buildings."

The play of consistency and differentiation is exactly what creates a system of art, and it is the recognition of a formal vocabulary that guarantees the systemic character of the ensemble. This is an art of composition, in which there are pre-ordained limits set by the artist for himself, which determine the degree of differentiation that is permitted. Clearly, this is no timid artist, and the self-confidence to deal with, and accept, unexpected intrusions is high. But there is also a clear ordering sensibility that judges, in any instance, when the limit has been reached. It allows the inclusion of organic elements (fish shapes), craft processes (boat hulls, carpentry), and manufactured entities (binoculars), provided that, in the last resort, they fit with the general rule, complementing and setting off the more conventional requirements of building a waterproof shell. The intrusive element either "works" or it doesn't. If it "works," it's in!

The claim is sometimes made that Gehry is a "deconstructive" architect. His work certainly has a deconstructive slant, in that it breaks away from convention and questions normalcy. It is unusual, often disquieting. It experiments with the limits of the ugly and the beautiful, and rejoices in intrusions, collisions, rotations and displacements. Of the Wagner residence, which had to follow the slope of the site without touching it, the architect has said: "I wanted it to look like the box was precariously perched on the hillside, almost sliding down." The Wagner house is a combination of rectangular and trapezoid shapes, recalling in some respects the Axonometric

House of Peter Eisenman. However, Gehry's comment reveals a very different attitude from Eisenman's, more sensuous and physical than metaphysical and intellectual. His intention is to disturb normal expectations without tearing the web of sensual fulfillment. However much his forms are tilted, skewed, tortured, distorted, they never lose the sense of where they came from, what they were before incorporation, and so the full recognition of what has been done to them. They retain a minimum of representational function.

For example, in one wall of the Wagner house—a regular parallelobiped that follows the slope—there are two rectangular windows: one is tilted, following the slope; the other remains aligned to the horizontal axis. One suggests the tilt as a normal condition; the other accentuates the tilt as an anomaly. In any case, they act together to squeeze the maximum recognition of the contradiction, to get the most joy out of the event. Similarly, in the Design Museum, the principal rooflight is cruciform in plan but tilted to the vertical in two axes. The act of tilting is thus recognized, but at the same time the identity of the motif is reinforced. In its rectangular identity, its angling is part of the dance of the external solids, but also a reassertion of the classic architectural apex, like a transformed Byzantine crossing. Internally, its tilt acts to disorient the natural light and animate the spaces; but it also acts to unify the two rectangular spaces of the plan, above whose junction it is balanced. The same attitude is evident in so small a detail as the display cases in the 1980 installation for The Avant-Garde in Russia exhibition. These are simple rectangular boxes that have been tilted, almost casually, looking as if they could fall off the ledges on which they are placed.

This preference for identity within unity is more dramatic than is the universal denoument of typical expressionist deconstructionists like Coop Himmelblau. The wish to reassure of identity while submitting the object to unseen forces does not seem to partake of the deconstructionist preference for infection or contamination, or dissolution and dismemberment. It is altogether more robust and confident in a future shared by the architect and his audience.

In Gehry we are always aware of actions and decisions taken, and hence of a moral climate containing those choices, between ugly and beautiful, between bad and good. However complex, his compositions contain a variety of dramatic possibilities. They do not contribute to a universal disengagement nor to an aesthetic of fragments. Paradoxically, they escape altogether the sense of being purely decorative that attaches to deconstructivist works where the invariant destruction produces a homogeneity of effect. In Gehry there are clear distinctions of parts, and their distortions do not presage final disaster, but a fresh accommodation. We are reminded of Robert Venturi's seminal phrase, the architects' duty "to the difficult whole." Gehry's architecture is not apocalyptical, and he leaves us in the land of the living.

Originally published in *OTTAGANO*, February 1990.

16   SAINSBURY WING, NATIONAL GALLERY: LONDON, ENGLAND
Venturi, Scott Brown and Associates, 1985.

SAINSBURY WING, NATIONAL GALLERY, LONDON

ARCHITECTS: VENTURI, SCOTT BROWN AND ASSOCIATES

So much spleen has been vented by various commentators on Robert Venturi and Denise Scott Brown's postmodernist style that the qualities of their buildings, and particularly of their first building in London, have virtually been ignored. What good could there possibly be in the outcome, if the style is wrong to start with? The judgement is supposedly a moral one, but is usually pursued with the fervor of a football fanatic: style is equated with game, and there is an uneasy sense that Venturi is playing cricket and baseball at the same time.

So most critics, it seems, would have felt more comfortable with an unreservedly 'modern' building, identified broadly as being made of glass and metal and having a revolving restaurant on top. This preference is noticeable particularly among cultural mandarins, experts on Italian art or university education. The hi-tech "style," unreservedly of its age, presents no awkward comparisons with masterpieces of previous ages, avoids tangling with issues of authenticity and taste and, like engineering, can be patronized as a matter of cultural indifference. In terms of taste, which is the unspoken name of English criticism, postmodernism is identified with studied irreverence towards the past, and is therefore condemned as essentially vulgar.

Only one voice, that of Martin Pawley, has been raised in defense of the Venturis, and it is significant that, for him, the name is a plural. Robert Venturi's populism is not in doubt, but it was clearly the advent of Denise Scott Brown fresh from the Architectural Association, the Smithsons and the Independent Group, that sparked the change in tone from a scholarly interest in the continuity of architecture (*Complexity and Contradiction*) to excitement about the on-going nature of visual communication (*Learning from Las Vegas*). In architectural terms, at least, the Venturis were clearly meant for each other. Denise has acknowledged this:

> "Our collaboration has worked because we both bring a rule-breaking outlook to aesthetics—we like the same 'ugly' things—and we both think that rule-breaking should be not wilful but based on the demands of reality" [1]

Whatever their current roles, and in spite of her expertise in planning, as she points out with some asperity that she, too, is an architect, it is evident that their collaboration has gained in strength from the need to accommodate two viewpoints, as well as a whole range of polar opposites, such as the recondite and the obvious. In sum their theory—a theory that aims to reconcile architectural order with messy vitality—is squarely aimed at the central problem of combining continuity and change. Architecture is incontrovertibly a social art that has to appeal to a consensus in society if it is not to stand (as it can do) for a minority position. We are therefore to be congratulated that after a long and devious route, the Trustees of the National Gallery have finally found a way to present us with a building that is both serious and populist. It is a building in which one could hope to find that Dame Myra Hess has been persuaded to give an extra lunch-time concert.

To have stated a theory that employs a fundamental dialectic, and to continue to practice it in ways that are demonstrably consistent over a period of some thirty years, is altogether a remarkable achievement, one that should bring them honor, not reprobation. The attempt to bring the inherited qualities of architecture into fresh contact with the on-going realities of life, especially when one considers the sources of their ideas, might have been expected to interest English taste—that taste which, in 1989, Adolf Loos appealed to as offering accommodation with the new forces of life, the direction of convenience and freedom. One of these sources, as Robert Venturi has acknowledged, is the idea of verbal play—the metaphysical poets (John Donne), the New Criticism (Eliot, Cleanth Brooks, Empson). Thus it was a verbal tradition that nurtured his interest in concepts of ambiguity and multiple meaning. Another important source—the strongest modernist influence in his work—is the example of Alvar Aalto—a modernist who never considered it improper to ornament his buildings with fine materials, both outside and in, and whose commitment to the possibilities of his own moment in time has never been in doubt. It is Aalto who provided Venturi with a role model by visualizing an architecture that, starting from functional principles, proceeds by an intuitive incorporation of rule-breaking features—formal inconsistencies, breaks in regularity, and empathetic episodes from everyday convention, like crafted door-handles, decorative light fittings, fancy plywood linings, or whatever.[2] It may be worth recalling that this deliberate mixing of rational and empathetic was a part of Aalto's own theory of architecture:

> "It is significant that even the best rationalist achievements of modern architecture are incomplete in respect of demands . . . that are closest to man and among the needs to which we give emotional name."[3]

> "If we look more closely at the progress of human life, we find that technology is only an aid and not a final and independent phenomenon in itself. Technical functionalism cannot achieve ultimate architecture."[4]

If we turn now to the Sainsbury wing, we can ask: how is the philosophy of reconciliation represented in this work?

Let's start with the interior, the origin of functional form in the modern tradition. Here we find the product of an intense collaboration between architect and curator.

What the curator required was a series of smallish rooms, each one of which could be differentiated and made individual to suit the unique works on display, yet remain consistent enough as part of a series to provide a composite setting for the mainly religious art of the early Renaissance. This Venturi has achieved through a play between three sets of elements: first, the vertical walls, defining room size, with the exact placement of the openings as part of the sense of identity; then, by way of the usually canted planes immediately above the hanging walls, an additional definition of the room as unique or partitioned off in a sequence; then, the clerestory windows, which follow a variety of spacings of mullions and glazing bars, adapted to the size and shape of the rooms. The variations between all these elements ensure that one is always in a system, but always in an individual room as well: another example of Venturi's principle of inclusion, of 'both-and.'

To these forming elements add a consistency of materials and a hierarchy of architectural details around the openings, so managed that in any one view the openings are as likely to appear different as the same. The predominant color—gray—was Venturi's suggestion, but became the curator's choice, with a view to setting off the almost invariable use of gilt in the frames of the pictures and altarpieces. The stone moldings, executed in Italian sandstone, are beautifully crafted, at once precise and sumptuous, and the result is a system which allows each room in turn to become, for the moment, the center of the universe, while prompting a constant interest in the next. It is clear that Neil MacGregor, the Director, is delighted with the outcome of this close collaboration. It is his vision which predominates, but the architect has interpreted that vision with imagination and skill, mixing long vistas with short ones, frequently contriving oblique or slanted views across the gallery ranges which direct the eye to important pictures, and creating a constant sense of expectation through the many variations of room shape and size.

A couple of special points are worth noting: the light is a mixture of artificial light and daylight, precisely controlled by hidden louvers and shutters so that the light level is maintained at the desired level and color. No modern museum is built today without such precision of control, but equally, no modern museum that I have seen makes so little stir about the science of light control. Technology is exploited, but is not permitted to invade the space of contemplation.

Secondly, there is something notable about the uses made of the architectural enrichment employed at the openings. Where the main cross-axis impinges on the enfilades of new rooms, we find pairs of engaged columns set into the reveals, sometimes nearly free-standing, sometimes nearly buried. They are of an order not previously seen in the world (the very concept of "an order" allows us to make this statement) (fig. 16). Vaguely baroque, vaguely romanesque, with bulging base molds that seem to be inherited from the age of Pepin the Bold, these constitute a free invention, in no way a pastiche of the classical. There are also, above the openings, pseudo-arches, formed by the vaulting, which are vaguely Soaneish, but would not be out of place in a Bavarian monastery. As examples of the "classical" these details will offend young fogeys and hi-tech boys alike. What makes this ornamental detail especially apt, aside from its literary quality, is the effect it produces on one's sense of space. The three parallel ranges of gallery follow a line slightly oblique to the axis of the main building. The existence of this angle, which in classical terms is an anomaly, is revealed by the play between the line of the axial space and the architectural details, which are set in normal fashion against their respective walls. The openings alone, without the benefit of the robust projections of the ornament, would not be sufficient to make this clear. The result is that, when we look back along the axis towards the main building, the walls seem to stir and flutter by the almost imperceptible contradiction between their planes and the inclined plane of the axis. It is an entirely novel effect, and one that puts the principle of ornamented detail into conflict with the principle of functionally ordered modern space, enlivening our sense of the twentieth-century vantage point at the intersection of traditions. What is completely absent is the dead-pan Beaux-Arts axiality that kills everything in its path.

As an extension of gallery space, the Sainsbury wing provides continuity along with a clear sense of orientation, identity with difference. It provides a worthy setting for an art that is far from the extroverted exploitation of private emotion that is characteristic of today's art, but that for us depends rather on the recreation of the devotional mood of its religious origins. This it does superbly, virtually cutting us off from the messy vitality that engulfs us. One can see why Venturi thought it would be appropriate to break his own rule and allow an intervention of messy vitality by the window which he proposed to open at the south end of the central enfilade, offering a view down into the foyer and an indirect glimpse of the buses in Trafalgar Square. This was forbidden: from the Director's point of view this would puncture the devotional setting and be a scandal. For Venturi, it is equally a scandal that the architect is not allowed to complete his concept of the experience offered by the building. This episode seems to be the only one where he has been defeated by the conservative view of his clients.

So, in the gallery floor, the curator's vision has prevailed. Thereafter, the ball was handed to Venturi for the completion of all the ancillary spaces which are necessary to enable the public to move from the contemplation of art to the enjoyment of experience. In the lower floors a more populist atmosphere is encouraged, with the addition of all those items which the National Gallery has been unable to provide over past years and that now allow it to move into competition with its rivals at the level of entertainment: a spacious foyer, shop, coatrooms, auditorium, restaurant, together with the new galleries for temporary exhibitions; and above all the social display possible with the dramatic new staircases. I venture to predict that these sites for messy vitality will rejuvenate the National Gallery and make it as popular in the new age as Stirling's fireworks have made the Staatsgalerie in Stuttgart.

The architect has really made something of the two grand staircases, one mounting to the galleries against a fully-glazed wall, one descending to the auditorium by a series of dramatic plunges marked by the purely ornamental moldings. The up staircase is reminiscent of the staircase in Baker House, the Aalto dormitory block in Cambridge on the Charles River. In Venturi's terms, this staircase brings into the interior some sense of civic scale appropriate to the setting adjacent to Trafalgar Square, London Town's meeting-room, to which its strong frontality returns us. But the provision of an internal movement system paralleling a public sidewalk immediately outside (here the alley through towards Leicester Square, open during normal gallery hours) is clearly a theme that Venturi has been exploring for some time: it appears in both of the museums recently completed in the United States—the Laguna Gloria in Texas and the Seattle Art Museum. The adjacency of internal and external circulation is clearly a generator of animation, once defined to me by Colin Rowe as the quintessential source of social enjoyment, an endless spectacle of human foibles. The critic might have expected a more direct connection between this staircase and the street, but Venturi has clearly preferred to develop the dramatic aspects of the view east towards the old building, part of the inflexion imparted to this extension as ancillary to, and a growth from, the main building.

It remains to say a word about the exterior, hitherto the only visible part and the part that has drawn most of the criticism of the building on stylistic grounds. It is really difficult to see this aspect of the building as "essentially vulgar," the inevitable consequences of the adoption of a postmodern style. It is full of contradictions, evidently: the Portland stone south front yields suddenly to the totally glazed elevation facing Wilkins's building, and somewhat less dramatically to the brick walls on the west side. Far from conveying vulgarity, the external sheath is a model of good manners and circumspection, to the point where one might have expected it to be more provoking. For those who can read the signs, however, it is full of provoking moments: the contradiction between the fullness of the ornamental moldings and their sudden cessation repeats the discontinuity between the facades, and reveals the architects' sense of irony, which extends equally to thin facades and fat moldings. Everything in the postmodern age has to be treated as provisional, and at this level the building refers us not to the postmodern style, but to the postmodern condition. The play of Corinthian pilasters adjacent to the main entrance is both from Wilkins and against him; it is contradicted by the stark, unmolded outlines of the main openings below. The enameled-steel Egyptian columns are another ornamental feature introduced to provide relief for the pedestrian in his close view of the building. They make an oblique reference to certain effects used by Greek Thompson, but that is to refer to their origin, not to their evident meaning. In a building that wants to work with a consensus view of architecture there can still be some mysteries of origin and multiple levels of meaning, without compromising the whole, which for the Venturis has always meant the "difficult whole," combining urbanism with the art of architecture, combining the popular and the mysterious in a single entity, whose contradictions mirror the world.

Today it is no longer possible to order a facade entirely with classical pilasters, but one can show appreciation. Yet the pilasters celebrate the inheritance very much in a jazz, or populist mode, rather in the way that the original Beatles songs celebrated madrigals and Elizabethan modality. No one chastised them for their eclecticism, or doubted that they had created something new.

Originally published in *Architecture Today*, June 1991.

NOTES

Denise Scott Brown: "Learning from Brutalism" in *The Independent Group: Postwar Britain and the Aesthetics of Plenty*, ed. David Robbins: M.I.T., 1990.
See Demetrios Porphyrious's view of Aalto's "heterogeneity," not merely personal but also part of a Scandinavian tradition.
Alvar Aalto: Lecture: "Rationalism and Man," 1935.
Alvar Aalto: Lecture: "The Humanizing of Architecture," 1940.

THEORY

ARCHITECTURE AND IDEOLOGY

17   CIVILIA

Photomontage from *The Architectural Review*, June, 1971.

THE FAILURE OF TOWNSCAPE

"Townscape" is a word that has become inseparable from a policy—the policy advocated by the *Architectural Review* more or less continuously since the war.[1] The first appearance of "townscape" was in the issue for December 1949, where the word was used as the title for an article by H. de Cronin Hastings, writing under the pseudonym of Ivor de Wolfe.[2] This long and somewhat convoluted article was a plea for an English visual philosophy founded on the true rock of Sir Uvedale Price, that is, it was a polemic for a national school of picturesque design. In this article the word occurs only once—in the last paragraph—where it is used to introduce the next section of the polemic, called a "Townscape Casebook." Compiled by Gordon Cullen, this was a casebook of examples to illustrate the workings of townscape from precedent rather than from principle (another English specialty).

The sub-joined disclaimers went so far as to describe the article as merely "hinting at a kind of theory" which this missing visual philosophy needed, while the Casebook, according to de Wolfe's introduction, would try "to demonstrate in a purely token way" an application of this theory to town planning as a visual art "termed by Thomas Sharpe 'civic design,' and by the review, I think, townscape."

De Wolfe's tentative use of the word "townscape" suggests that its adoption resulted, in an organic way, from conversations occurring in the lower regions of the *Review*'s premises in Queen Anne's Gate, where another English institution—the pub—had been installed in the basement as an engine of affability to encourage the cultivation of conversational philosophy.

In any event, it would appear that, at the time of going to press, Gordon Cullen was more familiar with the term than de Wolfe, and sufficiently enthusiastic, moreover, to run on happily into wallscape, roofscape and floorscape as extensions of the idea. All of these scapes were offshoots of landscape, defined earlier by de Wolfe as the "field of vision."

De Wolfe's "field of vision" puts an immediate emphasis on the act of perception. It is clear from the context of the article that the act of perception is crucial: it is the essential activity for bringing de Wolfe's proposed visual philosophy to bear on reality; at the same time, it is the means by which the national temperament exerts its characteristic bias for arguing from precedent to principle.

The theory of the picturesque, as adumbrated by de Wolfe, deals in a general way with these various issues. It is based on the assumption that there is a missing science of man that could ultimately explain the laws of behavior exercised in the making of aesthetic judgements. Gordon Cullen's Casebook was based on a similar assumption: that the disembodied eye moves in a not altogether mysterious way its wonders to perform.

The disembodied eye emerges, in the ensuing examples, freed from the cultural baggage of associations which attends any ordinary mortal's view of the world. That is, freed from the associations that blinded the eyes that Le Corbusier condemned as "eyes which do not see," blinding them to the beauty of everyday objects such as grain silos or ships. The disembodied eye acts in another way—the objective way—in which objects are seen as they really are, detached from the web of associations that locks them into the human system. Thus a front door no longer means home, but becomes a rectangle of color. According to Cullen, seen "objectively" and using a concept called the "art of ensemble," the door could fit into an entirely different scheme of things. This was an art in which forms would exert their own modifying influence on our feelings—the argument being that an understanding of this would enable feelings to be understood and brought into play.

Two ideas are thus compounded in Cullen's system: that there are laws of perception to which the objectively seeing eye can be rendered sensitive; and that a knowledge of these laws could be used to stimulate and communicate feelings. Cullen's system—a townscape glossary—is thus a mixture of compositional and psychological effects. Taking the objects in view in an urban setting, this glossary deals both with their physical characteristics and their applications in terms of a psychologically structured analysis. The system is entirely artificial because it denies the complexity of actual perceptions and the extent to which they are governed by cultural and social conditioning. A neater and more strictly coded language is necessary. Thus, in a particular sequence of architectural elements, closed courtyards exert pressure, openings promise release, incidents delay and intricacy intrigues. Thanks to this ascending scale of implications, the civic designer could create drama by the juxtaposition of forms, using his understanding of their regular effects on the eye. A skilful manipulation of form would thus add an enriching psychological aspect to the customary ingredients of normal associative vision.

Such a system would indeed constitute a rhetoric: that is, by orchestrating architectural elements it could cause an extensive, and in some respects insidious, modulation of the individual perception. Recent arguments in semiology have demonstrated the existence of such a rhetoric in the public arts of journalism and the media, particularly in advertising and the creation of consumer markets. It is also to be found, at least in embryo, in the faked historicism of Port Grimaud and the unnaturally harmonious ensembles of shopping malls.

Most people are familiar with the dream voice that accompanies the ad for a well-known bedtime drink, infusing this liquid with a strength far beyond its actual capabilities. The tone of the voice modulates the content of the message—its general dreaminess being associated by the viewer with the image of the steaming cup and the name on the packet. We are so used to examples like this that we discount them: they are almost reassuring in their banality. But a critic like Roland Barthes can justly claim that this very banality is a source of self-deception. Barthes argues that these unconscious perceptions operate in every walk of life, at every level, and that this blindness to our unvoiced assumptions distorts our understanding of society.

So far as I am aware, neither Cullen nor the *Review* have pursued the matter into such levels of theoretical explication as might be applied to the art of landscape, preferring just to accept that the art exists and that sensitivity to it could be cultivated by the few, if not the many.

To be fair, though, de Wolfe was hesitant about an art which he still thought of as an art in embryo, as yet unable to exert its control over the world out there. The landscape as it exists is the product of collision and accident, rather than assembly or collage (to anticipate another argument). It is "a mighty dustbin in which the various humanities, elegances and art lie buried alive." The *Review* had hoped that there was a particular kind of sensitive eye that could exploit irregularities as well as regularities, dissonances as well as assonances, intrusions as well as exclusions, the unexpected as well as the wanted.

The virtue of a philosophy of the picturesque, as expounded by Uvedale Price, lay in the fact that it was not bounded by beauty, but went in search of character. Long before Claude Levi-Strauss's bricolage was proposed as an alternative to engineering, de Wolfe was on to the art of bric-a-brac assembly as the only way to put visual coherence into our "brickish-a-brackish mid-century world of barbed wire . . ." Because our landscape was the product of unhappy accident, the happy accident had to be cultivated.

The strange assortment of objects, styles and characters thrown together by the operation of modern planning techniques are in themselves to become the raw material of the new art: ". . . the principle is that you love them or try to love them instead of trying to hate and rid yourself of them . . . from such assortments the radical planner has to produce his practical surrealist picture." This, for Robert Venturi fans to note, was 1949.

It must by now be evident that the *Review* and its townscape proposal have been dogged all these years by the limited premises of its philosophy. The problems faced by Uvedale Price were quite different from those confronting the *Review.* Price was suffering from a surfeit of harmony produced by Capability Brown's all too successful cult of beauty—hardly an ailment of today's environment. As antidote to his too elegantly regulated world Price introduced an element of irregularity into his designs. His response was limited to the professional world of the landscape designer. This is of an order quite different from the *Review*'s attempt to contain and convert the chaos of consumerism and bureaucracy that is apparent in our everyday landscape.

There is something disarming and at the same time hallucinatory about the *Review*'s advocacy of a policy for improving the quality of the environment, because on the one hand it looked to an inspired surrealism as the main resource of the radical planner and, on the other, hoped to eliminate the destructive effects of commercial and bureaucratic exploitation of the land by raising the level of public taste. This policy is somehow hung on a hope that our national temperament will keep us nicely balanced between idealism and pragmatism; between the false promises of utopia and the unbounded exercise of opportunism; between the uncomfortable dialectic of the superego and the id—with its endless conflict between cultural directives and insensate urges.

During all these years the *Review*'s program has appealed to architects and influenced planning policy: an art of the ensemble which successfully exploits variety and picturesque incongruity has been successfully counterfeited by François Spoerry at Port Grimaud. However the elimination of incongruities and variety has rendered our pedestrianized centers almost entirely odorless and certainly far removed from the spirit of Cullen's personal vision of a lively and varied townscape. As a policy, townscape has failed because it has defined the radical planner as a purely visual man. Whatever the merits of a picturesque eye for making the most of strange conjunctions, it cannot address itself to unwanted irregularities: its juxtapositions must be willed. Surrealism works not just through incongruity, but by suggesting a hidden meaning. The aim of the policy, "the cultivation of significant differences," depends on principles of rigorous selection which may be right for an individual artist but are impossible for a County Planning Officer. "Not any old differences. The significant ones." But the *Review* has steadfastly refused to consider the implications of a theory of signification, with all that implies of the uncovering of the arts of social control.

Civilia (fig. 17), a project previewed in the *Review*'s special issue of June 1971, is an imaginary city where everything is regulated by visual considerations. Taking from Port Grimaud, it is based on a marina over which the city towers and hovers in an entirely hallucinatory way. Tower blocks, service towers, arcades, *pilotis*, walls of giant prefabricated capsules—fragments culled from ten years of images, are picturesquely juxtaposed by the art of graphic collage to suggest a quality of high-density city life based on happy accident. The result is a kind of Welfare State Monte Carlo, a principality in which the act of consumption is celebrated in the name of an anonymous and invisibly dispersed Production, the nature of which is not to be offered for scrutiny. This reduction of architecture to cliché is justified in the introductory philosophy pronounced, as ever, by de

Wolfe. In essence it states that the art of ensemble can bring together the visual appetites of tourist and citizen to make every day a series of occasions for snapshots and living fun. In Civilia, any thought about the division of labor (and all that implies) is presumably anaesthetized by the British sense of fair play.

I suppose it is natural to expect some show of impatience from the editors of an architectural monthly. They exact their revenge for the pretensions of countless architects and create, in camera, a series of *tours de force*—such as the building hung out on its side, or the unexpected appearance in yachting gear of Colin Rowe. Irony there plays its part.

However, since Ivor de Wolfe proposed a picturesque theory of planning, things have gone on getting worse. It seems that to maintain a balance of beauty and incongruity in our landscape was to expect too much of the disembodied eye. Perhaps we are now better able to understand that the disembodied eye is in a highly privileged position; that visual detachment is a technique, not a policy; and that prescriptive casebooks cannot be segregated from social realities. I imagine we are now more aware of the way in which an individual's perceptions occur, and of the social content of the superego and the id—of the you in the me. At any rate, there must be no longer any hope that we could ever succeed in substituting an eye for an I.

Originally published in *Architectural Design*, Vol. XLVI, September 1976, as "An Eye for an I: Failure of the Townscape Tradition."

NOTES

1   The Oxford English Dictionary (1926) cites its first use of 'townscape' as by Lord Gower in 1880; and specifically in the current sense as by Hissey in "Tours in Phaeton:"(1889) "some of the quaint townscapes (to invent another word) of our romantic, unspoiled English towns . . . "

2   Reyner Banham revealed the name behind the pseudonym de Wolfe in his letter arguing that de Wolfe prefigured Colin Rowe's application of bricolage to town planning in "Collage City:" see *Architecural Review*, August 1975.

MANFREDO TAFURI:
THE ROLE OF IDEOLOGY

Architects are very conscious today of living through a period of crisis, not only in terms of the reduction of investment in building, but also in terms of important and perhaps irreversible changes in the conditions of professional practice. Would the return of investment put all to rights again—restore confidence? For some, the problem remains solely at this level. For others there is a residue of guilt to be purged or lived down—guilt for the corruption revealed so recently in British architectural practice, guilt for tower blocks, guilt for urban motorways. Such responses still hover around the issue of public confidence in the profession, as if it were a matter of simply restoring its public image, or locating a fault in the machine.

Some of us feel that it may be a good moment to draw back from the professional attitude and its relatively short history, and place it in a wider perspective; to attempt to gain a deeper understanding of what architecture is and has been in society; and to pay more attention to the history of cities and of society. Some of us feel, in addition, that before a "fresh start" can be proposed it may be salutary to reconsider the limitations of the fresh start.

Few would now maintain that architecture is a closed shop, or that a contract with the client justifies an exclusion of the user. But amid the ensuing rush to include the user and to exhibit at least the image of participation, few have paused to examine the wider uncertainties which surround the definition of a pure professionalism. The historian has long insisted that the architectural product of a given period is molded not only by inescapable social and economic conditions, but also by an accidental element which derives at least in part from the attitudes and discoveries of individuals. This creative element is limited in its scope as it is framed within the prevailing ideology and has to struggle to free itself from all its unrealized assumptions. This is why individuals who are not content with prevailing conditions must band together for mutual reassurance and support. The status quo is not necessarily pernicious in itself. On the whole it functions benignly in perpetuating the global system of beliefs on which society depends for its morale against danger, as much as for its hope for betterment and survival. Beliefs lose conviction in face of the uncertainty of the future, and have to be endlessly renewed. There is a general process of expressing the future now, a process which extends throughout science, philosophy, politics and art: a process from which architecture is not to be excluded.

Our obsession with technical levels of action has blinded architects to the wider dimensions of our political and cultural frameworks. This technicity is itself the expression of a belief in technological progress as a sufficient justification for continued practice. There is a reluctance, especially in England, to even become aware of the indications of the existence of the political and cultural envelopes within which we function.

To do this implies the development of a wider critical method which would take in its compass both the interpretation of history and the construction of a future; an elucidation of what has actually happened and of its problematic in terms of some kind of rational structure for taking action to improve the likely future, or at least avoid disaster.

Unfortunately neither the elucidation of the past nor the construction of a future can be produced by the human animal without introducing some taint of belief. Belief seems to be a necessary part of conviction. It is the effort to achieve an "effective" level of objectivity which makes this task so difficult, and which tends to leave a void at the very point where knowledge should inform action: a void that is all too readily filled by the purely operational techniques of management, with its pseudo-objective standards of efficiency.

The only coherent body of criticism that has laid claim to fill that void is, not surprisingly, the one that has been premised on a complete rejection of society in its present form, that is, the criticism made from the Left. This may be an unpleasant fact for many of us, but it has to be faced. There is too much truth in Marx for us to expect that liberal capitalism could regenerate itself without accepting fundamental changes in the structure of society. To say this is not to imply, however, that utopian Communism has found the solution to the woes of society: on the contrary, it seems to degenerate in practice into a centralized authoritarianism in which criticism and the search for an objective basis for constructing the future become no less difficult. There appears nevertheless to be a distinct opportunity to benefit from the opening of a dialogue with the Marxist position, and this is particularly so in architecture, now that there is a fresh impetus on all sides to define what architecture is and what it does.

There can be little doubt that Manfredo Tafuri has in a very short time established himself as the most interesting architectural critic of the Left. He is the most interesting because he discusses works of architecture, not just as examples of style or invention—of aesthetic or technical innovation as such—but as steps in an absorbing historical process. What he is concerned with, as a Marxist, is the way in which successive works produced within the capitalist framework preserve and perpetuate it against the pressures of economic and social reality. They have done this by projecting the beliefs and assumptions without which capitalist life could not continue; that is, by creating the necessary myths that put the system beyond question. The key to understanding how they operate is to expose how they contribute towards the reinforcement of an ideology of capitalism. This ideology advances as true, natural and irreplaceable a set of values that are in fact false, artificial and arbitrary, and whose whole purpose is to preserve the privileges of the ruling class. Seen in one way, this ideology is a deliberate mask for the exercise of power. Seen in another way, it is a set of illusions by which rulers and ruled alike hope to maintain their beliefs in the rightness of the world to which they were born.

By treating works of architecture from this viewpoint Tafuri elevates them to a position in no way less important than all the other products of intellectual thought or artistic endeavor. Thus, for example, the works of Piranesi become as important for an understanding of the insights of the rationalist enlightenment as are those of Descartes or Diderot. Moreover, Tafuri is concerned with ideas, so that drawings, projects or even verbal descriptions are as potent as built works, and often more so. Even if his analysis tends to show each and every manifestation as no more than overall steps in a process of decline and disintegration, it draws out the anguish and the achievement of each step in turn. The result is to establish the right of architecture to be taken as an integral part of culture, and to dispel any disparagement of it as mere technology or utility. Indeed, insofar as architecture is both a consumer and a symbol of wealth and the means by which land is articulated and partitioned, it qualifies as one of the more important languages by which social relations and aspirations are expressed.

This is a kind of scholarship which is as exhilarating in its impetus as it is cleansing in its action. By evaluating each work in terms of its ideological purport every one is, as it were, rubbed out, eliminated, but not before its essential qualities have been subjected to a ruthless and discerning analysis. Tafuri thus does for architecture very much what Roland Barthes has done for literature, emptying out the ideological contents of each work before putting it back on the shelf.

Perhaps this is the reason why one senses in Tafuri a respect for the essential bases of architecture. Architecture is a medium like any other, capable of powerful expression in the hands of a master. While all, or nearly all, of architectural production since 1750 is in a sense beyond redemption, much of it is admirable, even stupendous, as expression. Tafuri shows the extent of his admiration for works which are clear or pitiless in exhibiting the reality of capitalism, such as Le Corbusier's Obus scheme for Algiers; or which remain, in spite of all, deeply ambiguous and problematic, such as Piranesi's fantastic "reconstructions" of ancient Rome; or, perhaps, most of all, so formally tautological as to appear already emptied of all symbolic intent, such as the work of Aldo Rossi. In Rossi we are confronted with an architecture which seems deliberately to mix the formal language of functional mannerism with archetypical memories in such a way as to neutralize signification itself. This may be seen as constituting the end of the series, the final denial of bourgeois imperialism, and the razing of the *tabula* for the final act of political redemption.

But exhilarating as this process is, and in spite of the insights we gain into the steps by which consciousness is changed, there remains a deficiency in Tafuri. To share his interpretations, we must share his beliefs. If his beliefs appear as dogma, we have to grant the dogma before the meanings he elucidates are clear and unequivocal. If we do not share the dogma, the story becomes too complete. His system is an axiomatic one with all the virtues of extreme clarity and partiality.

Tafuri nowhere discusses the question of how, within Marxism, the dialectical process of history is to be continued, and what will be the relations between ideology, criticism and science; problems which have been occupying Louis Althusser at some length. Nor does he deal satisfactorily with the general problems of cybernetic control in an open system, and with the question of who controls the managers once goals have been defined. We are left to assume that such problems are peculiar to capitalism.

But perhaps more important is the lack of discussion, in Tafuri, of the role and significance of ideology as such. He finds it sufficient that its operations can be detected and unmasked. He seems to be running a course parallel to the Barthes of *Mythologies*, but without analyzing the mode of operation of ideology itself. As Althusser has clearly enunciated, all societies are bound together by ideology, which necessarily extends into every aspect of life, and poses a never-ending problem as to how it can be evaded. Barthes proposes that poetry alone escapes from rhetoric, the latter being identified as the medium of ideology—the "art of persuasion" by which the status quo wins back belief in the face of the unexpected. That poetry in some sense familiarizes us with the unexpected may reduce the validity of Barthes's exception. In its generic aspect as an excess of insight over belief, poetry may occur in any art, even in architecture. So poetry may not be so exceptional. Yet it would appear that potentially scientific objectivity and poetic subjectivity both rely on insights that lie outside of rhetoric, and therefore outside of ideology.

In his suspicion of the apparently endless duplicity of bourgeois ideology, its ability to absorb each and every criticism through its strangely unlimited reserves of liberal confidence, Tafuri has been led to reject the semiological initiative as nothing but another ploy of the old order, another postponement of the final reckoning. Formalism, by its obsession with syntax, devalues the semantic reference, but does not entirely remove it. Even Eisenman's "syntactic architecture," however deliberately abstruse in itself, is open to interpretation as part of a historical sequence. But Tafuri is describing a supra-historical process—a somewhat headlong one—and tends to undervalue that content of every form which is not immediately subsumed under the heading of ideological purpose. He has little to tell us, therefore, of that element which Paul Ricoeur calls the surplus of meaning in a tradition. He has little to say about the unexpended part of architecture, its fundamental qualities as a medium and as a language, and its potential for the future.

But this would be to expect too much. The distillation of a coherent and powerful criticism is a vital step in providing a theoretical base. It helps in the rejection of worn-out attitudes and in the generation of new possibilities. As we have seen, Tafuri combines a condemnation of bourgeois ideology and the impasse of its culture with a positive and even hopeful attitude towards the pragmatic tradition of Dewey and others.[1] He thus paves the way for others to attempt to carry Marxist theory into action. Whether and to what degree Tafuri would underwrite the production of Maurice Culot and of Leon Krier we do not know. But there is little doubt that they have drawn strength from the power of his critical method, particularly in his view of history and tradition as a thread which cannot be broken and which should not be dishonored.

Originally published in *Architectural Design*, Vol. 47, March 1977.

NOTES

[1] His approval of the pragmatic tradition is clearly spelled out in *Teorie e Storia dell' Architettura*, Laterza, 1968 and 1976.

ARCHITECTURE, LANGUAGE, AND PROCESS

THE WORK OF MAURICE CULOT AND LEON KRIER

The debate on the present condition of architecture can be conducted on a number of levels, but in England it seems to center anxiously on the single issue of public confidence. Until this is restored, architects are well advised to keep a low profile and apply the same to their buildings. Context is all. While the architectural philosophers canvass yet again for signs of a new sensitivity to the *genius loci*, individual firms, crying "snap!" claim to have already discovered it—a claim that seems to rest, for the most part, on a liberal use of such devices as pitched roofs, bay windows and indented facades. There is not only a lack of speculation about architectural possibilities, but a sort of horror of any gesture that is not purely empirical in its reference, anything savoring of an interest in ideal form, anything that might revive the image of the architect as a formalist ogre. It is almost as though an interest in form were seen as incompatible with a dedication to people. People, formerly omitted from photographs of new developments as obscuring the brilliance of the design, are now admitted in such numbers as to suggest that we are overpopulated on the scale of a developing country. The swing to an undiscriminating populism may be cynically seen as the ploy of a profession suddenly deprived of willing clients, and the hypocritical layers would no doubt be quickly steamed off by a return of investment. But some degree of cynicism towards at least the sentimental aspects of the popular revival seems entirely called for.

It is a pleasure, then, to review the work of Maurice Culot and of Leon Krier, two innovators who between them define a region of theoretical practice dense with new possibilities. It is not the purpose of this essay to describe and evaluate either contribution in detail, but rather to attempt to show how, between them, they clarify the problems facing architecture, or at least facing the development of an architecture that could encompass the functional, social and ritual requirements of urban living during the next phase of western society.

Both of them start from a perception that architecture is a social object, acquiring its value from acceptance and use. Both enjoy architecture and appreciate the specific benefits that it can confer on social intercourse—not only as an enabling system, but also as a system of expression—a system that in the past has often been a means of confirming, both practically and symbolically, social cohesion and shared values. Both have been led into a radical appraisal of those divisions in society that now appear to block this ideal state of affairs.

These divisions stem from an ingrained assumption on the part of bourgeois society that competition is a law of nature and that society benefits in the long run from a firm opposition of capital and labor; an assumption that does not prevent the growth of bureaucratic rigidity, but that does invite and accentuate the class struggle, with an indefinite prolongation of divisions and waste within the social body. Perhaps it is true that only by this means can Capital dispel attention away from its opportunistic nature and assure a dynamic disequilibrium within which its necessary "opportunities" will continue to arise.[1]

Awareness of these obstacles has apparently led them both into a position of intellectual Marxism, a position that accepts the reality of the class struggle and looks to some kind of social and political revolution as a prerequisite for a healthy society and a return of coherence to the public realm that architecture hopes to articulate. This position sharpens their arguments, but does not seem to conduct them into a dogmatic impasse, in which architecture is rendered silent and impotent during a long twilight, while the slate is wiped clean.

On the contrary, both convey a sense that the revolution is already happening, that the change is as much a revolution in consciousness as a struggle for power, and that architecture, as a tradition that combines and has always combined a theory and a practice, is in a position to contribute decisively. Both, I think, see architecture as not only a reflector of social and economic relations, but as a means of suggesting what those relations should be. By its very coherence and diversity, architecture can enter into the social reality, helping to identify, actualize and confirm the conditions of life.

Both therefore treat architecture seriously as a primary element of production and as a system of articulating the use of land. They also share a serious attention to history, without which no identification could be made, no reality could be constructed, and no future could be assessed.

Where they differ, in the first place, is in the action that they propose in order to demonstrate the importance of architecture as an activator of a socialist future. Whereas Krier sees architecture as an immediate source of ideological values by means of which the new conditions of life may be envisaged, Culot looks rather to its established ideological values as a source of political clarification and confrontation, and hence as the occasion for political action. One sees architecture as a value to be conserved and recuperated; the other as a resource to be expended in the political struggle.

Maurice Culot is Director of the Archives de l'Architecture Moderne in Brussels, an enterprise that he, and some others, founded in 1968. In only a few years it has already build up a valuable collection of books and original drawings. His work on Pompe, Bodson, Sauvage, and others shows him to be a talented historian and critic, and his respect for architectural scholarship and his love of the early buildings of the modern movement are very evident to any who converse with him. Yet at the same time he was a founder member of ARAU—*Atelier de Recherche et de l'Action Urbaines*—an agency dedicated to the task of intervening in city development on the side of the indigenous populations who are threatened with disruption or dispersal.

This formidable combination of scholarship and activism is rare, yet it follows logically from his Marxist beliefs and the idea that history has to be both understood and made. It is a position that sees theory and practice as together indispensable for material progress. The result of this approach is to clarify the extent to which the process of technocratic development and the process of maintaining historical continuity are in confrontation.

It is a curiosity of the Brussels scene that the big developments of the last fifteen years have almost invariably resulted in the insertion of isolated slab blocks into the city fabric. These buildings, some of which have been the product of English finance, are dotted insanely around, wherever sites could be found, but tend to cluster in the area of the Gare du Nord. Their architectural character is uniformly bureaucratic, mechanical and soulless. They introduce a measureless scale that plainly disrupts the existing scale of three-, four- or five-story houses, so that the displacement they effect in terms of loss of dwellings, shops, workshops and local ties of all kinds is accentuated by their character. Small wonder, in a way, that Culot has been able to unite all shades of local opinion and sentiment to resist further incursions and to bring several of the more recent schemes to a full stop.

His method is to demonstrate the true cost of these developments in human terms by putting forward alternative schemes. These counter-proposals make every possible use of architectural thought and ingenuity to make clear to ordinary people what they stand to lose and what they stand to gain.

In preparing alternative schemes, Culot has employed subtle tactics: aware that the officially sponsored plans invariably involve a degree of grandiosity and the bravura of indefinite growth, with the assumption of a bull market, he has been able to demonstrate that lower, tighter and more traditional forms of development could be more economical, and also more effective in contributing to an overall city plan. Without in any way conniving in an exploitation of real estate, he has been able to show convincingly that the alien proposals were not good value for any except their promoters, quite apart from their disruptive effects on their surroundings. By producing more reasonable alternatives Culot has avoided being accused of being merely obstructive, of wanting to halt all progress. But he has shown how moderate development could be allowed, while at the same time extending and consolidating the existing grain of the city. The way he has done this has brought into focus the possibilities inherent in architecture of staging quite self-consciously an art of city living. Camillo Sitte is being revived and given new tasks.

These alternative schemes are produced in great variety, by the contributions of different individuals or through group efforts, and Culot has never been concerned to define a pure architectural material for his purposes, but is content for it to be hybrid, variable and opportunistic. Its general tendency is to reinforce and intensify the existing street network. Instead of high blocks and wide, windy spaces at the scale of the automobile, he has low chains with spaces layered, filled and enclosed, at the scale of the pedestrian. Because he sees the existing city fabric as a territory over which the local residents have primary rights, he is able to present the advance of business architecture as a straightforward invasion and to expose in the clearest terms the conflict on interest between those who finance building and those who use the city.

The two values become very obvious: the new blocks are wanted in the city mainly for reasons of prestige, to promote a business and to make a presence. The very fact that it is in the city that they must make their appearance shows that it is a place to fight for, and therefore worth fighting for. Then, also, the alternative schemes are all directed towards showing the city as a responsive and joyous environment where life is not only possible but advantageous. City blight may take many forms, but an old and established community is generally full of life. In such areas blight, if it strikes, may well be the result of a deliberate wasting process whose purpose is to pave the way for cheap land acquisition and exploitation. It does not occur when the inhabitants have access to land and buildings and can identify with their quarters as home and workplace, even if they are not owners. Apart from exposing links between changes in ownership and exploitive intentions, Culot's researches are of special interest to architects in showing what aspects of city form are conducive to the formation of group identity and attachment to places.

It is here that paradox enters in. It is easier to change the face of a quarter than to entirely restructure its patterns of ownership and use. The two may go together, or they may not. Many of ARAU's schemes have a certain improvised or theatrical quality. They can involve, for instance, masking views of an existing tower block by judicious infill around a little church,[2] or lining a boring old building with new house fronts.[3] In the latter case the old pattern of individually distinct houses is imitated at a smaller scale. Effectively what is reproduced is a reflection of burgher row houses, with their happy blend of emulation and conformity, such as we find most completely in Amsterdam. As the object of the exercise is not stylistic in intent, but political, style becomes expendable, a means of interesting the consumers. Pastiche and kitsch are treated as weapons lying to hand.

Reproached with this, Culot is unrepentant. Capitalism, after all, has no scruples in using these same weapons. And it is true that in London we have already seen the return of the mansard as a way of pushing up the disposable floor area in conservation areas, or the simulation of old tourist alleys in order to increase the frontage for shops, as in the well-known group in Heath Street alongside Hampstead underground station. And perhaps the most notable of all is that spurious imitation of an entire old town by Francois Spoerry at Port Grimaud, where a fictitious historicity is fabricated as a means of interesting consumers. If these games can be used for commercial purposes, they can equally well be used for social purposes.

As Culot is engaged in an active process of political confrontation, it is not surprising that many of his schemes should have the quality of a provocation, since the invasion of a living quarter by a horde of tower blocks may also be seen as a provocation. This ironical, sometimes satirical and occasionally ribald vein of comment shows up more plainly in the work of students associated with ARAU. But this does not mean that we should dismiss these results as a mere counter-exploitative rhetoric. It has always seemed to me that Spoerry's success at Port Grimaud is a standing reproach to our municipal housing and its unfailingly antiseptic approach. A touch of consumer hedonism and the risk of spreading the bacteria of personalization might make the task of providing homes easier than building houses. At any rate, Culot's alternatives are useful in suggesting what contributions architecture can make towards making a city quarter more livable and more loveable.

If this seems to lead back to a facsimile of bourgeois consumption, and hence merely tends towards a further disintegration of bourgeois society through proliferation, it is hardly reasonable to reproach Culot with this result, which must after all be considered perfectly consonant with the ends of a Marxist activist. The question is posed rather for those of us (if any exist) who still feel that liberal bourgeois society is capable of correcting social injustice and of evolving new mechanisms for control of production and investment that would limit managerial privilege and put a stop to exploitation.

In purely expressive terms this quandary seems to be a simple issue, but of course it is not. It is unlikely that a complete socialist revolution could accommodate a petit-bourgeois heaven and a legitimation of a moderate scale of private consumption. It is difficult to judge the real terms and conditions of life in a country such as Cuba or China, but insofar as their art gives an indication it shows the rhetoric of consumption replaced by the rhetoric of production. The pressure goes into reverse, but the human tendency underneath does not seem to vary so much. The general militancy of communist government, especially in China, is not to be explained solely by the negative pull of market forces at world scale (the forces that at present curb public expenditure in England): the dialectic of cultural revolution and bureaucratic retrenchment wears a more fundamental aspect, the result of an endemic conflict between individual and group—so clearly described by Durkheim—with all the attendant problems of controlling society while animating it. These problems are in my view not solvable by ideology alone, but involve a history and science of human affairs as well as a philosophy of knowledge.

The image of a lived-in architecture, with its aura of bourgeois consumption, that we receive from Maurice Culot's projects must be seen as a purely heuristic device for carrying out a political practice in architecture within the framework of bourgeois society.

To see it only in these terms, however, would be to do Maurice Culot an injustice. There is a genuine curiosity in his program and a willingness to experiment with a variety of forms, that indicate a level of cultural interest going beyond the adventitious. In some of the proposals[4] we see a search for an architecture that is not purely one of consumption, but that proposes a fresh blend of present interest and historical antecedent, and this return of architecture to its historical base seems now the only sane way to advance it and to make progress. As Culot has said: "The Culture-machine doesn't ever turn uselessly when it mixes history into the present."[5]

Mixing history into the present and making a new synthesis is precisely what Leon Krier appears to set out to do. He is not involved in political action, other than by making drawings of a possible architecture. These drawings must speak for him, and if they influence only other architects, they may still have an ineluctable effect on the future of architectural practice. The drawings represent a labor of creative thought and discovery that could justifiably be described as intellectual production. Krier's wish is to establish this activity as legitimate and potent. Instead of aiming to clarify the conditions of consumption, he tries to clarify the relationship between intellectual and material production, again on the premise, on which Marxists rightly insist, that there is no practice without a theory, and no theory without a practice.

If Culot's talent is directed towards social relations and the heroics of confrontation, Krier's lies undoubtedly in a mastery of draughtmanship and the dedicated stoicism of solitary work. Mere drawing would be nothing, though, without the passion that animates it. The drawing can be pitched at different levels of reality: the epigraphs, for example, are both witticisms and mirages, situated in an imaginary realm, but immediate in their effect; while the elaborated perspectives, such as that of the High School at Echternach (1970), are all-embracing in their actuality, with old and new reconstituted together in the same painstaking delineation. But the new proposals are characterized by an ideal configuration, skillfully adapted to local irregularity, but making no secret of their normal intent.

In these more realistic drawings the architecture is not to be seen as totally introspective and empty of social purpose, and this is true in spite of an element of surrealism that comes to the surface from time to time. On the contrary, the aim of the drawings is to define a possible architecture—one that could answer the variety of functions, both practical and poetic, which we recognize readily enough when we encounter them in old cities. The aim is to establish in visual terms the form of a matrix for fresh city life. For the body of his city, Krier would have ordinary city blocks defined by ordinary city streets, the correct dimensioning of these units being itself a key to the opening up of the territory and the regulation of the sizes of building sites and hence of building operations. Mixed uses, working and living, recreation and social ritual—all would be acknowledged as a set of patterns of human behavior, not as abstracted and physically isolated activities.

Krier's approach constitutes a polemic against the over-specialization and functional determinism of modern "urbanism," particularly as defined in the era of CIAM. In that dogma, the universal application of rigid zones, together with an obsessive treatment of buildings as uniquely generated from internal functional pressures regardless of their relation to their surroundings, has been responsible for a total disintegration of city form. A neutral zone of undifferentiated space separates everything and murders both place and occasion.

This philosophy has been taken even further in post-war planning for indeterminacy and indefinite expansion.[6] These tendencies, developed in the Modern Movement as part of an excitement about function and control, have now lost their curative aspect and have delivered to the city the operation as much of bureaucratic regimentation as of business exploitation. From rather different points of view, Culot and Krier join in their defense of the "quarter," the close-knit locus of community life and loyalties.

With Krier, these intentions can be most readily appreciated in his entry for the competition for La Villette. He has gridded the entire area with a hierarchy of streets based on a small block, which could itself be subdivided as required into smaller building plots. Although certain functions are localized—as for example the concentration of industry along the margin of the motorway ring—the important thing is the non-specific mix over the majority of the area.

It is against this matrix that we read the differentiated elements, which consist not only of individual buildings, but also of spaces: *Mairie*, school, hotel and so on, but also (from Krier's own list) piazza, colonnade, arcade, passage, mews, court. Simultaneously, he shapes space as well as building mass, and this combination is particularly stressed in the case of the two spatial elements by which the individual quarters are aggregated into a segment of Paris—the grand boulevard and the park.

I have deliberately come to these elements last because they are the most striking, indeed audacious, from a formal point of view, and tend to monopolize the attention. What we see in this studied formality is a refusal of those strictly functional typologies generally adopted today (as, for example, in Mathias Ungers's gridded systems) and the embracing of a deliberate rhetoric of public events. Along this boulevard both the *Mairie* and the *Square des Congrès* are nodes that combine building and public space into a single entity; while the *Place Centrale*, at the intersection of park and boulevard, is an event simultaneously at the scale of the locality and of Paris as a whole.

The plan, then, is about the definition of place and identity within the matrix of a city. It is against this central purpose that we must read the significance of individual episodes like the *Glacis de l'Industrie*, the *Colline des Vents*, the *Grand Hotel de Babylone*, and other singularities.

By an opposition between episode and background, figures and fields, Krier is creating a systematic web of relations, a syntax of the city, freezing the process of pragmatic development in order to neutralize the diachronic movement and distributing values according to a strict subdivision of the whole in order to display synchronic relations. These relations are not those of an emptied formality, but are dependent on an attribution of social functions, like the "meanings" of the dictionary. By joining together elements that simultaneously activate syntactic and semantic links, he is, effectively, creating a language.

Much nonsense has been talked in recent years about a "language of architecture," for the most part nullified by the failure to understand that the process of signification involves a simultaneous segmenting of the fields of thought and of expression. Instead there is an obsessive insistence that meaning is aggregated from fixed units that are independently accessible to every individual. Krier's synoptic view of a total field and its subdivisions avoids this solipsism.

To project this totality, Krier has nevertheless been forced to undertake quite arbitrary steps in both the diachronic and synchronic dimensions. Paradoxically, in order to give depth and character to his statements and avoid construction of a mere architectural Esperanto, he has had to tie them back to the language of architecture as it is, with all its contingent poignancy and confusion. Normally architect and planner alike face this problem by ignoring it. The planner deals in statistical abstraction which necessarily disembodies the material and destroys all meaningful relations except those established, in abstraction, by the original model and its axioms. The architect takes the general persistence of the "language" for granted, going through it to the particular contents he wishes to define or to modify. Such an injection of isolated content, like the coining of new words or the projection of a personal style, can change the general form of the language only by slight degrees, if at all.

To recognize the vast scope of Krier's intention and ambition is to put the idiosyncrasy of his more singular episodes into perspective. We should not suppose that if he were to undertake an individual building commission he would take the opportunity to build any one of these episodes out of context.[7] We should not take any of the proposals too literally, while recognizing that they are about the world of real possibilities, and not a completely fictitious realm.

In relation to his project for housing at the Royal Mint site, he pointed out that the somewhat grandiloquent colonnaded frontages were thought of as expressing a range of diverse functions, rather than what he regarded as the overspecialized brief for housing alone. What we are meant to see is the potential for generalized public meaning, and to condemn any particular element as an unsatisfactory model for immediate imitation is once again to mistake the trees for the forest.

However, what is especially enjoyable about Krier's world is precisely the extent to which, after all, it escapes from a purely axiomatic and abstract approach, and sets up resonances at many levels, precisely because it recognizes the impossibility of creating meanings outside of our established cultural tradition and its rather agonized history. There are frequent references to previous episodes in the history of architecture, particularly from Le Corbusier, Boullée and Ledoux. He is aware of the history of projecting whole cities as visual models, of the efforts of Sitte, Garnier and Le Corbusier.

It is the combination of rationalism and historical reference that gives his world authority and independence as a statement in that sequence. It does not amount to a mere didactic exercise (though that is what it is) but has a life of its own within the language of our times. He has commented on the form he gives to the *Mairie*, in the scheme for La Villette, that it is a "reflection" on a plan of Ledoux. He thus gives us an indication of how the individual architect, by selecting his models and working on them, may secrete new characters from the insertion of past into present. But this process is work, the product of mental effort, and is not to be confused with the superficial slapping on of "vernacular" emblems so widespread today.

Moreover, in doing this work, he insists on the autonomy of architecture, endlessly in need of renewal as it may be, but not to be deprived of its own essential contents, nor under any absolute compulsion to borrow contents from other disciplines. This means that the fundamental acts of defining space by means of walls, columns, roofs, suddenly take on new life. Familiar elements they may be, but suddenly capable of new juxtapositions and fresh meanings. By this faith in the autonomy of architecture, Krier effectively devalues the whole gamut of purely analogical form generators, from organicist eccentricity through to machine aesthetics and the obsession with the aleatory states of mechanical systems. He opens instead the search for archetypical roots within architecture: a celebration of the art and wit of architecture.

And further on this line we have to accept his frequent use of irony and wit, at the very least as a defense against the boredom of undertaking a daring yet laborious task. The shadows of De Chirico's arcades and of Böcklin's cypress trees fall frequently across the images, charging them sometimes with an apocalyptic intensity—a comment perhaps on the insanity of the technological ratrace—or with a whimsical disclaimer—as in the deliberate confusion of the outlines of statues, lay-figures, people in various period silhouettes, and, quite often, an aghast Jim Stirling in woolly pullover. If we wonder why the animation in the perspectives is provided by cars, airplanes and figures taken from Le Corbusier's twenties drawings, we should ask ourselves how the author could do otherwise than attempt to distance us from these utopian evocations. To have put in the animation in strictly contemporary fashion (as in a Peter Sainsbury of Helmut Jacoby rendering) would be to risk being taken for a mere Letraset technician: although the perspectives are meant to convey an actuality, they are not scenes from everyday life.

Krier and Culot thus come to architecture from almost opposite entrances, but they join within it. For both of them it constitutes a range of social objects and a territory that by its organization reflects the reality of the social order and so creates and confirms meanings. Both see these meanings as inseparable from tradition and history, because both language and the social reality are in a continuity of evolution through time. The terms by which this process could be understood and even managed have still to be discovered. It is a task of enormous complexity, but one which we at least know cannot be expected to be simple. The danger of delivering the task of directing our future to any group of managers or rulers is too evident to need pointing out. But at least we are now aware of the false promises of objectivity by which the Modern Movement was originally dazzled, while noting that the more axiomatic any system is, the more it is open to the methods of operational research. Current difficulties of explaining and correcting our economic situation may be taken as hopeful signs that every part of our culture shares in the complexity and autonomy of language. The hope to somehow manage our future, in the sense of avoiding the worst disasters, does not mean that we are justified in disregarding the historical process or of putting ourselves "outside" it.

Whether or not we share the (to me, touching) belief that the substitution of a Marxist for a bourgeois ideology will instantly transform the social realm and suffuse it with clear meanings, we must be grateful for work that makes such a positive contribution towards clarifying what architecture is and yet can be, and what actions could lead to the unfolding of its potential. The dialectical process of history is unstoppable, but its direction and momentum can only be measured against synthetic statements proposing ideal conditions. As Georg Simmel emphasizes, it is through such "forms" that we measure our progress. The understanding of the nature of the dialectical process is an essential step in the rectifying of some mistakes.

And to recognize the city as a theater of action and of reflection provides the only framework for the uncovering of a practical future for architecture.

Originally published in *Architectural Design*, Vol. 47, No. 3, 1977.

NOTES

1   As, for example, in the current tendency of multinational corporations to invest in agricultural land. See Richard Norton-Taylor: "Why Britain's farmers need a new Domesday Book," *The Guardian*, May 2, 1977.
2   Aménagement du quartier des Brigittines.
3   Rehabilitation of the Rue de Rollebeck.
4   Such as the fifth-year ENSAAV studies of the area of Porte-Louise, Bas de Ville, and of the extension of the Telephone Exchange.
5   Speaking of the Krier/Scolari maquette at the New York Institute of Architecture and Urban Design, in 1976.
6   As in Milt Webber's "The urban place and the non-place realm" in Webber et al: *Explorations into Urban Structure*, Philadelphia, 1964.
7   What he would do in such a case may be partly surmised from his collaboration with James Stirling on the Derby Civic Center Competition.

THE JUDGEMENT OF IDEOLOGY

Demetrios Porphyrios, in his formidable discourse, has demonstrated the futility of heterotopia, of *lebensphilosophie*, of typologies, of metaphor, in their quest of recovering a cultural aura for material civilization under capitalism. All these have failed because they are concerned in some degree to project a false consciousness of reality. At the end he asks: "—must we not start again?"

However this question, as the termination of a deconstructive criticism, poses a problem: it seems to constitute another rhetoric, in implying that there is a possible fresh start that will not only succeed in avoiding the errors already exposed in our four philosophies, but that will solve, without error, the same problematic that they have raised. In the context of the examination of four defective philosophies, this raises the hope of an effective philosophy that is not only a critical deconstruction of those others but a positive hypothesis in its own right. We are left guessing, however, what this more objective account would be.

The fresh start, in any case, is a well-known formula in human affairs. In the despair of false conclusions it offers by implication not only freedom from the culture of culture, the clearing away of rubbish, but the creation of a *tabula rasa* against whose clarity all false logic, unjustified assumptions and simple irrelevancies will stand out and be eliminated. We should be wary of the fresh start, however, insofar as it raises the hope, not only of avoiding error in our logic, but of being this time able to apply our logic correctly to the empirical situation. The second hope certainly carries the danger of an arrogant assumption of objectivity. The death of a million people in Cambodia is not ineffective, politically, but certainly does not create a *tabula rasa* from which error has been eliminated. Let us beware of the fresh start which promises, this time, an especially successful outcome, and recognize that such fresh starts are themselves instances of a type of rhetorical inspiration.

This is not to deny the importance of the desire to start again— it is probably an essential dynamic component of western thought, underlying the whole cumulative shape of western philosophy and science. The Greeks called *pothos* the unattainable, and the longing for the unattainable might be a description of western man's hunger for truth. Where the hunger for truth gives way to a demand for certainty, however, and then the assertion of dogma, it produces an unphilosophical and unscientific element that we can identify as ideological. The ideological arises when the wish for assurance exceeds the evidence to provide it. We may suspect that in order to avoid errors that are essentially those of serving the predominant western ideology of capitalism, we shall be offered as alternative a prescription that falls into other errors, the errors that are produced under a Marxist or proletarian ideology, since these two systems of consistent beliefs constitute the main choice that is before us today.

From within either of these two ideologies a system of analysis can be achieved that satisfactorily correlates certain value judgements with a logical pattern of description. From within either it is possible to be convinced that logic and belief not only support each other, but together reveal the true state of affairs in the world. At the same time, if one of these ideologies is to be accepted, the other must be wrong, and can be shown to be in error.

Is this what Demetrios Porphyrios has done? Since he has deconstructed four attitudes from the point of view of revealing their "true" political motivation, we must suspect so; yet in exchange he has not elaborated an alternative attitude, an explicit attitude that might lay itself open to deconstruction from a capitalist or liberal point of view.

Or is it indeed possible to assume that at a certain level deconstruction itself has a salutary, neutral ability to genuinely expose ideological error, while itself being free from error precisely so long as it refrains from construction? In this case deconstructive criticism would be to an extent analogous to the type of hard-working and fact-oriented conceptualization that, in the realm of the natural sciences, acts as the corrosive test of all hypothetical propositions that aim to bring nature and logic into a fresh clarity—what scientists refer to as the empirical test.

Or is it impossible to eradicate the traces of our beliefs from even our deconstructive criticism, so that we are forced to envisage the further deconstruction of deconstructive criticism, and so on in infinite regress? Is true objectivity a myth, taking on the elusive quality of Reyner Banham's "entirely radical architecture"?[1] In this case, in order to avoid an infinite regress, we should be forced to accept an initial ideological stance and proceed as if it constituted an acceptably neutral framework in which the values of a world-view correspond to a representation of the world-as-it-is. Many do this, and are forced to anathemize everyone who does not share their initial premise.

This problem is not only a political one, but a philosophical one. Since Kant first insisted on the contribution made by the observer's own intelligence in discerning meaning in the world-as-observed, we have seen the development through the work of Hegel, Husserl, Heidegger and Merleau-Ponty of a phenomenological philosophy that broadly accepts a teleological drive in human perception, the sedimentation of experience both as lived events and as accumulated history, and the role of culture as a many-layered framework within which, and only within which, meaning is secreted.[2] In this case the role of deconstructive criticism is extended: either in the aim of achieving "true" objectivity, it must take as its task the deconstruction of the cultural framework itself; or, if this is seen to be impossible, it accepts a limited and purely asymtotic approach to objectivity, accepting incompleteness, and leaving the further, and never complete clarification of problems to the dialectic of history within the cultural medium.

By his analysis of the term "culture" as employed in capitalist society, Demetrios Porphyrios implied that he is prising open the cultural envelope itself, exposing us to the cold of a natural explanation. But while the word "culture" is indeed subject to ideological use, it is at present the only word that we have to express the unspoken ground of perception itself, and it seems to me that we must accede to the Kantian notion of a transcendental source of judgement, the notion that

law must . . . rest on a purely transcendental, and not on empirical grounds. For in the latter case it would come later than the systems, while in fact the systemical character of our knowledge of nature is produced by it.[3]

A crucial question of critical analysis, then, is to consider whether and to what extent it is able to avoid ideological error, either by struggling with ideology from a basis within a transcendental cultural envelope that we can never define from outside, or from a defined ideological position, which, however, is to be put to the test, not by the critic alone, but by the dialectic of history. In either case, it seems to me that the results of critical analysis can never partake of an absolute judgement, but—as in the role of hypothesis-making and—unmaking in the literature of natural science—must proceed on the basis of only ever producing conditional results, that are open to "correction" by further steps in the dialectic of history.

I pose these alternatives because it seems to me that if ideology is in some sense unavoidable, it may be better to admit than to deny one's ideological commitment: admitting too that one's own presentation of one's ideological framework may itself be offered for deconstruction. Certainly, his degree of commitment to Marxism has not prevented Manfredo Tafuri from exercising a discrimination that exceeds the demands of his ideology:

> "To ward off anguish by understanding and absorbing its causes would seem to be one of the principal ethical exigencies of bourgeois art."[4]

Such a passage can be read as part of a project of deconstructing bourgeois culture and revealing the political motivation that underlies it; but it can also be read as a sympathetic revelation of the teleological drive in a human culture (which happens to be a bourgeois one), and hence in Culture generally. Tafuri's criticism seems to me to conceal an elision that consists of shifting from a position where angst is discovered as the mark of a divine discontent, to one where it becomes the mark of a mere hypocritical materialism. Tafuri's discrimination between ideologies, which has preceded his choice of a defined political stance, is exceeded by his discrimination between the meanings and their representation that arise within culture. And as he never, to my knowledge, demonstrates or proves any hypothesis about Marxism as a constructed explanation of the world-as-it-is, we are able to accept his criticism for what it produces, not within Marxism, but within the cultural envelope that includes the whole story of Marxism.

This means, however, that his conclusions are not to be accepted at the same level as his analysis, because they are, by his own admission, politically motivated; and it is indeed not surprising that all his evidence always leads to the same conclusion, whatever interest his analysis has revealed along the way—the one he has already decided is right. In this Tafuri resembles other critics of a positivistic cast: for example, Gombrich has pointed out about Josef Burckhardt that his innate Hegelianism caused him to believe in the abstraction "Spirit of the Renaissance," so that everywhere he looked he found evidence for its existence.[5]

If there can be an admitted value in such criticism, made from a clearly defined ideological base, it must be because the ideological base is itself defined only within a wider base that admits both of this ideological interpretation and of other, contrary or different interpretations. There was a time when the common factor that lay outside of specific advocacy was called God, or Providence, or Nature (Newton was one who did a great deal towards substituting Nature for God), and was itself conceived as both belief, requiring an act of faith, and truth, in that no other ground of knowledge could be imagined. Since the "Death of God" we may feel exposed to an existential abyss, and I believe that much of the fervor that today attaches to ideological stances is a kind of compensation for the loss of certainty which followed from the outbreak of skeptical thought released by the Enlightenment—through its development of an experimental science located within a continuum of rational thought.

Like scientific thought in general, ideology is a compound of the ideal and the logical. Insofar as it purports to identify and explain true causes it is a construction of scientific interest. Insofar as it asserts an ideal or final truth it becomes locked into error and passion, which it cannot either avow or disavow. The clash between ideologies today is similar to the clashes between sects which characterized the development of Christianity. Insofar as Christianity itself was a defined creed, separate from any merely inchoate set of feelings about the existence of God as first principle of human life, it too acquired the characteristics of an ideology, susceptible to the sort of concealed political motivation that underlay both the Reformation and the counter-Reformation.

The role of ideology is always obscured by the very fervor by which it offers its interpretation as true, natural and complete, where in fact it is consistent, artificial and incomplete. In this sense ideology always tries to hide within the larger teleological motivation that constitutes the cultural envelope and that so satisfactorily ensures that wherever we look we find a universe measured in human terms. Phenomenonology has drawn attention to the non-pathological, even essential role of culture in assimilating nature to human history. In terms of those who benefit from its hidden work, an ideology is considered as both benign and non-existent, while those who suffer from it can see its existence very clearly and are in no doubt about its malign influence on their lives. But to the extent that an ideology benefits classes of men at the expense of man, it reveals its motivated and partial nature. Given the widespread role of ideology, and the difficulty of removing it from criticism, whether consciously or unconsciously identified with ideological positions, what then should be the role of criticism?

Criticism, in its attempt to recover objectivity (not an aura, but an efficacy) must attend to the way in which the New is produced, as well as to how it is assimilated. That there is newness in the world, I would assert as a matter of practical observation. Helicopters may have existed on earth in some prior moment of time, but there is no evidence for this. In the absence of such evidence I must conclude that there are helicopters today where there were none before. Within natural science, and its dependent technology, we find an example of a system of thought which offers up to the observed world a set of hypotheses that both structure that world and explain it, and at the same time lead to the uncovering of new possibilities that did not previously exist. However positivistic rational thought may be, and to whatever extent it is tainted with ideological error, it succeeds—through its submission to the experimental method—in producing predictive models that permit it to interfere with the workings of nature and even, to a degree, the possibility of control over natural processes: a presumption that may not be without its nemesis. In doing this, it also succeeds in producing unexpected information which in turn leads over time to change in the hypotheticizing structures. This dynamic procedure does in a sense exemplify Hegel's proposition of dialectical struggle and change in human history, but without the need to postulate either absolute values or any final state. The experimental method operates by an alternation between transcendental *a priore* logic and empirical observation, and contains within itself impulses that are both realist and idealist in direction, each capable of "criticizing" the other, and not artificially bound together into a complete and exclusive system, but open to further change and knowledge.

Insofar as criticism deals not with nature, but with human nature and its products (a sub-class of nature that in many respects we consider unnatural because of the apparent opposition between nature and design), its task is much more difficult than that of natural science: but it has no other model than that of the experimental to go on. One who has thought deeply about this problem is Tomas Maldonado:

"The human world is our realization ... phylogenetically and ontologically, the making of our environment and the making of ourselves has been a single process. But if that work is a factor in self-realization it is also a factor in alienation. It is obvious by now that the particular mode in which consciousness takes hold of environmental reality has a decisive influence on the ultimate configuration of that reality ..."[6]

As a reflective being, whose gaze is not only bent upon the world, but upon his own gaze bent upon the world, the human animal has set itself the task of understanding itself and the world together; the difficulties in even taking this decipherment as possible indicate the extent of the objectivist and rationalist assumptions with which rational discourse is saturated. The gap between understanding and existence is moreover paralleled by a corresponding gap between the modes of thought that are even possible to man: on the one hand, logical construction based on the perception of relationships that can be abstracted from observations; on the other, intuitional judgement based on the invisible sub-stratum of sedimented experience. These modalities of thought are formally contradictory, yet they are both taken together in all thinking, each acting in turn as supplement, and finally as corrective, to the other. While one offers "truth-value" (to be verified by inspection within the logic of the abstracted system, which is, finally tautologous), the other offers "truth" (to be verified by empirical observation outward from the initial system).[7] The understanding that the "true" is no longer always one and the same, but has two aspects, is one that represents a recent gain in systematic thought, part of the Einsteinian legacy, and not yet part of ordinary thought. More importantly, while each mode offers in itself a source of authority, neither in practice is ever free from the taint of the other. It is this assimilation of one to the other that accounts for the endless variety of configurations, the play of metaphor, the alternation of abstract and concrete, of generality and particularity that characterize human discourse. Finally, there is no Science that has not some art in it, and no Art that does not in some measure contain a positivistic something notionally accessible to all. Why otherwise would artists keep on going?

The activity which I postulate as proper to the avant-garde is to mediate between the objectivity towards which natural science directs itself (while accepting its own instrumentality) and the subjectivity from which artistic products emerge (which attempts to refuse precisely its own instrumentality). The tool of the avant-garde is criticism, dealing both with the conditions of knowledge and judgement, and with the exercise of knowledge and judgement. The artist, strictly speaking, I remove from the avant-garde—except insofar as he accompanies his unexpected work with a commentary which provides in some degree a theoretical framework for its consideration (as did Duchamp). But in general new and creative art is not part of the avant-garde until it is theorized. In this sense, the critic battens on the creative artist, and uses the material he produces as the occasion for his own work. In general the critic will take into consideration the products of both art and science, seeking to relate them to a continuum of theory and practice. The critic's duty is to explain the unexpected qualities of new art and science, thereby assisting their assimilation into culture.

Hannes Meyer, in his 1938 lecture at the San Carlos Academy in Mexico, had this to say:

> Architecture is a social manifestation and indissolubly linked with the structure of society at a given point in time. Once separated from the society of its age, it becomes an empty sham and a toy for the infatuated followers of vulgar fashion. Today, in an epoch of the greatest social confusion when one social system is merging into the next, we should not be surprised if architecture itself displays the heterogeneous forms of the transition.[8]

Already we can see, only forty years later, the assumptions that lie within this short text. For Meyer, the transition to which he so confidently looked forward, as if to the transition from night to day, was the transition from Capitalism to Socialism. He was in little doubt as to the inevitability of this transition. It is a transition, however, that we are still experiencing: and who today could be so confident that it is the only or even the main characteristic of impending social change? Still less, that one could allocate, as Meyer did, distinct styles of architecture to the two phases of social reality? This is not only a matter of the difficulty of "freeing" society from the mechanisms of capitalist investment, in a world where market forces, imperfectly understood, still constitute the underlying structure within which all countries must perforce operate. It is also a matter of recognizing the disparity between our models of society (including the just society) and the complexity of what actually happens. Our naivety is somewhat still that of H.G. Wells, who predicted the emergence of a scientific mode of government for the world as a single enterprise—the "cybernetic world state." The remoteness of this possibility today must teach us to be more scientific in extending the study of empirical reality from sub-atomic nature (the hydrogen bomb, considered instrumentally, is a success), to social and economic man, where no comparable success has been attained, and where technology can be seen to be generating as many fresh problems as it has solved.

Given this disarray in social man and his environment, we must ask, if not for a fresh start, at least for a fresh impulse in the renewal of critical thought. If critical thought is to escape the debilitating effects of ideology, it must learn to recognize ideology and describe it whenever it occurs. As long as ideology is secretive and suppressed, it flaws the argument and undermines the power of criticism. Where it can be named and defined, it can be allowed for, forcing either an abandonment of ideological content and a gain in truth, or the emergence of a re-statement that can offer the benefits of another trial. (I include the benefits of always, again, starting again!) The cumulative value of criticism is, then, of as much import as the steps, often painful, by which criticism must seek to free itself from its own hidden ideology. The cumulative story of criticism, contributed by many voices, becomes in due course a part of cultural history, along with the events and objects which it tries to construe.

In his essay "In Search of Cultural History," Ernest Gombrich draws attention to a basic dilemma caused by the breakdown of the Hegelian tradition, with its belief in the teleological shape of historical development. This dilemma—

> stems from the chastening insight that no culture can be mapped out in its entirety, but no element of this culture can be understood in isolation.[9]

This dilemma, in a general way, underlies all anthropological study. De Saussure showed that although we have no difficulty in speaking in our own native language, we never possess it, either as formulated language or as speech. Our experience of both is always incomplete.[10] In many ways language can stand for culture as a whole. In the considered act of criticism, in a critical text, we cannot expect to do more than to sharpen, momentarily, our sense of the particular in the general, giving sense to the particular by relating it to the general, without ever hoping to empty out its content completely.

From the side of *a priori* and logical truth the critic will draw frameworks on which to extend and measure the particularity of the phenomena he takes as his source material. But only if he can respond to its opacity, its resistance to any scheme of order, will he succeed at the same time in giving a representation of the unexpected and unknown subjectivity that resides in all aesthetic activity. For this alone he will have to be as creative with metaphor as he is rigorous with law. The only tradition of criticism that is open to the unexpected is the creative criticism that was first defined by Coleridge.

Paper contributed to a symposium of the *Colegio Oficial de Arquitectos* in Valencia, Spain, April 23, 1980. Published in *9H* magazine, No. 2, London, 1980.

NOTES

1   The phrase "entirely radical" was applied by Reyner Banham to the concept of Buckminster Fuller's Dymaxion House in *Theory and Design*, 1960. See also Charles Jencks: "History as Myth" in *Meaning in Architecture*, 1965.

2   Ferdinand de Saussure, followed by Louis Hjelmslev, insists that "meanings" are not autonomous but arise only within a cultural framework that also provides a context.

3   Kant: *Critique of Pure Reason* (1781) see English translation by Muller, Anchor, 1966, p. 434.

4   Manfredo Tafuri: *Architecture and Utopia*, 1973.

5   E.H. Gombrich: *In Search of Cultural History*, Oxford, 1969.

6   Tomas Maldonado: *Design, Nature and Revolution*, New York, 1972, pp. 2-3.

7   This separation may be observed by tracing the specificity of truth as it must be defined in order to apply within logical systems—requiring that it is operational only by the application of rules. See R. Carnap: *Meaning and Necessity*, Chicago, 1947. For an examination of the strict limits of logical systems see Nagel and Newman: *Gödel's Proof*, New York, 1964.

8   The quotation of a passage given in the lecture given by Meyer in 1938 at the San Carlos Academy, Mexico, is taken from Claude Schnaidt: *Hannes Meyer*, Niggli, 1965, p. 55.

9   E.H. Gombrich: *In Search of Cultural History*, p. 4.

10 See F. Saussure: *Course in General Linguistic*, McGraw-Hill, 1966. According to Saussure a natural language is in a state of dynamic balance, evolving between the corpus of its formulation (*la lange*)—which is never complete, and the sums of all the utterances in the language (*la parole*) which is also incommensurable. Language is both an agent of culture and a constituent of culture. Its synchronic stability within continuous diachronic evolution may be taken as a model, or at the very least, as a metaphor for culture.

REYNER BANHAM—HISTORIAN

In this essay we follow a methodology devised by Demetrios Porphyrios, in his role as editor of a special publication on historiographical issues within architecture. The aim is to assess the quality of historical writing, in this case by Reyner Banham, with particular reference to a piece of Banham text that can stand as a sort of biological sample, but also as an object of study that is offered to the reader along with the criticism. The reader can thus see the point of the criticism directly, and is also free to differ from the critic on the basis of the evidence available.

On Nikolaus Pevsner:

"Pevsner's success as a stylistic talent-spotter could be due to a number of things; luck, undue influence on later events, or a true perception of how things happen in history. All three are indeed there; he was clearly fortunate to be set on course by Gropius almost before he knew that such a thing as a 'Modern Movement' might exist; he certainly was influential in shaping the ideas of two if not three generations of architects, historians and critics, so that all were inclined to make his prophecies come true. And at least one of the reasons he was so influential was that his historical generalizations looked true at the time, and in many cases still look good.

Anyone who believes he can find direction and purpose in history must be capable of producing comprehensible pictures of the historical process and they will be comprehensible only in so far as they can cut through the glitter and confusions of 'the Brownian movement of random events' to reveal patterns (true or false) that lie within. The discovery and delivery of such generalizing patterns is one of the services that historians render to the lay members of society. Indeed the ability to generalize convincingly and usefully is one of the tests of a great historian and is also one of the reasons historians' reputations are so perishable since changing circumstances will undermine the conviction and utility of any generalization. But it also explains Pevsner's impact in the 1930s, 1940s and even 1950s, when architects and lay-folk alike needed help in understanding what was going on.

Given such generalizations it is, admittedly, very easy to endow them with personalities, parts and passions, and it is—alas—not a very long step from such glib observations as 'The Roman Baroque prefers elliptical floor-plans,' to more sinister historicist rhetoric about 'the architectonic mission of the German volk.' Yet their utility persists, and Watkin avails himself of them as much as any historian: "the historicist and Zeitgeist-inspired historian will tend to regard modern collectivist ideas as right; he will be ever anxious to deal wholesale with humanity, to label individuals as types, to identify them in classes . . ."—a sentence in which he himself labels individuals as types and identifies them in classes.

The relative blackness of pots and kettles is not the point at issue here: Pevsner's performance is. He got it right. He got it more right than Giedion or Henry-Russell Hitchcock. It behooves any of us who disapprove of his methodology, or dislike his particular favorites and are concerned at the omission of our particular favorites, to recognize that he produced a picture of the architecture of his own time which was useful, applicable, and had demonstrable predictive power. If it was Whiggish historicism, or the kind of moralizing that comes naturally to a self-made Lutheran that made it possible to do that, then so much the worse for Butterfield and Popper.

Indeed, a good Popperian, I feel, should salute rather than abuse Pevsner for having offered a falsifiable hypothesis about the main style of twentieth-century architecture in the Western industrialized world, and having seen that hypothesis resist falsification for forty years. It is, of course, only one of the many historical services he has rendered us, but its success should command respect, and give pause to those who would deprecate any of his methods."

Reyner Banham, 'Pevsner's Progress,' *Times Literary Supplement*, February 17, 1978.

The excerpt cited is from the review Reyner Banham made of David Watkin's book *Morality and Architecture.*[1] It is a short text, and it may seem invidious to reproduce just part of it. However, what I have omitted is largely taken up with the polemics of reviewing, whereas the passage quoted, being mainly a defense of Nikolaus Pevsner, is one of the few passages where Banham addresses himself to the job of the historian. It has the advantage of being recent, and of dealing with the Modern Movement as a single event of history. This essay is not an attempt to summarize Banham's achievement, but to clarify his method: I will thus amplify the excerpt chosen by references to his more important books.

The polemical passages are in crisp *TLS* manner, not so much avoiding beating around the bush as simply eradicating it. Banham identifies Watkin's book as a piece of Butterfieldian-Peterhousey anti-Whiggery; an attempt perhaps at an academic 'take-over of the current fashion for knocking modern architecture.' Apart from affording us a glimpse of a Banham who is basically 'for' modern architecture, this also shows us a Banham who, in spite of being an academic, does not wish to be in any way associated with academicism. Confined, as most historians are, to the rear-wards view, Banham has a quick eye to grasp the actuality of events as they swirl into the field of vision. His interest in the virtually unchanging profile of the distant mountains is as low as his trust in the redeeming power of the Phileban solids.[2] Whereas most historians work to dislodge past events from the dust which has already immobilized them and which might efface them, Banham seems to prefer events which are still in motion, on which the dust has not settled. His view of culture emphasizes its inertia, its accumulation, and suggests that, like all accumulations, it constitutes clutter. His telling phrase—'the history of the immediate future'—reveals much of his motivation and his writing has the intrinsic interest of revealing a picture for the first time.

This combination of virtues has certain journalistic consequences like the danger of being 'wrong,' or simply of mistaking the momentary for the momentous; but I would be the last to reproach him for his tone of light banter, or take exception to the occasionally portentous result of bending his mind to minutiae like clipboards or alternative neckties. What is refreshing in him is especially his refusal to reject apparently light-weight evidence, since this increases our awareness of the historical dimension in our own lives 'as lived.' If his achievement as an academic has been no more than to employ more frequently the normal lens of the amateur in preference to the wide-angle or telescopic lenses of the expert, we are already in his debt.

And yet there are still some doubts to raise about his method. Banham is, after all, a writer. The eye for fast-moving objects, which we have attributed to him, is only a metaphor. What is the controlling framework which allows his roving camera-work? My guess is that we should seek this control in the form of his work, rather than in its content. Yet his reputation has been so strongly linked to his concept of a history of 'the immediate future' that we must first try to unravel his method from his purpose—which appears to be prediction: prediction is the quality he singles out in Pevsner for praise. His confidence in handling fast-moving objects seems closely related to his confidence in the Zeitgeist-ian motion of the train—his anticipation of a future increasingly focussed on the possibilities of technological development—which is the direction he wants the train to be headed in. We, the architects, have been constantly chastised by him for our backwardness to the point where we appear to be more concerned with the past than is he, whose job it is as historian to analyze the past.

> "The architect who proposes to run with technology knows now that he will be in fast company, and that, in order to keep up, he may have to emulate the futurists and discard his whole cultural load . . ."[3]

In the pain of receiving this admonition we have perhaps failed to question its assumptions: did the Futurists discard their whole cultural load? They reacted against it, certainly, but did they shed it? Like Abbé Laugier's prescription for a fundamental architecture, their designs now seem quaint, locked into their moment in history, and Futurism was to remain an 'ism' and not become the model for architectural advance. But then we, the architects, have perhaps been too pained in general with Banham's admonitory tone to notice that his own preferences suggest the idiosyncrasy of a sensibility rather than the regularity of a dogma. He has on the whole been soft on the Futurists, hard on the Purists, soft on Fuller and hard on Le Corbusier, soft on Parkhill and hard on the Unité, soft on Archigram and hard on the Pompidou Center, soft on Philip Johnson and hard on Venturi; soft on his friends engaged in the practice of architecture, hard on the profession as a whole. And, in the example under examination, hard on David Watkin in condemning him for adopting concepts that Watkin names only in order to criticize them.

The question then is how this kind of variability can be related to the constancy required in a historical method. Here we must be careful to detach Banham's preferences, as a critic of architecture, from his assertions as a historian. If we do this, we will find that he makes no wild claims, but remains anchored very close to established fact. His preferences, as a critic, are disciplined by his professional responsibility as a historian. The motion he imparts to facts affects them very little, but affects our view of them considerably.

Notice how, in the last quotation, he does not demand that all architects should shed their cultural load, but only those who propose to run with technology: a strong assertion that has the unassailability of a tautology. Yet it insinuates the idea that not to be in the select group who want to run with technology is not to be in the running at all. This passage well represents the Banham style: at once rigorous, self-evident and seductive.

The matter of prediction is dealt with in our quoted excerpt. Here Banham is concerned to show that Pevsner correctly predicted the success of the Modern Movement by defining it not simply in visual terms, but in terms of its basic attributes: functionality, honesty to materials and structure, and social responsibility. Broadly speaking, an architecture with such characteristics did take shape and is still with us. The revolutionary theoretical ideas that emerged from the Great War did indeed result—not in a short-lived 'ism'— but in a normative practical sequel, as 'the main style of twentieth-century architecture in the western industrialized world.'

> "Now, Pevsner's success as a stylistic talent-spotter could be due to a number of things; luck, undue influence on later events, or a true perception of how things happen in history. All these are indeed there …"

Pevsner, says Banham, was indeed lucky in being set on course early by Gropius, but most important was his performance as an interpreter of history. His interpretation amounted to a selective definition of modernity, as much by its hypothetical characteristics as by the chosen exemplars. It involved an action of generalization, in order to make the pattern perceptible and comprehensible and this involved a risk of leaving something essential out, of getting it wrong.

This judgement raises some interesting points, starting with the acknowledgement that the telling of history involves making an interpretation. The individual historian cannot completely avoid bias, but he can be proved right, or at least not entirely wrong, by the subsequent march of events. His rightness is a matter of correctly predicting outcomes. His subjectivity must, however, be illuminated by a 'true perception of how things happen in history;' a revelation, presumably, of the real forces determining the immediate future. Hence the capacity of predicting this future as by the operation of science, with the possibility of having the predictions falsified by the outcome.

One wonders indeed if Banham takes seriously the proposition of refutability encapsulated here. Are we to take it that he means that Pevsner showed conclusively that, given the premises of functionality, only thus could architecture evolve? Or was it rather that Pevsner perceived that the new kind of architecture, free from traditional constraints, was more responsive to actual conditions and therefore more acceptable and more likely to endure? These points are not dwelt upon, and indeed there is a suggestion that it was not so much the operational hypotheses, but the stylistic characteristics, which Pevsner got right: that he anticipated merely the broad outlines of the look of a kind of architecture, largely emanating from the Bauhaus and approximating to the International Style.

In any case one may doubt if Pevsner's work, however important in other ways, was effective as prediction. The discovery that modern architecture was from the start less functional, less honest to material, less responsive to people, than its protagonists claimed, has been going on for almost as long as the Modern Movement itself. Reyner Banham has played an important part in that discovery, just as he has been right in insisting that style alone does not bestow functionality. The modern is now a compendious style embracing many practical and stylistic transformations which suggest a process of adaptation to economic and social pressures. This process of change in real time has little relation either to the intellectual process by which a set of hypotheses may be refuted by argument, or to the empirical process by which they may be disproved by experiment. To suggest that Pevsner, as historian, has established the fundamental premises of the new style in refutable terms is a large claim, and one which skirts the extreme complexity of identifying and defining the role of causality in history. Admittedly, we should not expect to find these questions laid to rest in a review article, but we might expect to find them raised, if only in the form of caveat. By 1936, when *Pioneers of the Modern Movement* was published in England,[4] the main lines of the new architecture had already crystallized, Johnson and Hitchcock's book had been out for some four years, the key masterpieces built, Weissenhof Siedlung was dispensing its influence, and layouts of white-walled housing by Gropius, Scharoun and others, were already lived in. It would have been more convincing to present Pevsner as a percipient critic, won over to a set of ideas already embodied and communicated in a style by architects, a work of acculturation largely accomplished by 1925. The view of him as a propagandist (presumably of an ideology) was, according to Banham, not unacceptable to Pevsner himself—conversationally at least.[5] And in spite of the talk about prediction, it is the picture of Pevsner which we are effectively given.

It will be seen that Banham's defense of Pevsner, while communicating sympathy with the latter's achievement, does not amount to an endorsement of his method. Still less does it commit Banham himself to a deterministic view of history. The historian stands well back from the risks cheerfully accepted by the critic. His description of an historian's job, which in the context we may take as applying to Pevsner, we must not take as applying to Banham. All that we can assume is that the discovery and delivery of generalized patterns within the random motion of events—just one of the services that historians render to the lay members of society—is an essential part of the job of the historian. It is one which happens to describe very aptly most of what Banham himself does. His generalizations have indeed been effective in their aim of sweeping the here-and-now into a comprehensible story, a story often admonitory, often controversial even, but issuing from his sensibility as a critic rather than from the rectitude of a historical methodology. If his comprehensible generalizations arouse doubts, it is not in relation to the historiographical questions which they offend, but to the critical view of architecture which they enclose. This has always been bent in one direction, towards an 'other' architecture, one that would be light, adaptable and responsive, technologically progressive and therefore of the immediate future, and in the words of his own *Guide to Modern Architecture*, stronger in space and function than in form and structure. While, according to Jencks,[6] Banham believes in the possibility of an 'entirely radical' architecture that would once and for all put paid to the architects' persistent tendency to monumentalize, he has not projected this architecture as historically inevitable, but as morally desirable. "It is Banham's strength [(said Rowe)] to be the possessor of a crucial and simple idea . . . [he] has believed, and continues to believe, that modern architecture should be, and can be, exactly what it was claimed to be, i.e. an objective approach to building deriving from the unprejudiced scrutiny of facts."[7]

This position appears to stem from belief rather than from a reasoned position, and to be in that sense beyond attack. It has enabled Banham to criticize all contemporary architecture as in various crucial ways failing the test of being entirely radical. His hope that architecture would consistently evolve closer to engineering technology and away from formal games, is not invalidated by the fact that it seems in the seventies to be reverting to formal games and antitechnological attitudes. History, since the energy crisis, has provided Banham—and all of us—with a few surprises.

And yet, in spite of Banham's enthusiasms, and they are many, it is his disappointments that come through. In *Theory and Design* there is no concealing his disenchantment with the failure of modern architecture to match the early promise of the Futurists. In *The New Brutalists* he is confronted with a sad decline from ethic to aesthetic, a promise laid to rest before he even takes up his pen. In *Megastructures* he again records the story of an idea which had already degenerated beyond hope. Since these writings all involve the story of a promise unfulfilled in the performance, one marvels that expectation can stay high. He is too perceptive and too sympathetic a critic to ascribe these failures merely to the pigheadedness of the architectural profession, even though architects do collect a fair share of the blame. This built-in capacity to be disappointed could be explained as endemic optimism: a temperamental bias to be grateful for in good times and bad times alike. But it could also be explained as an ontological blindness to the fact of culture; to the processes by which culture accumulates its clutter and to the way in which the individual delves in this clutter in order to identify the points of criticism and hence of renewal.

By characterizing culture as primarily "a load which must be shed," Banham seems to disregard the dialectical nature of history. Does he really think that culture only clutters? It surely has both negative and positive effects. It keeps enmities alive, and the home fires burning. But is it not also the source of divine discontent? The entirely radical idea is the one that has not yet been assimilated into culture, that has not even perhaps been communicated. Obviously there is a meaning to be attached to radical, but the truly radical one may suspect is a myth.

But where we may feel that Banham's critical view of architecture is unjustifiably optimistic and his experience of it unnecessarily disappointing, it would be wrong to see this as invalidating his approach as an historian. On the evidence more of his books than of our excerpt alone, Banham appears no fantasist, but straightforwardly a pragmatist. An exponent, one might say, of the British Brutalist view of history, a view that prefers the brute fact to the smooth story, the evidence to the interpretation. There is a distinct air of Dr Johnson in his view of ideality and his refutations are likely to take the form of kicking out at something solid. This preference for solid evidence can intrude at levels concerned purely with imagination. In his discussion of Archigram's 'Walking City' (in *Megastructures*) he praises its wealth of graphic detail as if this were evidence of its essential practicality. Earlier megastructuralists had been excessively vague about detail:

> It is noticeable—alarming even—how few of them actually offer any nut-and-bolt proposals as to how the transient elements should be secured to the megaform, or what precise devices and services are required for the physical activities of *homo ludens*.

Archigram, on the other hand, produced reassuring images that not only had a certain verisimilitude, but indeed provided a wealth of technical detail verging on the production of working drawings. The look of technical detail, perhaps; but is 'Walking City' really concerned with the idea of technicity as part of an essential practicality? Surely its purpose is to project us into a fantasy where walking cities are already commonplace; we are brought to accept the fantastic as if it had already been actualized. The diminishing telescopic legs are not involved with technical questions but with rhetorical questions: anyway, to be truely telescopic, they should have been made up of pieces of uniform cross-section, like a camera tripod (fig. 18). Rather than expressing a nut-and-bolt attitude, it looks as if the artist could not resist the expression of legginess.

Such a rhetorical use of graphic detail has nothing to do with making megastructures real, but with making fantasy realistic. It

18 WALKING CITY
Ron Herron, Archigram Group, 1964.

does, however, have the effect of effacing the ideological basis of 'Walking City,' by focusing on its actuality. One can but agree with Banham when he comments:

> "The reasons why the British alone seemed prone to finnick over detailing are diverse, and often personal, but do seem somewhat connected to a national tendency to take refuge from ideology in pragmatics."[8]

Though conversational in tone, as always, this passage suggests that Banham indeed believes that pragmatics are, or can be, independent of ideology. The pragmatic is his base for the criticism of architectural ideologies, and the fact that it is always identified by a concrete instance obscures the critical role it plays as a category. Thus in *Theory and Design* Bucky's Dymaxion Ground-Taxiing Unit was rated as pragmatically superior to Gropius's Adler Cabriolet, and the Dymaxion House to the Villa Savoie. As Colquhoun has pointed out,[9] Banham has ignored or preferred not to see the ideality present in both Fuller products, just as he has passed over in silence the Beaux-Arts content in Sant'Elia's Futurist cityscapes. His blindness to formal and rhetorical content in his own preferred examples suggests that, like the Smithsons, he believes rhetoric to be both reprehensible and avoidable.

Yet is Banham himself not a master of rhetoric? Is it not as much his presentational skill as his insights in selecting the hard evidence, that constitutes his strength as a historian? In saying this, I do not mean to call in question his good faith nor his use of the facts. But it seems to me that the conviction of his narrative stems not from the facts as pragmatic evidence alone, but from the impact these facts create within the empire of his text. In shying away from epistemological questions, in limiting the use of generalizing frameworks to the duty of communicating true perceptions of history to a lay audience, Banham is asserting the primacy and immediacy of the fact, thereby diverting our attention from the text to the event outside of it:

> "As far as can be ascertained, the phrase 'Fun Palace' was coined, and applied to the project Cedric Price was designing for Joan Littlewood, on the sidewalk in 42nd Street during a visit they paid to New York (in 1962)."[10]

In such passages it is we who become eye witnesses to the making of history; and we are astonished to find that history is real, not bunk.

In 'Memoirs of a Survivor,' the concluding section of *The New Brutalists*, Banham states his involvement with the events described more categorically than would have been possible with *Theory and Design*:

> "The reader will have deduced, if he did not already know, that this book is the work of someone fairly deeply involved with the events it describes. I have in fact been personally acquainted with most of the British Brutalists and Quasi-Brutalists mentioned . . . The book, therefore, has a built-in bias towards the British contribution to Brutalism: it is not a dispassionate and Olympian survey, conducted from the cool heights of an academic ivory tower."[11]

In projecting the immediacy of the events, what is being stressed is the role of the historian as eyewitness. History in these terms becomes a question of access. The further away we are from the event, the less we know about it. The event itself is unequivocal. It has an intrinsic reality which validates the account by the degree that the account is close to it. It is the plenitude of presence that authenticates.[12]

But the historian cannot be close to every event he describes. In *Theory and Design* the majority of the events described took place far away and long ago. It is a problem not unknown to historians, and there is a well-known answer: quotations from historical sources are themselves pragmatic facts, and when inserted into a text, they take on the aura of real events. Some historians emphasize and enjoy the dust-stained aspect of these documentary relics, like the Clerk-of-Works records that figure so largely in nineteenth-century historical works. Banham has a different method. In him these quotations speak with the vibrancy of key people interviewed on television. Quotations are a hefty chunk of the text in *Theory and Design*. Far from deadening the narrative, they sustain it and give it life.

Banham's power of narrative is based on the skill with which he uses these quotations to create a rhetoric of actuality. A framework of relations is set up, by which the writing animates and is animated by the events that it takes as its ostensible content. Thus, what real events are to the author's project (the subject of the book), real quotations are to the author's narrative (the text). We see the event—the quotation—but we don't see the text. Events and quotations are evidence of life; they indubitably exist as facts and, being outside of the author's purposes, they impart to the text an authenticity which is that of life. Viewed as parts of writing, however, they are events which are breathed into new life by the way in which they are sewn into the congruity of the text.

This amounts to little more than saying that Banham is a damned good writer: true, but in the context of an historiographical debate it enables us to locate him in an array of other talents and other methods. As a pragmatist he will tend to ignore the framework by which he works; yet this framework does constitute a method and a way of valuing the subject matter of history. Banham remains suspicious of comprehensive classifications and ideological frameworks, and prefers reality as found. That this reality is not tainted by the very act of grasping it, Banham does not appear to doubt. But, despite his seductiveness, his 'rhetoric of the real' often fails to convince us that he has achieved a true perception of how things happen in history. It is his performance, not his promise, that has us in thrall.

Originally published in *Architectural Design*, No. 8/9, 1981, as "The Plenitude of Presence: Reyner Banham."

NOTES

Times Literary Supplement, February 17, 1978.

The Phileban solids may be included in Le Corbusier's list of *les constants humains*—regular human preferences which link us to our distant ancestors and provide archetypes for the immediate future.

From the concluding admonition in Reyner Banham, *Theory and Design in the First Machine Age*.

Pioneers of the Modern Movement was published in England in 1936. The suggestion that Pevsner himself was a pioneer is but a suggestion. Banham's text reads: "... conversationally at least he [Pevsner] has acknowledged himself a propagandist for that kind of architecture which was pioneered from William Morris to Walter Gropius."

Charles Jencks: "History as Myth," in *Meaning in Architecture*, ed. Jencks and Baird, 1969.

Colin Rowe: "Waiting for Utopia"—a review of Banham's *New Brutalism* and Venturi's *Complexity and Contradiction* which appeared in *The New York Times*, 1967.

Ibid., p. 85.

Alan Colquhoun: "The Modern Movement in Architecture," *The British Journal of Aesthetics*, Vol. 12, No. 1, January 1962.

Reyner Banham, *Megastructures*, p. 84.

Reyner Banham, *The New Brutalists*, p. 134.

The position from which I have approached the work of Reyner Banham is clearly influenced by the Jacques Derrida of *De La Grammatologie*. Derrida discusses writing in relation to speech: truth can never be grasped in a text, but only glimpsed in the relations conveyed. In this view, rhetoric is not an avoidable weakness, but rather the main vehicle by which communication is effected. Rhetoric is capable of recreating the illusion of presence; and the plenitude of presence is the experience which all writing tries to shadow. The question of the theoretical position of this critic is more closely examined in Chapter XXX.

REYNER BANHAM — THE MAN

Journalist, architectural historian, scholar, guru of students, scourge of the gratuitously monumental, pedant of the commonplace, lover of the transient and the incidental, optimist and thoroughly futurist, Banham, alas, is no more. And it is strange—is it not?—that this sudden cessation seems unnatural, *à rebours*, not the way things were intended. For in the story of Banham, that is to say, in the telling of his project, the last chapter was about to be written, the final act was about to open, and we were all, friends and enemies alike, tensed for it. His appointment as the Sheldon H. Solow Professor of the History of Architecture, at New York University's Institute of Fine Arts, had set the scene for this fifth act, had offered him an authoritative platform from which he could once again operate as the Arbiter of Large and Small Things.

Can we doubt that he would have used this opportunity to the full? As postmodernism dissolves into the sub-normal, as modernism begins to assume a nostalgic appeal, can we doubt that he would have resumed his close examination of the immediate future, that he would have leaned forward resolutely into it? And, whatever metaphysical doubts may have arisen through the adoption of Derridaean analysis, that he would have continued, like Dr Johnson, to dismiss certain kinds of arguments as one would kick away a stone in one's path?

Certainly we should have hung on his comments on the show of Deconstructivist Architecture at the Museum of Modern Art; the sort of event that seems to be made for his judgement, and it is almost unbearable to be deprived of it; it's hard to see him, as a futurist and an empiricist, endorsing the negative message at its core, but he would no doubt have enjoyed its irreverencies. His judgments were often surprising, indicating a flexibility in his own position, and we can only speculate in this case. But with the shifts and adjustments presently taking place around the world, we can be sure—both that he would have felt the necessity to re-examine his positions, and that we should have benefited immeasurably from this operation.

If we found his opinions so interesting, and often surprising, it says something for his reputation as a scholar and soothsayer. The scholar was always there, in the background, hidden behind a genial-assumption of omniscience; the soothsayer was inclined to take precedence. It would be true to say, I think, that Banham was relatively careless of his reputation as a scholar: his first book, _Theory and Design in the First Machine Age,_ based on his doctoral thesis, was his most scholarly, and I do not suggest that it is anything but impeccable in its scholarship. All the other books, while not ever being unscholarly, are directed towards a view of life which he believed in, not towards the fulfillment of a scholarly career. _Theory and Design,_ however, is an essential book for the understanding of the Modern Movement in architecture. It makes the most of the knowledge imparted to him by his advisor, Nikolas Pevsner, while quietly undermining Pevsner's orthodox way of looking at the Modern Movement. While the thesis was under way, Banham was working as a journalist at the _Architectural Review,_ through the basement bar of which, at one time or another, passed just about every famous architect of the day, the only exceptions (he said) being Robert van t'Hoff and Mies. It must have been a great boost to his research that a lot of it could be undertaken _viva voce_ rather than by delving in the libraries.

At the same time he was enjoying a full life as the focus of a number of intellectual circles on the London scene, of which he was the intersection. There were, first, the architects, most of them neighbors: Sandy Wilson, the Smithsons, James Stirling, Sam Stevens, Alan Colquhoun and myself. Then, the artists Eduardo Paolozzi, Bill Turnbull, Richard Hamilton, with Nigel Henderson, the photographer, and Laurence Alloway, the critic. Less well-defined at that time, but taking on increasing definition over the years, was a small group of inventors: Cedric Price, Bucky Fuller, and Peter Cook, the inventor of Archigram. These circles intersected, but only Banham was equally at ease with all of them.

Arguments were lively and frank in those circles, and—though we didn't use the expression—ideologies were revealed and concealed, formulated and reformulated, in quick succession, as a means of trying out ideas. Among the architects, the main excitement derived from the realization that Le Corbusier, for all his rational arguments, was an artist of power in whom classical archetypes were visible to those who could read the signs. Thus arose a kind of practical hermeneutics whose aim was to apply the insights gained from analysis to the opportunities of the day. The idea of combining critical analysis with critical design probably owed a good deal to the *eminence grise* of the group—Colin Rowe—whose comparison of Corbusian and Palladian villas had permitted a way of discussing architecture of all periods as if its qualities were always directly accessible to the designer. We didn't realize at the time that Rowe had introduced the modern genre of formalist criticism to architecture, nor did we have any inkling that Robert Venturi would exploit this vein of criticism to entirely different effect some years later.

The perception of archetypal constants in Le Corbusier, which so excited the architects, had a different effect on Banham. Although fascinated by design, and a keen do-it-yourselfer, Banham had no professional outlet in design. He distanced himself from the architects's perhaps naive excitement, and continued throughout his career to be extremely suspicious of them as automatically inclined to the monumental. A sort of Banham-Rowe axis declared itself, with Banham taking an anti-formalist and inherently historicist position. Yet his position was far from being academic, but was formed from a fusion of intellect and the thrill of recognizing history being created now—at this very minute. In this spirit he records the very moment when the phrase "Fun Palace" was coined, on the sidewalk on 42nd Street in New York, in a conversation between himself, Cedric Price and Joan Littlewood. And in this spirit he relates how his interest in the Futurists, and in their attitude towards the automobile, was kindled by picking up from a book barrow, outside the Brera in Milan, a bound volume of the Futurist Manifestos. His interest in the immediate future was only partly a yearning for new design, for a different kind of design, it was also an aspect of his chosen calling as a journalist-historian. To such a person, the future was forever impending. Temperamentally this made him process-oriented, since every product is doomed from its inception to be marked with the inadequacies of its moment. It also made him inherently suspicious of temporary resolutions and bland surfaces.

But the critical idea that modern architecture, at least in the Corbusian interpretation, was as much concerned with surface appearance as with spatial organization and functional efficiency became the principal theme of his book: a theme with which he was to wrestle for the rest of his life. The machine aesthetic became an ambiguous term for him, for he loved the look of Bugattis as much as any of them, but could not content himself with mere promise: performance had to follow. Indeed, it had to lead, and the cultivation of appearance independent of performance became for him the over-riding danger, and the besetting sin of his architect friends. So in a way his friends, the architects, were inclined to see him as a traitor, revealing to the world their intimate aspirations to archetypal resonance and classical continuity as though these were nothing but pretensions to monumentality; unfair, really, but to be expected. In professional terms, Banham had done only what every good journalist needs to do: he had supped with his sources.

So we find him, almost from the beginning (and probably from the beginning, if we knew all the facts), possessed of an exquisite eye for the appeasements of appearance and image, but also of a hunger for actuality, for the solidity of performance. This opposition at times appeared to take on a Manichean intensity in him, giving him the flashing eye and floating beard of the Ancient Mariner, a prophet of doom; while at other times allowing him to appear as the most genial and entertaining of impresarios, with a nod and a wink for every conceivable position.

The anti-monumental stance he adopted with the architects translated into something more immediate and sustaining when in the company of the artists. It became a polemic in favor of popular art, against the art of the Courtauld Institute (where he had taken his Art History degree) and the art of the museums in general. Banham's optimism and enjoyment of immediate results, his do-it-yourself enthusiasms, must have contributed to the inspiration of the English group of Pop Artists, institutionalized to a degree by the formation of the Independent Group at the Institute of Contemporary Arts, when it was still housed in a cramped first floor apartment in Dover Street. Richard Hamilton, Eduardo Paolozzi, John McHale and Bill Turnbull were the performers, but Peter and Alison Smithson, with Nigel Henderson, were crucial members of the circle, and the Smithsons' exhibition "Parallel of Life and Art," mounted at the I.C.A. in 1953, was a notice to architects that art, radically reappraised as a quasi-biological force, had a positive part to play in the new "social" architecture. Their contribution, in collaboration with Paolozzi and Henderson, to "This is Tomorrow" at the Whitechapel Art Gallery in 1956 proved to be the most telling exhibit of the show, completely anti-institutional and improvisatory in feeling. By this time Banham had become scribe, propagandist and tutelary deity to the Pop Movement in Britain.

The Archigram group was related to the Pop group, but in a special way. It grew out of the freelance activities of a number of architectural students in London, starting around 1960. It may have been a happy accident that its principal progenitor, Peter Cook, came to live almost opposite the Banhams' apartment in Aberdare Gardens. Banham's comment on their history is characteristic: "Archigram is short on theory, long on draftsmanship and craftsmanship. They're in the image business . . ." Their fantasies of an immediate future where the capabilities of high technology were no longer restricted to military projects, but available to all, appealed to the mechanic in him. In some way their realistic rhetoric was translated in his mind into an empirical competence with nuts and bolts. Their concern with image was essential to their business of promoting a technological view of the future, and so did not come under the blanket disapproval with which he regarded the neo-platonic tendencies of the architects. Above all, the image they projected was processal in nature, full of happy accidents, but never reaching any final point of rest. It corresponded to Banham's own restless nature.

In some ways, while Banham propagandized for Archigram, Archigram became propaganda for his own point of view. As the renown of Archigram grew throughout the sixties, so did Banham's. By the end of the decade he was a world figure, well known on the American lecture circuit and in Japan. The International Expo '70 in Osaka marked the apogee of this influence, with a main pavilion designed by Arata Isozaki that confirmed the Archigram vision of a high technology liberated from military rule.

But 1970 was also the year when the new ecological militants attacked. In an interview with John Maule McKean (*Building Design*, August 27, 1976) Banham confesses: "The Aspen [Design] Conference in 1970 was the most bruising experience of my life . . . I could suddenly feel all those changes running together in a spasm of bad vibrations that shook the conference. We got ourselves together again, but an epoch had ended." Concern over wasted resources, pollution, and world poverty had suddenly made Archigram fantasies look self-indulgent and exploitive, part of a militaristic and capitalistic system. The energy crisis of 1973 added a more immediate economic factor to the situation. In the course of the seventies it was to be discovered that a low-energy conventional house with improved insulation was the universal need, not a high-energy "environmental bubble" with elaborate and stylish life-support systems by François Dallegret. Weight and mass were suddenly re-valued, and the monumental threatened to become environmentally respectable. When Banham decided to abandon his post at London University and head out west, there was a palpable feeling that he had gone into voluntary exile.

At Buffalo, where he had hoped to set up a new PhD program, he found himself instead recording for posterity the relics of the first machine age, in the form of the very factories that had inspired Gropius, Le Corbusier and Moholy-Nagy. As a historian of the immediate past, Banham still had admonitions for the architects: it was those Europeans who had needlessly idealized these pragmatic inventions and sent architecture on a course backwards to the platonic past. America was thus justified as the source, not only of the skyscraper, but of the empirical tradition with which he himself was aligned. In the same way, the ultimate expression of the free empirical spirit was to draw him inexorably westward to Los Angeles, the idol of his own idealizing tendency. From the margins of the Pacific Ocean he was able to survey with some detachment the depredations of postmodernism and the egregious career of Charles Jencks, and survive, like General de Gaulle, until the Call would come. It didn't come in time. In a profound sense, we are all at a loss.

MODERN AND POSTMODERN POSITIONS

19   CITY HALL (MODEL): THE HAGUE, THE NETHERLANDS
Richard Meier & Partners, competition entry, 1986 (completion date: 1995).

RICHARD MEIER:
PURITY AND DANGER

"...The architect found himself to be an enthusiast for speed and for sport; for youth, sunbathing, simple life, sociology, Canadian grain elevators, Atlantic liners, Vuitton trunks, filing cabinets and factories. And his buildings became the illustrations of these enthusiasms. But they became also the outward and visible signs of a better world, a testament in the present as to what the future would disclose; and there was always the proviso that his buildings were the agents of this future, that the more modern buildings were erected the more the hoped for condition would ensue."

C.F. Rowe: Introduction to *Five Architects*, 1975

The style of modern architecture around 1930 is by no means the style of modern architecture today, and the hoped for condition has clearly not arrived. The actual history of the last sixty years provides an invaluable commentary on the horizon of expectations that opened to architects then—say in 1927, after the modest success of the exhibition at the Weissenhof Siedlung. For many, the pure thirties style, viewed retrospectively, has been seen as merely the prelude to the International Style, widely adopted for business purposes, as a result of which modern architecture was debased in the same measure as it became accepted. For others, it is only with the process-oriented phases of modernism that unrolled in the sixties that the modern project took form, and finally shed its covert classicism. But then, as Venturi showed, brutalist accentuation of construction was another route by which artifice had re-entered, and artifice was perhaps better controlled by admitting to it in decent amounts; a formulation which in turn has led to the excesses of postmodernism, a style that is artificial and illusory to a degree, and which has even opened the door to classical revivalism, revivalism being the sin against which the virtue of modernism was originally defined. Could this continuation of the battle of the styles have been anticipated in 1930, when the promise of being functionally correct was equivalent to being freed from the burden of style altogether? Richard Meier's architecture is so evocative of the originating phase of the modernist style, in all its purity, and particularly in the depth of its Corbusian loyalty, that it does not strike one as simply another manipulation of images. By a hallucinatory effect, the sheer consistency of the manner suggests that it has not been adopted arbitrarily, but is the application of a rule of measure. Consistency takes on the force of a principle.

One great advantage of this approach is that it restores a consistent relation between form and function. The play of large and small openings, of glass walls and windows, of canopied entrances and unmarked exits, of ship's rail and solid-fronted balconies, all works to ensure that the formal importances are made clear. Because these small differences are strictly controlled, they take on meaning as coded markers of the building's function. It is as if Richard Meier had renounced self-expression, client adulation, image-mongering, whim, and all accidental effects, in order to purify the material of architecture and render it transparent to the function. That, to do this, he has had to seize arbitrarily on a predetermined style, seems a small matter. In one sense, we may think that he is taking advantage, as with a take-over bid, of another's achievements. In another sense, we may be grateful to him for purging architecture of excessive levels of noise and disturbance, allowing us to see, as it were, the underlying realities of building. By a strange paradox, the narrowness of his preferred choice, and the limited range he allows himself, have resulted in his style being perceived as extremely personal. In the American marketplace, his "product" is readily identifiable. As pure white buildings are rarely found, it has a rarity value, yet the client has some preliminary idea what to expect: there is plenty of mileage in this.

As Richard Meier's work extends from private villas to institutional buildings, and moves from idyllic landscape settings to gritty urban streets, from the dynamic building lots of American real-estate to the confined sites of Europe, it will face new challenges and will perhaps suffer some inroads. It is not that he is unprepared for these, but it is also true that the older projects on difficult sites, such as the public housing and the medical center in the Bronx, do not share in the pristine vulnerability of the pure thirties style, and do not provide the same sort of evidence as to the viability of a consistent language of architecture. Both of those projects, although belonging to the seventies, seem to be historically indebted to the brutalist canon of the sixties. With the Atheneum at New Harmony, and the High Museum at Atlanta, however, a new path was opened by which whiter than white architecture, previously associated with privileged private clients who could do what they wanted within the confines of their property, was now offered as a serious contribution to the public realm. The High Museum has been an extremely popular building, and its reception by the general public is part of its potency as a solution for the dilemma of architectural style. Both of these projects, along with the Museum at Frankfurt, effect a transition from private to public scale without sacrificing the intensity of formal elaboration, the acute measuring of accent and incident, that confers meaning and authority. In the exhibition that took place in the 9H Gallery to coincide with Meier's receiving the RIBA Gold Medal, it was possible to study in detail the means by which the same crossing of the gap between private and public was effected, comparing the Westchester house with the City Hall and Library for the Hague (fig. 19). In its pristine whiteness, the model of the City Hall seems to leap across with verve. The less abstract rendering, with its glow of light sources, converging crowd, and wet reflective streets, reminds us of the inherent surreality of the cubist vision, and alerts us to the magnitude of the task which Richard Meier has undertaken.

In a sense this task is also like the recapitulation of the history of the Modern Movement. We see it moving from the creation of new objects of discovery and vision to repeated applications within recurring social and economic constraints. The great Corbusian villas represent a unique fusion of reason and unreason. While offering the seeds of a new language of architecture, capable of expansion into huge institutional enterprises like the Centrosoyus or the Palace of the Soviets, they also demonstrated their uniqueness and inwardness as objects of contemplation. While illustrating the five points of a rational architecture, they also gave architecture the possibilities of depth, figurative meaning, self-contradiction and ambiguity. These qualities were lost when their language was institutionalized.

20 BRIDGEPORT CENTER: BRIDGEPORT, CONNECTICUT
Richard Meier & Partners, 1989.

At another level, and in a very different setting, Richard Meier's houses also exhibit an inward quality; a self-awareness of their object-hood, a distancing of their banality as objects of use through an idealization of function in general; all this in conformity with the over-reaching aim of evolving a language. By their use of porcelain facings, along with steel frame, masonry enclosures, plywood skins, they are well adapted to their different conditions of production and to their particularity in place and time. In this respect, while they are a-historical in their formalism, they also appear to be free from nostalgic sentiment. The general self-isolation of so many American buildings allows us to view the Atheneum and the High Museum in terms of the privileged domain they define, and their projection of a guarded inner life: they are still objects surrounded by space. What is really challenging in Richard Meier's work is the attempt to retain the inner mystery while opening his buildings up to a more intensive invasion of function and use. The project at Bridgeport (fig. 20) seems to have suffered from this invasion, and to have lost the virtue of consistency. It is to be hoped that the projects at the Hague and at Ulm will, when realized, prove to have retrieved for us the sense of measure and meaning which is his hallmark.

Originally published in *Building Design*, September 16, 1988.

NORMAN FOSTER –
THE SACKLER GALLERIES

The twentieth century will surely go down in future history as the age of the museum. It is somehow deeply ironical that, at the very moment when technological development has become a threat to the living environment, and the conservation of nature becomes a vital part of the value of civilization, the conservation of the patrimony becomes dependent on a mass public. Objects of art now have to be made increasingly accessible to large numbers of people, an exposure which also increases the problems of their conservation. From this condition results a need to modify existing galleries of art, either by introducing a new organizational structure, as with Pei's pyramid at the Louvre, or by providing ancillary but essential accommodation to a higher standard, as with Venturi's new Sainsbury wing at the National Gallery in London.

A consequence of this need to expand physical facilities is the secondary need to be seen as up-to-date. Museums and galleries now exist in a competitive milieu, each one has to attract its share of the public. As Umberto Eco has shown,[1] the public expects entertainment as well as education: art galleries are competing with Disneyland as well as with each other. The gallery must become concerned with its public image.

In London, where the Tate and the National Gallery have both acquired a new wing, one can sympathize with the situation of the Royal Academy at Burlington House. The popularity of the annual

21 THE SACKLER GALLERIES, ROYAL ACADEMY OF THE ARTS (INTERIOR VIEW):
LONDON, ENGLAND
Foster Associates, 1991.

Summer exhibition has kept the gallery high in public esteem, but at the same time has confirmed its image as forever fixed, sentimentally untouchable, inevitably *vieux-jeu*. The situation of Burlington House—behind a formally exact fore-court giving on to a congested frontage in Piccadilly—simply does not allow space for a new wing. At this point, it became advisable to consult one of the architect Members, and we are fortunate that this led to Norman Foster being commissioned to solve the problem by modern methods, including the creation of space from nothing.

This indeed is the miracle that the architect has wrought. There was some hardly used spare gallery space at the top of the building, virtually inaccessible, since the staircase leading to it became visible only at the moment of leaving the tea-room. These galleries have now been re-constructed and given a new character, but the miracle lies in the new space of access, made out of a disused light well lying between the front and back portions of the existing building. There are two routes: either by slipping behind the main staircase by a passage on either side at ground level, or by making a single right turn at the top of the grand staircase, at the *piano nobile*. In either case one comes into a new lobby containing a machine—an elevator, on closer examination. This new lobby, contrived out of lost space, seems to have been conjured out of nowhere. It is nowhere space, a genuine piece of Utopia. Bathed in a diffused light from above, the elevator presents itself as a sort of time-machine by which one may escape into the fourth dimension and cheat the constraints of the everyday world (fig. 21).

And indeed, the machine rises into another world in which reality has been transformed. The cornice of the rear building, once a remote and unregarded relic, now becomes a Scarpa-like, hovering stone plinth on which sculpture is displayed, the new floor level being fixed at a convenient height below it of just under a meter. One retains a sense of being in a strange dimension. The lobby at which one arrives expands across the whole length of the building, becoming "lobby" as well as "sculpture gallery," but remaining at the same time a special space that exceeds its merely functional designations. It is a moment or two before one realizes that this new world in which one has arrived is simply the world of modern design, and that breathing may continue uninterrupted.

It is the quality of the light, as much as the unexpectedness of the space, that continues the sense of rebirth. It is controlled by a special kind of milky white plate glass, discovered only after a long search, which trans-

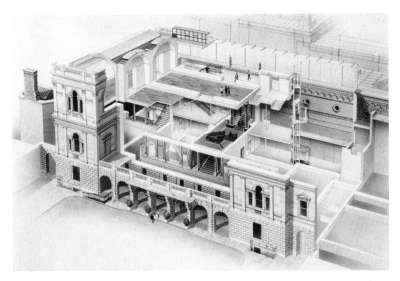

22   THE SACKLER GALLERIES (CUT-AWAY PERSPECTIVE RENDERING)
Foster Associates, 1991.

mits an intense but diffused radiance in all directions. At the same time this glass is impenetrable, firmly excluding the banal universe of roofs and gutters. One remains in an ideal world, clean, clinical, scientific.

The means of constructing this newly recovered dimension of space is an almost invisible set of Corbusian columns, running down the center line, and supporting the horizontal surfaces by cantilevered brackets, hardly touching the adjacent walls—wall surfaces which were once exposed, real and useless, now fossilized, unreal. The staircase and its landings, by which one may return down to the real world, is constructed from segments of thick glass, allowing as much light as possible to penetrate to the nether regions (fig. 22). It has the same formal precision as the elevator at the other end, and the same sense of being a machine that will work some strange effect on the body. Again, surprisingly, one survives its use without undergoing actual bodily harm.

By comparison with these intimations of mortality, the galleries themselves are reassuring and familiar. Here the surprise is to see how modern a barrel-vault may look when it is painted stark white. But of course the sense of absolute control persists in the precise proportioning of vertical and curved, in the thin line at the springing containing air-conditioning inlets, and in the groove at the base which divides the wall surface from the stone plinth without change of plane. The light, coming from the apex of the vault, is controlled by a set of moveable louvers set to the curve of the vault. There is a sense of fine-tuning which involves not just the physical characteristics of the light, but the psychological aspects of the space. There is no need here for the rather heavy reflectors which Kahn had to introduce with his pseudo-vaults at the Kimbell Museum in Texas, but one retains a sense of that precedent—this is probably the source of that feeling of familiarity. It seems that the generally rather clinical setting has been modified by an acknowledgement of a strictly "modern" tradition into which there passed, by way of Louis Kahn, an atavistic conscience, a further intimation of mortality that far exceeds the physical threat of daring construction. However this may be, the galleries are calm spaces which allow the art to come into its own.

One cannot but admire the way in which Foster has renovated the Royal Academy, not only by the ingenuity of his spatial planning, but by its psychology. It makes a utopia out of a lost space, and it makes a modern gallery out of an old familiar one. One may cavil at certain aspects, the inevitable consequences perhaps of the dominant ideology: the dead light of the sculpture gallery does not flatter the pieces of neoclassical academic work by John Gibson, which are difficult to see against the glass walls behind them; while Michaelangelo's *Tondu*, mounted in a beveled recess behind glass, is flattened into virtual invisibility (a concealed side light might return it to some degree of *chiaro-oscuro*). The concept of "modern," expressed by way of control of light, has produced the cliché "top-lit sculpture gallery." In the same way the necessary modernity, expressed in the clinically white walls of the galleries, has produced the cliché of "neutral setting," white being thought to be equally indifferent to all displays. I suspect that these aspects in the end are allowed to dominate the setting to a point where they obtrude an ideology. The concept of modernity is in this view mandatory rather than permissive, military rather than humanistic. One is grateful for that familiarity of the gallery form, which, whether or not a reflection of Kahn, leaves us with a sense of being human.

Originally published in *Casabella*, October 1991.

NOTES

1   See Umberto Ecco: *Travels in Hyper-reality*, Picador, 1987.

**23   MIXED DEVELOPMENT, PATERNOSTER SITE, ST. PAUL'S (SITE MODEL):
LONDON, ENGLAND**
Foster Associates, 1987.

NORMAN FOSTER–
THE URBAN DIMENSION

In the realist tradition of writing, "a novel will be deemed successful if the reader is persuaded that the picture is not the writer's composition but life itself, making its appearance on its own authority."[1] In exactly this sense Norman Foster's version of functionalism is realist in intention, aiming to present a view of design in which the solution has emerged from the raw material of circumstance. To this end he labors indefatigably to sift the raw material of circumstance in search of certain advantages by which space and structure may be defined in relation to stated needs and goals. The needs and goals stated are generally those of the client: those of the architect are subsumed and have to be inferred from the work as a whole.

The extreme formal precision of Foster's output makes it clear that this emphasis on the program is counterbalanced by some principles of design that derive more from the ideal than the circumstantial. The decisions about exactly which circumstances will contribute to the final solution remain hidden within the operational mysteries of the office. At the same time, there is no reason to doubt the architect's good faith, nor his dedication to the hard work of program analysis, nor his sensitivity to social aspects of architecture. If this sensitivity has a spatial dimension, that after all is the architect's expertise, his professional contribution. For example, in his design for a Special Care Unit for spastic children (1972), his analysis of needs focussed on the incontinence of the children, for which the remoteness of standard toilets was little help. He then produced an unusual layout where the core of toilets, divided only by low screens, is more readily accessible, and allows for both supervision and privacy. Along with improved functional efficiency comes a benefit in terms of a sense of spatial continuity and communal lightness. The "solution" is not typologically unique, but partakes of a general approach to the fitting out of activities derived from Miesian and Corbusian concepts of the free plan. It is analogous to the use of shoulder-height dividers to define architects' work-stations in the "office landscape," providing a carefully measured mixture of individual privacy and competitive continuity in the work environment.

One can speak, then, of a constant search for a formal order that is presumed to be initially hidden within the raw material of the program. One must also be allowed to speak of a search, within recognizable formal solutions, for certain variations and transformations that will sharpen these forms with new programmatic life. This dialectical relationship is not essentially different from that identified by Le Corbusier in his famous essay "In Defense of Architecture." Nor is it very different from the dialectic expounded by Louis Kahn as the conflict between the will-to-form of an object and its embodiment through a process of design that adapts to circumstance. Le Corbusier and Louis Kahn are important influences in Foster's development, and if he is not original in terms of the theory by which he operates, he is certainly unique in the degree to which he subjects the ideal object to circumstantial stress and distortion. Yet this never reduces the object to a mere accessory to the program; as the product of a well-defined process, it always radiates an intensity and a self-awareness that speaks of aesthetic closure and stylistic measure. It is necessary therefore to go a little further in attempting to define the ideal qualities which he pursues through his designs.

Within the tradition of modernism where Foster has placed himself, there is clearly to be found the retention of a certain machine aesthetic. This is no longer the somewhat abstracted aesthetic of the heroic modern period but more a latter-day imitation of machines, an imagery of some literalness which can also be, on occasion, quite surreal. In his most extravagant building to date, the Hong Kong and Shanghai Bank, there are intimations of the bridge, the engineer's shed, the space rocket. In probably his least extravagant building, the Air-supported Offices (1970), there are intimations of the airship. Foster has repeatedly stressed the need to seek technological means outside of the standard building tradition, with its reliance on wet trades and weight, and this search has led in the direction of light-weight materials and flight technology. If the oil-rig is the paradigm of the braced platform, the helicopter is the paradigm of power in reserve. But perhaps most attractive is the glider, the paradigm of minimal power, of beauty produced by circumstance (wind currents, clouds). This image is potent in Foster, insofar as it suggests an energy efficiency derived entirely from shape and structure. It is significant that Foster's longest-standing partner, Loren Butt, is an engineer specializing in energy. The ideal of energy utilization is the principle of elegance, as it is the ideal of mathematical proof, and it is elegance of the object that Foster pursues in the aesthetic dimension. For this reason the play of circumstance is an essential part of Foster's method, and Banham is correct in stressing in his work the ideal of "appropriate technology" rather than any doctrinaire addiction to the attractions of "hi-tech."[2] No Foster building can be adequately explained without regard to the circumstantial, whether this be located in the program as such, or in the detail accounting whereby the program is represented in form.

We come now to the question of the urban context: clearly the physical context of a Foster building is part of its circumstantial genesis, and also dialectically of its circumstantial aura, and the definition of appropriate technology cannot proceed without taking into account the whole idea of appropriateness to the site. As a maker of elegant objects, which draw at least part of their unexpectedness from some internal principle of organization, Foster has a peculiar responsibility in dealing with the external pressures present in the urban context, the more so as these are as much social as physical, and he has always presented himself as sensitive to social factors.

This is almost a novel question, since the greater part of Foster's work to date has been on isolated or "greenfield" sites. But with his office building for Willis Faber Dumas (1975) we come squarely up against the urban context.

The *Architectural Review*, in publishing a review of this building,[3] was concerned that it introduced a negative factor into the townscape, since its entirely glazed walls offer no incident of scale or character, but blankly reflect the surrounding buildings in a fractured, surrealist manner. What would happen, the *Review* asked, if the adjoining buildings in turn were replaced by similar reflecting glass objects? It is true that Willis Faber Dumas is disconcerting in that its appearance fluctuates between two contradictory extremes: when the internal lighting is stronger than the outside light level, it displays its structure as a three-story building; at other times the glass wall becomes a reflecting barrier, as impregnable as granite. However, before dismissing it as entirely negative to the townscape, it is worth asking what it does, if anything, in recognition of its urban setting. The positive aspects may be summarized as follows: the building reinforces the given street pattern; in avoiding the conventional organization into "podium" and "tower," it conforms to the planners' preference for a three-story envelope (a partial fourth story is virtually invisible from the street); and the face towards the old Unitarian Church, and its garden setting, is classically orthogonal in disposition, creating a pleasant civic square on the side facing the mediaeval town. Since on the opposite side, the mediaeval street pattern no longer holds, and a loose suburban pattern takes over, the offense offered by the glass fortress is hardly egregious. Nevertheless, it is startling to come upon, and it embodies, in a novel form, the conflict between the internal world of the client and user, and the external world of citizen and shared convention. Foster is in the habit of seeking advantage for his client, and he enjoys rejecting conventional wisdom, so we shall expect to find other instances of this conflict.

The Radio Center (1983) is such an instance. The glazed mall which bisects it diagonally is positioned to provide a pedestrian link between the north-east corner of Cavendish Square and the bend in Regent Street at Langham Place, doubly articulated at this point by the curved front of the old BBC building and the circular portico of John Nash's church. The internal system of office layout is made orthogonal to this mall, with the advantage that this produces considerable variation of depth within the envelope, giving cross axes of different lengths. At the perimeter, just as at Willis Faber Dumas, a secondary columnar system parallel to the street elevations sews the edge to the street pattern. The use of a diagonal geometry is only apparent at the points where the transverse axes meet the periphery with fire stair exits. The internal layout has thus been conceived in order to make sense of the pedestrian flow through the building, and to orient the building as a whole towards the civic register of Cavendish Square, All Souls Church, and the "parent" building.

It is characteristic of Foster that the civic dimension should be recognized in terms of pedestrian flow, a factor both social and operational, but also physical and measurable. What is absent is the use of figuration by means of traditional architectural motifs that gesture towards the civic context as a historical continuum. There is no trace here of the postmodernism of facades, and this is clearly a point of honor with the architect, an expression of his ideological commitment to functionalism. This is not to say that we are dealing here with an architecture of degree zero, that the objects produced are devoid of ideological stance and are in some sense objective correlates of the program. As we have seen, the program is as much penetrated by a selective sensibility as are the formal means adopted. The approach encompasses both an apparently objective web of circumstance, and a circumstantial aura that expresses contingency as an absolute value. For this reason, the resulting architecture is not manifestly "civic," even in the reduced sense allowed by Giorgio Grassi, but remains in some way hostile to the historical context and reformative towards it.

The conflict between internal program and civic context is perhaps at its most poignant in the case of the Médiathèque at Nîmes. The program has all the potential provocation of a populist demonstration, a provincial Pompidou Center, but it is pointed irrevocably towards the flank of the Maison Carrée, the most perfect relic of antiquity in France. All of Foster's studies for this commission reflect a certain agony in dealing with the tension between these polar references. It is not surprising that one senses here the shadow of Louis Kahn, who in his own work made a change of commitment between the claims of the future and those of the past.

In Foster, the issue of spatial direction, of longitudinal frontality, is tied up with the concept of the industrial shed. The shed is one of the recognizable types in his repertoire, since it embodies the principle of serial construction with regular structural elements, as first demonstrated in the Crystal Palace. The shed in its pure linearity is the prototype for the Modern Art Glass Building (1973) and the Sainsbury Center (1977), and it reappears in other projects, most surprisingly perhaps, in the high-rise format of the Hong-Kong and Shanghai Bank (1986). While the form is generated from the need to reconcile serial structure with the rational disposition of the service elements, it does have the inevitable consequence of producing directed space, and this quality of space appears to be actively sought and enjoyed for its own sake. At Sainsbury, the ends of this spatial flow are marked by external recesses which have the feeling of being porticos, even in the absence of formal entrances. One can make a direct comparison between the "portico" at the outer end of the Sainsbury Center and the evident portico at the outer end of the Palazzo dei Congressi at E.U.R. Both have similar spatial properties, and both recognize the technological counter-motive in their lattice-work, in the main structure in the former, in the window mullions in the latter. There is a further irony in this comparison, in that Libera was forced to insert an order of giant Tuscan columns in his portico (in the corresponding one at the other end of the building), whereas at Nîmes, Foster was narrowly able to avoid incorporating an array of classical columns surviving from the old Municipal Theater.

In any event, the overhang of the roof at the outer end facing the Maison Carrée has all the qualities of a civic portico, if not a classical one. Moreover, as we can see from the four intermediate steps by which the design evolved, the architect was not only concerned with his civic duty towards the monument, but with the need to recognize also the bias of the civic space as determined by the frontality of the Maison Carrée. This is reflected variously in the use of splayed sides, and in the off-center placement of the glazed atrium which extends back through the space. A further reflection of the civic role of the building is evident in the adoption of a monumental form in the serial staircase which joins the main public floors and confirms the directionality of the space. This is far removed from the mechanical aspect of the external escalators at the Pompidou Center. The Médiathèque thus reveals in Foster a sensibility towards civic convention, even if his method constrains his response.

Urban design is not a major factor in the case of the additions to Burlington House for the Royal Academy, since the effect on external space is minimal, although the changes will allow the public to use a new entrance courtyard and appreciate an unfamiliar aspect of the building. What strikes one about these proposals is the efficiency and discretion with which the new elements have been incorporated, while allowing a better use of the existing features, such as the main monumental staircase, to be enjoyed. With the small Thames-side development at Chelsea Reach, there is a delicate balance struck between the symmetry of the three elements of the plan, and the asymmetrical dominance of the higher volume alongside the river. This plan enables us to see the essential rationalism within Foster's sometimes sensational images.

In the case of the building for the Royal Thames Yacht Club, in Knightsbridge, the rationality is compromised by the sensational accent placed on the two elevators, brought forward and exposed outside the main entrance, although approached in use from within —a play reminiscent of the escalators at the Pompidou Center, similarly displayed on the outside, but approached from within. In such cases one senses the architect's need to balance discretion with physical vigor, like reasserting youth against age. But one may certainly question whether the exhibition of moving parts is not already falling into the category of cliché. In this case it appears to diminish unfairly the status of the small neoclassical building standing on the left of the entrance.

The scheme for Paternoster Square (fig. 23) has something in common with the Radio Center, in the way in which office space is broken down and differentiated by the use of top-lit access elements. Since the site is irregular anyway, there was no inhibition against allowing these channels to run north-south, in varying lengths, reinforcing a directionality towards the public space around St. Paul's Cathedral, and incidentally towards the river Thames, Europe and the sun. The south face of the new complex would clearly be a place of public amenity, with a certain democratic aspect as each section of offices reaches its place on the barrier facing the Cathedral. The building height is moderated, as with Willis Faber Dumas, and the result is more like a kind of casbah than the mishmash of standard office buildings that is due to be replaced on this site. Yet one may be forgiven for questioning the adequacy of such a organizationally systematic complex as a setting for the City of London's greatest monument.

St. Paul's itself is, in Foster's terms, a dishonest building, since its entire upper story has no other function than to screen the essentially gothic organization of the nave and aisles. The honesty in which the modern architect takes such pride, his constant efforts to be transparent towards the program, seem in this context to be trivial and somewhat puerile. The selection of what is to be given significance remains hidden and doubtful. The approach allows an organizational order, certainly, but is organization a sufficient principle of art, as Hannes Meyer proposed? It is interesting that among the architect's analytical sketches there is one that shows some diversity of character among the pieces, suggesting that the layout is a masterplan, or structure plan, capable of providing "a basis for individual identities and separate design responsibilities." In that admission there is a whole world of adjustment still to be made. It expresses a dissatisfaction with the implied uniformity of corporate offices, but it also limits the scope of individual identity to what is consonant with the dominance of an organizational system. It is the pressures of the functional tradition, with its emphasis on transparency towards the program, that limits the accommodation with the flow of history and civic convention. Yet, such is the eagerness with which others have all too readily embraced appearance, dissimulation and accommodation that our impatience with Norman Foster is mixed with gratitude.

Originally published in *Casabella*, No. 557, May 1989, as "The Urban Dimension in Norman Foster."

NOTES

1   Denis Donoghue: review of John Updike's *Memoirs*, in *The New York Times Book Review*, March 5, 1989, p. 7.
2   Reyner Banham: Introduction to *Foster Associates*, RIBA Publications, 1979, p. 5.
3   *Architectural Review*, September 1975, editorial p. 131.

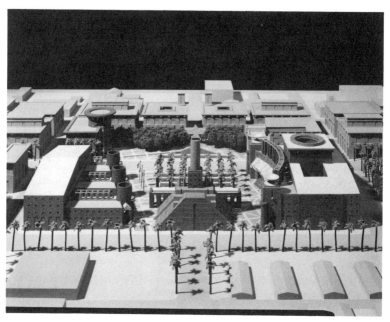

24   PHOENIX MUNICIPAL CENTER (MODEL, VIEW FROM SOUTH): PHOENIX, ARIZONA
Michael Graves, Architect, 1985.

MICHAEL GRAVES: COMPOSITION AS A TEST OF LANGUAGE

Recent projects by Michael Graves share a theme: the re-discovery of an architectural language that is both learned and learnable, at once recondite and open to interpretation. The mastery with which a limited array of elements and figures is combined and recombined in Graves's work should not deceive us into seeing this architecture as facile: it is experimental. The choice of elements no doubt reflects the architect's taste—how could it not? However, the interest is not simply in the specificity of his allusions, the clear traces of Ledoux, of Gilly, of Schinkel, the neoclassic aura; nor in the fact that the prominence of those historical references makes Graves a postmodernist in a world where this has come to imply the deliberate manipulation of images. The interest lies rather in the testing of this repertoire of elements to verify its strength as a system of composition.

If composition is again credible—that is, if it can be repeated indefinitely without loss of conviction—then it is possible equally to define a system of architecture that permits it, an architecture that takes as its goal not only the satisfaction of a social need, but the status of a work of art. Like all good architecture, it could be infinitely adaptable, it could register continuity but reveal the unexpected, it could function as a language that is already understood, and thus bring meaning to life, a goal that is incidentally also a social need.

Hannes Meyer stated the opposite position when he rejected composition within architecture as the activity proper only to art. "All art is composition and hence unsuited to a particular end. All life is function and therefore not artistic. The idea of the 'composition of a dock' is enough to make a cat laugh."[1] If architecture's purpose is only to reflect function, to become visible and have form only to the degree that it transparently reveals the program, composition indeed becomes impossible. The dominant mode in that case is one of organization which is, or tries to be, rational and logical, and whose only goal is to fulfill the conditions of the program. Buildings will then have no meaning other than that conferred by use and habitation.

To the historical avant-garde that was highly desirable: not only in the sense that architecture must be subservient to program in order to serve the revolution, but also in a contrary, indeed fundamentally contradictory sense, for only through the magnetism of the program by function could architecture be purged of its cultural sediment, freed from all convention, homogenized and thus delivered over as purely plastic material to serve the intentions of the new socialist architect. Those intentions were, naturally, propagandist, and the forms thus delivered to him were abstract. Paradoxically, this architect continued to work by intuition, to attend to the free movement of subjective emotion, in his sovereignty as abstract artist, in his power to abstract.

It seems that functionality was valued both as a goal, and as a method that produced unexpected results. By revealing the unexpected it became the equivalent of an avant-garde activity, capable of surprising and subverting. It conferred on the true functionalist the role of an iconoclast, the aura of an original artist. The true functionalist building was to symbolize nothing, as a value, other than its purpose. If, in Meyer's design for the League of Nations, there was no front door, but only specialized entrances from the car park basement, that was to be a recognition of functionality. Yet it was impossible for the absence of a front door not to read as a symbolic gesture. The logical system of the building is always enclosed in a social system that confers meaning willy-nilly by comparison with other forms and other conditions prevailing.

Graves, on the other hand, rejects the functional as the unique source of meaning. Meaning arises from use and habitation, of course, but also from the form employed, with its myriad links to the conditions prevailing. In his investigations of the potential of a reinvigorated rule of composition, Graves is seeking to recover an art of architecture. By testing the resilience and durability of his material he seeks to redefine architecture as an inherited cultural substance. For him the cohesive potential of his forms is as important as the divergent possibilities of expression that may be revealed incidentally.

By substance, I do not mean only the chosen material of construction, which is certainly the substance of architectural expression. I follow the Hjelmslevian distinction between the plane of thought and the plane of expression, in each of which a further distinction may be made between substance and form.[2] In this analysis thought and expression both possess a substance and a form, and form, common to both, becomes in Hjemslev the vital zone in which thought finds expression. Form in Graves is then a link between his expressive intent and a pre-existent substance of architecture. The act of composition, in which the formal articulation of that substance is achieved through the selection and rearrangement of the elements—column, wall, opening, grid, and so on—becomes the validating process by which meanings are re-assigned and meaning is retrieved.

All art involves a balance between polar opposites, as between order and disorder, diction and contradiction, simplicity and complexity. Where complexity has been seen as analogous to nature, it has tended towards the illegible, the mystic, the arcane, as in Eisenman. With Graves legibility remains crucial and so in place of a processal complexity he cultivates a formal versatility, essential to him as the antithesis to the simplicities of a fundamentally classical approach. It is enough to point to this dialectical balance in Graves to distinguish his architecture from the robotic simplification of Nazi neoclassism, and equally from the facile convolutions of commercial postmodernism.

Does Graves succeed in his aim? Certainly he demonstrates an extraordinary versatility. As his projects show, the elements of his art have been to a remarkable degree stabilized over the last ten years. To me the astonishing thing is not that he repeats himself, but that his repetitions should be so varied, so bold, so unexpected in their effects. This vein of richness is clearly far from exhausted.

As to the method of composition, this, it is true, retains a strong trace of its origins in the principle of cubist collage, for which Graves has a penchant. In its original form, as employed by Gris, Picasso, Braque, during the phase of synthetic cubism, the free choice of elements, whether of pigmented figures or applied materials, was balanced against the planar composition made possible through the use of abstraction. The incongruity of contrasting materials was contained by the synthesizing sensibility of the sovereign artist. In Graves's Portland Building the juxtaposition of figures is clearly analogous, in that the flat shapes are 'pasted' together: as for instance, in the main key-stone figure which is formed partly by color differentiation and partly by a substitution of strip fenestration in place of the adjacent punched-hole windows. That was shocking in its disregard for functional expression, since the juxtaposed surface figures are imposed across uniformly office-use spaces. The arbitrary choice of expression (arbitrary as regards function) may be justified here if both forms of fenestration are conceded to be at least adequate for the uses. This is perfectly consonant with the systematic view of function which evolved by the end of the design-method movement: there was no longer a claim that each function demanded specific form, but only that certain forms excluded certain functions. Defined negatively, functional proprieties may allow a wide variety of formal options, just as in the design of a beam, as Le Corbusier pointed out, many cross-sections may be dimensionally adequate, allowing the engineer to choose one that fits into other criteria. Graves, it may be said, is perfectly respectful of function, viewed in this way. His Portland Building met all the requirements of cost and economy, and his design for the Phoenix Municipal Center was not rejected on functional grounds—according to the jury's analysis, it met programmatic and economic requirements better than the designated winner.

The questions that arise about the use of collage as a method of composition are not so much governed by its relation to functionality, but rather arise in relation to the morality of forms. An artist like Eduardo Paolozzi justifies collage, or the re-assemblage of abstracted or dislocated parts, as something like a moral imperative: our age faces disintegration through social cancer and the destructive shadow of the hydrogen bomb. Only by bricolage may one assert a vestige of artistic wholeness against an over-riding cultural *déchéance*. His frequent choice of technological figures is itself an acknowledgement of the ambiguous nature of our successes, for technology is at once the source of futurist excitement and ecological foreboding. Venturi takes a less apocalyptic, but equally pessimistic stance. The entrance figure at Wu Hall, on Princeton campus, is a flat composition because it is emblematic of a lost architecture: we may express our awareness of that loss but we cannot restore it in its plastic richness and wholeness. Graves, however, seems to be attempting just that.

Increasingly, his juxtapositions are asserted not from despair but from ambition. The projecting lattice bracket on the front of his Humana Building is not an assertion of the power of steel construction or a denial of that of masonry, but a symbolic gesture by which the building reaches out expressively towards the river and its steel lattice bridges. In the same way the lattice structure proposed to tie together the segmented array of apartment buildings at 'Grand Reef' Galveston, does not carry a polemic about technology as an alternative, a challenging system, but seeks to add to the repertoire of forms by which grand scale compositions may be made, and, in this case, to create a kind of sea portal to the resort as a whole.

In his willingness to use technological elements as part of the lexicon, Graves asserts a typical American pragmatism. Unlike Leon Krier, who prefers to renounce the practice of architecture—as a form of protest against the present condition of society and its reliance on alienating mechanisms—Graves is keen to build. In the American context he has no especial difficulty in finding clients. However shocking architects found the Portland Building, it was not only constructed within a very tight budget but has put the city on the map as successfully as any futuristic design could have done. The Humana Building has also been acclaimed, this time not only by its users, but by visiting architects who can appreciate its contribution to the townscape; while the library at San Juan Capistrano has been highly popular with its users—adults and children alike. In Graves's professional stance, he reaps a bonus from an ideological position based on the retrievability of architectural forms, because all the conservative values of contextualism, of institutional continuity, of civic symbolism and pride, are on his side. His boldness lies not in technological innovation (to which he would no doubt assign a limited role) but in his power to reactivate old symbols. Many commercial architects are quick to jump on this bandwagon, but they do not usually display the inward sensitivity to the substance of architecture that Graves does.

In this respect it is noteworthy that Kevin Roche, whom Francesco Dal Co has singled out as the doyen architect of consumer opportunism, has had no internal problem in adapting to a movement that he sees as merely fashionable. So he can painlessly substitute a neoclassic model (as in the Morgan Bank headquarters) for a minimal abstraction model (as in United Nations Plaza).[3] Kevin Roche, in his determination to build and to serve society by building, accepts the complete normality of fashion as the instigator of consumer interest and the motor of the capitalist dynamic. His stance enables us to see that Graves, although he finds his opportunities within that same society, is not opportunistic in the same way. With him, the recovery of an architecture constitutes an ideal that transcends both technological and economic motivations, and looks to the reconstruction of wholeness rather than feeding on the incidence of change.

This may be best seen at the scale of larger complexes, where the issue of contextuality is important. Here one may voice a regret that Graves's design for the Municipal Center at Phoenix is not to be built. Within this design, a clear hierarchy is displayed which is compositional, in the artistic sense, but positional, in the civic sense (fig. 24). In the final design the council chamber is given the prime position, facing the principal street. Although smaller than the adjacent offices, it dominates both by its sculptural form and by its axiality. To this frontality the convex front of the municipal offices and the diagonal series of the opposing buildings offer a compositional counterpoint. Artistically speaking they convey a hierarchy, establishing the focus of attention in a composition of an admittedly somewhat cubist nature. Outside of that composition a frame is provided of consistent yet comparatively ordinary buildings, forming a smooth transition to the order of the street grid and its attendant accident and disorder. There is a clear advantage in the adoption of this essentially classical format, for it requires no elaboration of a boundary, or barrier, within which an aesthetic realm can only appear by redesigning the rules of normalcy. As the mode of composition is centripetal rather than centrifugal, it defines itself by its intensification towards the center, not by its dissipation of tensions to a limiting boundary. In this respect the compositional method seems to have dispensed with the edge or boundary which defines the realm of cubist space.[4]

In civic terms this represents a concept directly opposed to the Modern Movement concept of the object-building generated from internal forces. It is rather the combination of building and context that generates civic space, and hence civic meaning, and they are evidently designed together with this intention. The question for us is to what extent this intention and its implementation in real time represents a rejection of the principle of composition based on collage; whether collage is by its nature strictly confined to cubistic fragmentation, or apocalyptic disintegration, and whether it is not therefore an expression of dissent and cannot without contradiction form the basis for a more conservative and reactionary system.

A critical view of Graves's work would no doubt concede that a hierarchical and holistic approach has indeed been substituted for the more fragmentary approach that marked the transition from the cubistic, Corbusian phase of his work (as in Hanselmann, Benacerraf) to the figural, classical phase (as in Plocek). The increasing coherence of the work may be a mark of his increasing confidence in the ideal, or may be dismissed as increasing surrender to the scenographic. In any case the results will not be admitted as in themselves constituting a challenge to the dogmas of negative dialectic, nor as proving the existence of an alternative to collage as the only compositional approach that deals with pure surfaces and their differentiation.

It is here that one can look with further interest at the more recent projects of Graves, considering them as buildings. For it seems to me that at the purely tectonic level, where we are considering the transition between structure and surface, Graves's position is also experimental.

For all their evocation of a neoclassical past, these projects are securely within a modern constructional framework. Masonry is understood here, not in the sense of the cathedral builders of the twelfth century, but as a subsidiary technique for in-filling frames. Very few American buildings are built of anything other than frame: timber for small structures, steel or ferro-concrete for large. Modernity in the 80s is gauged largely by the sophistication of the surface skin which is held out from that frame, and this is as true of Richard Meier's High Museum as of Kevin Roche's projected glass-and-granite skyscrapers. In the High Museum, the white surface that recalls the constructional concrete of the International Style is just such a skin, and tectonically, it is hardly different from a Roche design where thin sheets of granite are combined with thin sheets of plate glass in an equivalence that has little to do, constructionally, with the organization of the structure into solids and voids. It seems to me that, given the resulting ambiguity of all surface systems, it becomes a matter of concern to determine by what architectural rules the surface may be differentiated; firstly as regards the stereometric image of solid and void, walls and openings, that is desired, and secondly as regards the hierarchy of differentiation that may be proposed.

In the cases of both Kevin Roche and Richardo Bofill we will find an aggressive play with architectural possibilities within this area. Bofill has found ways of "constructing" a giant order out of a service duct or a bow window repeated on many floors. Roche, in his Morgan Bank headquarters, will carry horizontal strips of granite and glass across profiles that adumbrate plinth, giant order and attic temple. In such schemes we see the figures as fugitive, expiatory, hollow, in no way offering any resistance to the exploitive aspect of capitalistic enterprise. I don't think this is the case with Graves. What is different is precisely the concern with vocabulary, with syntax, with the problem of fitting together.

If we compare the Condominium at Grand Reef Galveston with the Columbus Circle scheme, for instance, we find that both employ the flat Ledoux arch as a principle figure, cut out of the surface of the block. In both we find a lower block, thus organized, contrasted with a duality of towers rising above and behind, which exhibit a more planar, or more trabeated texture. There is a broad similarity of the compositional elements in the two schemes, but a marked difference in the character of each building. Those similarities are the means by which those differences stand out. They are evidence that what is happening is the testing of an architectonic system whose capabilities will extend far beyond the range of a single occasion, and in that sense are not exploitive but conservative.

Again, we must recognize a serious intent even in a commercial scheme like that for Blocks B and 9 at Stamford. Graves makes no bones about providing car park spaces, but those parking volumes do not find expression on the facades. Since surface has become a prime resource for differentiation, it can allow a civic surface to mask a civic utility. But this device is not in itself obtruded: it is simply taken for granted that the unity of the composition demands a combination of consistent elements. The concern is no longer with a naive revelation of function, but with a sophisticated attention to surface as the bearer of tidings, to connoisseur and to citizen alike.

Working at the super-scale of whole buildings (as do Bofill and Roche) Graves still accedes to the need for measure and decorum. These are the necessary logical consequences of a civic architecture that permits composition and that recuperates meaning.

It seems that in Graves's work, surface differentiation, though sometimes arbitrary in relation to function (within limits), is undertaken in the interest of establishing a larger unity. The juxtapositions are not intended to produce shock (as appears to be the case with Bofill) with the subsequent recognition of a non-human scale and order. Here human scale is exceeded only as a means of establishing continuity between different aspects of the building: its face to the sidewalk, its face to the street, to the river, to the distant view. Certainly there is a play with scale, and an element of strangeness, for that is essential to art, and to no art more than to architecture which risks being overwhelmed by the banal, but which suffers if exaggerated beyond what daily life will bear.

There is a real advantage in reviewing Graves's work through these recent projects. Every one of them is conceived within a concept of civic space, differentiated from the city yet bound up in it. They all bear an imprint that is instantly recognizable, yet none of them, if built, will contradict the actuality of the city, with the existing continuity of its streets and facades. They count upon that continuity for their own prominence and distinction, just as they count upon a continuity of culture for the perception in them of that which is old and that which is new.

Originally published in *Lotus International,* No. 50, Fall 1986.

NOTES

See Claude Schnaidt: *Hannes Meyer,* Niedertaufen, 1975.
See Hjelmslev: *Prolégomème à une théorie du langage,* tr. R. Lindekins, Hatier, Paris, 1975.
See Francisco Dal Co: *Kevin Roche,* Milan-New York, 1986.
It is interesting to note that the design of Legorreta, in the same contest, was abstract expressionist in approach, and attempted to make just such a boundary and establish such a distinction between its own space and the rest of the city.

THE DIALECTICS OF BRAIN
AND HEART

STIRLING AS A MASTER OF MANNERISM

25 STAATSGALERIE: STUTTGART, GERMANY
James Stirling Michael Wilford & Associates, 1984.

THE ARCHITECT AS ARTIST

It is gratifying, in retrospect, that James Stirling was awarded the RIBA Gold Medal no later than last year, an occasion that preceded his award of the Pritzker Prize this year. If the order of giving had been reversed it would have looked as if we were struggling belatedly to recognize merit where others had long discerned it. So the prophet is not after all without honor in his own country.

And yet, within Britain, while Stirling is dimly understood to be out of the ordinary, he is hardly accepted as great. The cartoonist Hellman's comment on the Gold Medal showed a heavyweight figure skating over thin ice. Skating—here equated with artistic endeavor—is inappropriate both to the character of the architect as a burly type and to the deceptive nature of the environment as a source of joy.

In England, in particular, there is a peculiar breath of scandal attaching to the pursuit of architecture as art. Criticism of architecture in the public mind is broadly associated with sociological or material failure, and these specters haunt the practice of architecture. Yet when such faults occur they are not thought to be really scandalous except when associated with high architectural aspirations. Aiming high, which must mean being concerned about something other than the avoidance of sociological or material failure, becomes itself the measure of an increased risk. To practice architecture as an art implies an idea of hubris. On the whole we feel safer if architectural aspirations are confined to the notion of building as a craft, using only well-tried methods corresponding to complete subservience to the social order. Even that approach, if followed closely, would probably appear as too radical in our consumer-oriented society, with its emphasis on good taste—usually degenerating into high-minded good taste. Stirling has repudiated such a limited role and has seen the need to actively avoid good taste. It was Stirling who said: "Let's face it, William Morris was a Swede!"[1]

The risks that Stirling has been seen to take are, paradoxically, of two kinds, corresponding to two major phases of his career: at the beginning he was thought to be manipulating form in the name of modernity; and then, when that was accepted, he suddenly appeared to be manipulating it in the name of history.

He came to public notice with the Stirling and Gowan masterpiece at Leicester University, in an uncompromisingly modern style that made no concessions to campus conformity but did express the forthright stance of engineering research. The general language of non-conformity used at Leicester had been anticipated in the firm's design for Selwyn College in 1959, and was followed by Stirling's own development in his buildings for the Universities of Cambridge (1964), St. Andrews (1964) and Oxford (1966).

The character of these three buildings is in different degrees a celebration of modernity. They are all conceived within a canon of form following function, and they all show evidence of technological innovation, as in the use of adhesive red tiles to match with brickwork in the vertical cladding, the use of cheap greenhouse glazing in large areas, or the development of large-scale structural units. They all fall within the concept of an orthodox modernity that, in Pevsner's definition, was expected to display "new methods and materials, the vital aspect of progressive architecture."[2] In this spirit, too, are the rounded plastic casings of the Olivetti Training Center at Haslemere—an architectural equivalent of the modern look of industrial design for which Olivetti typewriters were famous.

The search for technological innovation was obligatory, both as an index of modernity and as a mark of continuity in the tradition of modernity, since it was technological innovation that identified the new spirit in the first place, in its most British beginnings. It is clear that Stirling identified himself with that tradition, both in its Britishness and in its inventive enterprise, preceding as it did the subsequent transformation of it to an engineering aesthetic in the pages of *L'esprit Nouveau*. This nationalistic bias is revealed in Stirling's own words:

"One only has to compare the Crystal Palace to the Festival of Britain, or the Victorian railway stations to recent airport terminals, to appreciate the desperate situation of our technological inventiveness in comparison to the supreme position which we held in the last century."[3]

Reyner Banham, in assessing the History Faculty Building at Cambridge, thought that it made all other recent buildings in Cambridge look effete. There is a tough-mindedness, a robust self-reliance, not only in its use of materials and in its technological directness, but also in the derivation and organization of its forms and spaces. It entirely escapes the stigma of merely looking modern, it does not merely reproduce the modern "look," tied so often at this period to the excessive use of concrete or the image of mediterranean cells. If anything, it looks British. But in terms of popular image, it fulfills the Russian Formalists prescription for art: it makes the familiar strange. It has to be learned to be loved.

In the seventies, new tendencies began to appear in Stirling's work: a new interest in context, in symmetry, in historical allusion. For those who had learned to love the tough-minded analysis that characterizes his heroic style, with its aura of an entirely native tradition of modernity, these new tendencies seemed to imply a volte-face. They certainly imply a revaluation of architecture as an ancient art embodied in an essentially European tradition. Neoclassism is not an English invention, if England has in the past contributed its share of that development. Leon Krier, a good European, was undoubtedly an influence, or possibly a catalyst, but the tendency towards reviewing classical models was evident before he arrived in the Stirling office (the Runcorn housing, designed in 1967, shows as much neoclassism as does Siemens two years later, when Krier had arrived). Indeed the interest in classical models is evident long before, as in the Isle of Wight house of 1956, which owes something to Kahn (as well as to the contemporary interest in neopalladianism; and can even be seen in the Stirling Liverpool thesis design of 1950).

Do these new tendencies really imply a *volte-face*? Stirling has been at pains to stress the continuity between his phases. His early work, of more domestic scale and character, was nearly all designed within a simple discipline of brick construction, but it also drew explicitly upon vernacular elements and the native functional tradition of barns and warehouses, canal bridges and signal cabins, as much as upon ideas of high modernity. His initial empiricism had a sound basis in terms of overall economy and in terms of his own wish to acquire the rudiments of a constructional technique. Many aspects of early Stirling and Gowan have been absorbed into Local Authority housing conventions, and the resulting familiarity obscures the fact that they originally constituted a novel approach to the definition of a practical modernity that would suit the British climate. Nowhere in early Stirling do we come upon the conventional signs of the International Style, and indeed Stirling frequently inveighed against "shoe-box architecture," which he correctly saw was all too vulnerable to the mono-dimensional men, the developers who employed accountants to reveal the essential bottom line. From the beginning of Stirling's practice we are aware of a strong independence, and a depth of reflection on the nature of building and the relation of building to expression. Single-minded his architecture has been, but never simple-minded.

He has also been at pains to point out—in distinction to what he saw as the "arbitrary" interpretations of critics (such as Jencks's insistence on the presence of a marine metaphor in St. Andrews)—the regular and architectonic sources of design ideas in his work.[4] These add up to a wide collection of concepts and precedents ranging from sectioned machines (Sheffield) and Cotswold barns (Woolton House) to stately gate towers (Florey) and Inca stonework (St. Andrews). The wide range of his sources is the mark of an extremely intelligent and even erudite sensibility, and shows us that Stirling has always appreciated that form does not derive from function in a narrow sense, but only through the mediation of a tradition, that is, within a cultural envelope.

Agreed that his architecture shows a consistency in its very depth of cultural relativity, it is still evident that a marked change of attitude has taken place at the end of the seventies, and that modernity in its original sense of being technically innovative is no longer the sole aim of his work today.

It is tempting at this point to reconsider his debt to Le Corbusier. Stirling's work shows an awareness of all the great men in the heroic age of modern architecture, including Kahn, and he has learned something from all of them. But there is evidence that he has paid particular attention to both Wright and Le Corbusier, and in some way wanted to reconcile their qualities in his own work. Aside from their work in its detail, both these role models had careers marked by abrupt changes of style. Le Corbusier's career has had a particular importance here.

Stirling's main contributions to architectural criticism are contained in the two articles he produced in the mid-fifties, and these are both concerned with Le Corbusier's *volte-face*.[5]

With Jaoul, and with Ronchamp, there appeared to be an abandonment of a rational, technologically progressive modernity in favor of an emotional, technologically regressive vernacularity. Le Corbusier's change of heart, his acceptance of "Algerian" standards of workmanship, posed a problem, and at the same time opened a door. Stirling meditated deeply the consequences of Le Corbusier's having "gone soft with Ronchamp." Out of this meditation came a brick architecture that was not soft, but hard, hard in its precision of profile and in its ability to define taut abstract planes: empirical, but modern.

Stirling had always appreciated that Le Corbusier was an eclectic borrower, noting his debt to Mediterranean vernacular and his sensitivity to Indian forms, as evidenced at Chandigarh. But in the very source of Stirling's style there was a problematic: modernity was never more to be a simple matter of only following function. It involved choices that function alone could not determine, even within the idea of radically recasting the program. For many, and this included Stirling, it involved a necessary meditation on form, and on what I have called the two faces of form: the face that beckons on, and the face that looks back.

In a somewhat obvious way Le Corbusier's *volte-face* with Jaoul provided Stirling with a source of empirical freedom. It legitimated the flats at Ham Common and the subsequent explorations of a brick vernacular. It was the mastery of brickwork which permitted the greater adventurousness of the later university buildings. The modernity that was sought within the tough discipline of brick cross-walls was then released when larger commissions allowed a freer approach, including the vital element of technological innovation. But what was learned during those largely preparatory years was more than a constructional understanding of brickwork. It was rather a matter of how to extract from a recalcitrant material the immaterial and abstract qualities of a weightless architecture, of an architecture formed in the mind. Form, and its manipulation, becomes the source of possibilities that are not suggested by construction alone.

Peter Eisenman, in his analysis of Leicester Engineering, is able to demonstrate rather convincingly that constructional elements such as brick and glass are consistently played with as purely formal values in a game of ambiguity and reversal.[6] This sophistication of conception (which it needed an American critic to discover) indicates that Stirling has deeply meditated the question of architecture as an expression of its own articulations, that is, as language, by that fact alone confronted with all the problems that attend the use of language; not least, the problems of defining the language spoken in the act of speaking it. In the words of Manfredo Tafuri:

> "Stirling has 'rewritten' the 'words' of modern architecture, building a true 'archeology of the present.'"[7]

There is no "betrayal" of modernity in this, as some would have us believe, because the very terms of what is "modern" have been exposed as a kind of illusion, as constituting a concept that dissolves the moment it is taken into meditation. There is a new search for the locus of modernity in a non-utopian future. The appearance in Stirling's work of motifs that look back as well as forward, of motifs carrying an extrinsic meaning, are a necessary consequence of this new area of search. They do not prevent, if they make more difficult, the parallel search for intrinsic meaning; for meaning, that is, which stems from the building as a whole, considered as a meditated act of construction, as an artifact with its own rules of articulation, as an act of language that destroys trite meanings and extends meaning.

The re-conversion of a vernacular of brick and glass into a high architecture of modernity had already ensured, by the end of the sixties, a place for Stirling at the international table. The force of that transformation, especially in forcing a red-brick mode of building on hallowed university sites, constituted a first scandal. One suspects, however, that it is his second scandal, the scandal of historicity, that has supplied the element of notoriety and danger that now seems to attach to him. In this he has moved faster than many younger architects to place himself exactly where the action is. During the seventies events have also moved fast, and the concept of modernity as the inalienable property of the Modern Movement has changed inexorably. Modernity today is the problem, in many ways more demanding, of rediscovering a "now" within history and within tradition.

Le Corbusier's "going soft" with Ronchamp, his transformation of the rigid International Style into a fluid and potent material for the exploration of his own sensibility, thus secreting the seeds of a new expressionism—all this became a crucial influence on Stirling. It allowed him to develop his own somewhat British search for modernity. And when that had been achieved it still offered him the model, the provocation, for his further transformation into a grand master of the game. But of what game?

In spite of the range of his references, the subtlety of his allusions, the versatility of his models, Stirling's game is not a manipulation of our responses, but a meditation on his own. It is not an arbitrary accumulation of images, or a play with surfaces. It is wilful, perhaps, but also full of determination and discipline. It comprises syntactic as well as semantic dimensions; and the balance of these, within the artifact, conveys an inner coherence—the sense of a convergence, however oblique, to a new and unexpected whole. In this he exemplifies what Robert Venturi has asserted to be the goal of artistic endeavor in architecture: "the duty towards the difficult whole."

Yet this whole is not ideologically remote or inaccessible. It is not in the first place an enigma, intended only to be unravelled by the discerning scholar, although there will be much that only the discerning will see. It can be more simply read as the combined satisfaction of physical and psychological "requirements," the extension of function towards ritual and of ritual towards the spareness and bleakness symptomatic of our age. No longer utopian, in the futuristic sense, it still deals with the reduction of values to essentials—not to essences, but to relations. In this Stirling shows himself to be a modern, to be post-enlightenment, post-romantic, post-Darwinian, post-Einsteinian: the heir to a twentieth-century philosophy. As a modern he will continue to search for truth in the fundamental patterns of life, neither refusing the past nor trying to retrieve a lost glory, but enjoying the vantage point of his own moment and his own sensibility, which is to be found only in that moment's potential. In this he exemplifies Le Corbusier's dialectic of head and heart, reason and passion, between what is known and what remains to be discovered.

His stance is thus essentially constructive, and his game a game of discovery. His chosen means of expression combines semantic, syntactic and pragmatic dimensions: the three essentials in Charles

Morris's definition of language. What he discovers is communicated, adds to our resources. In Stirling's language of expression we find figuration combined with abstraction, as we do in painting today, showing how closely he locates in the spirit of our time (fig. 26). [8]

Stirling has not descended into historical allusionism. He has brought to maturity and made self-evident his long-standing search for "architecturality," the analogue to "literariness" in humanistic studies. That means the essential ingredient, or rather mode of being, that makes a building more than a utility. His search is important for the world because it demonstrates that modernity continues, that it has the scope and the duty to develop, although now prisoned within history, within tradition, within non-utopia. In spite of the apparent paradox his own comments on the utopian aspect of Garches may justly be applied to the new modernity implicit in Stirling's work, the modernity that revives the possibility of the monument. For, according to Stirling, Garches was:

> "a monument, not to an age which is dead, but to a way of life which has not generally arrived, and a continuous reminder of the quality to which all architects must aspire if modern architecture is to retain its vitality."[9]

Originally published in *Architectural Design Profiles*, 1982; reprinted in *Akshara*, Journal of the School of Architecture, Ahmedabad, April 1982.

NOTES

1 James Stirling, quoted in Paolo Portoghesi: *Dopo L'Architettura Moderna*, 1980, p. 194. In England, Swedish style is the acme of good taste, as exemplified in the products of IKEA.

2 The phrase is taken from the sentence: "An American middle-income family can afford a house built by new methods and materials, the vital aspect of progressive architecture." James Stirling: "Regionalism and Modern Architecture," in *Architects' Year Book*, ed. Dannatt, 1957.

3 James Stirling, "Regionalism and Modern Architecture."

4 His lecture at the Iran Conference of 1974, reported as "Stirling Connexions" in *Architectural Review*, May 1975.

5 "From Garches to Jaoul" in *Architectural Review*, September 1955; and "Ronchamp—Le Corbusier's Chapel and the Crisis of Regionalism" in *Architectural Review*, March 1956.

6 Peter Eisenman: "Real and English," in *Oppositions*, No. 4, October 1974.

7 Manfredo Tafuri: "L'architecture dans le boudoir," in *Oppositions*, No. 3, May 1974.

8 I am thinking particularly of Francis Bacon, the strongest voice in contemporary British painting.

9 James Stirling, "From Garches to Jaoul."

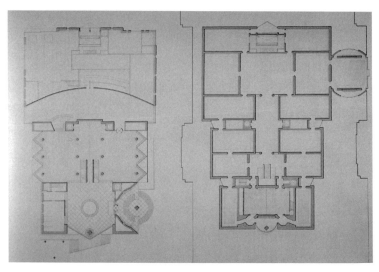

26 SAINSBURY WING, NATIONAL GALLERY (GALLERY PLANS): LONDON, ENGLAND
James Stirling Michael Wilford & Associates, competition entry, 1985.

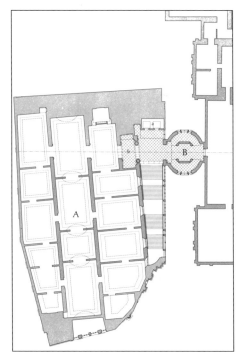

27 SAINSBURY WING, NATIONAL GALLERY (MAIN FLOOR PLAN)
Venturi, Scott Brown and Associates, competition entry, 1985; constructed, 1991.

JAMES STIRLING AND ROBERT VENTURI

The death of James Stirling has raised, prematurely, the question of his importance for world architecture: certainly, he was a world star, but has he been a major influence? The variety of the work has led to his being characterized in recent years as a postmodernist, not a label which he welcomed. In his own eyes he was and remained a modernist. Nevertheless, his work seemed to respond to changes in the world, and particularly with the series of buildings he designed for German museums—beginning with Dusseldorf in 1975—which deal directly with the question of the role of architecture in the city, placing functionality at the service of a larger view of architecture as civic art. This can be seen as a response to the times, and perhaps to the ideas of Aldo Rossi, rather than as a theoretical development for which he was himself responsible. At the same time, his work continued to assert a somewhat idiosyncratic view of architecture, remaining clearly in the path of a continuous personal evolution.

Like Aalto, Stirling has not been a force through his theories, but rather through the inner conviction which radiates from the buildings he designed. If we compare him to Robert Venturi, whose "gentle manifesto" provided a new theoretical approach to the problem of representation within modern architecture, we find no theoretical position as such. His arguments were always made from a basis of functionality and, after Dusseldorf, from a basis of contextuality. Compared to Venturi, Stirling seems lacking in ideology. There is a school of Venturi, but no school of Stirling. Yet in contemplating the future of modern architecture without him, one has a sense of irreparable loss.

The main thrust of Stirling's ideas seemed to remain within a purely architectonic discourse. The changes that arose in society, with corresponding changes in architecture's mission, were not of so much interest to him as the re-consideration of the internal balance of form and function within the work. Thus Stirling speaks to us in a limited way, not by verbal polemic, but through the works themselves. From the beginning he wished to practice a straightforward, even a daring functionalism, pursuing technical innovation along with a devotion to the logic of the plan. From the beginning, we see also a frank interest in the resulting forms not as an outcome, determined by the practical considerations, but as an opportunity to play with meaning. This playfulness, which some have seen as an expression of a sort of insubordination, and which resulted in his becoming a figure of suspicion on the English scene, is nevertheless the main source of our continuing interest in his work. While he preferred clear-cut and even classical diagrams, he always wished to apply a contradictory twist, which carried the implication of subversion, and as a result the work is never predictable, and never boring. From this point of view, it is interesting to make the comparison with Venturi, who invented a whole theory of communication to justify his use of contradiction.

Let us take a case where both architects made designs in answer to the same brief. If we compare Stirling's unsuccessful competition entry for the National Gallery Extension in London with Venturi's winning design, the point is made clear. Venturi's design is essentially Aalto-esque, asymmetrical, and systematic. There is no evident classical principle involved, other than the elementary one of having a brief episode of double-height foyer near the entrance at the south end—a remnant of Corbusian space-syntax. The large composite window in the south elevation remains as a trace of an intended visual connection from the main gallery enfilade to the representational facade facing Trafalgar Square, that might be held to substitute for an ordering axis.[1] Thereafter the classical exists only as fragments organized on non-classical principles, like the build-up of layered pilasters at the corner nearest to the main building.

In Stirling's design, there is an evident tension between classical and non-classical elements. The plan clearly organizes all the important spaces on a single north-south axis, orthogonal to the main building, and only the ground level departs from this by placing the entrance at right angles, leaving the central axis to terminate with a bay window. The turning of the axis is achieved within an axial convention. Where the classical element in Venturi is understated, elusive, in Stirling it is plainly stated (figs. 26, 27). The anti-classical aspects, such as the placing of a single square column on the diagonal in both the entrance bay and the axial bay window, and the method of massing the various elements of the volumetric layout, so that the volume nearest the street may appear wholly directed towards the main building—together with the use of the coved cornice for emphasis, as in the Staatsgalerie—all these elements are thus thoroughly organized around the classical parti, and have the effect of renovating it, whereas Venturi's collaged classical details, although respecting it, speak of its loss.

Here we approach the crux of Stirling's method, one that permeates all his work. Whatever the genre of the design under discussion, we will always find that he takes a position astride a dialectical opening between classical and anti-classical aspects. This is to define him as a master of mannerism. The National Gallery Competition entry is more evidently classical than, say, the Tokyo International Forum of 1989, but the latter is still organized according to an axial principle.

Let us take a closer look at this question. The competition design for the Cinema Palace on the Lido in Venice is completely without a normal central axis, but it occupies a position to one side of the old Casino, and is inflected towards its Beaux-Arts axis, in order to reinforce it. Like Venturi's National Gallery extension, the form is governed by its duty of inflecting towards the old building. Why does it not share in the mourning for a lost classicism, as Venturi's building does? The reason is that in its other aspects the Cinema Palace remains classical in a second-order degree, through its re-use of the prismatic geometries of Modern Movement forms as these emerged in the twenties and thirties. Thus, the stair-tower and sign recall Duiker, and the regular grid of cylindrical columns is in the spirit of Le Corbusier's *plan libre*, the whole being a classically defined field oriented back to its rectangular base lines to west and north. In this case the anti-classical elements are embodied in the large-scale zig-zag line of glazing, which suppresses externally all of the regular structural columns except for one. To this is given the heroic task of supporting the entrance canopy, apparently unaided, and engaging in a close dialogue with the zig-zagging ramp (this suppression may itself be interpreted as a form of mannerist inversion on a classical theme). For all the freedom of the facetted glazing and the apparently wayward gestures of the ramp, every element is closely controlled and precisely located by reference to the structural grid. Within this orthogonal system a new axiality appears—the unity of the two halls in combination finds its axial principle in the screen placed symmetrically across the north-west corner, from which it moves diagonally across the space to the structural bay adjoining the entrance.

In the balance of axiality and empirically organized planning, there is no withdrawal to a point outside the system from which it may be viewed as a quotation, identified as a relic, mourned as dead. Everything remains integral and spontaneous, as if modernity had just been invented, and was developing, not finished. The Cinema Palace thus appears to be an extension of the Modern Movement, not a reversion to it, just as Schinkel's Altes Museum appears to extend the uses of a classical vocabulary, not to exhaust them. Stirling's continued fascination with the positive role of modernist forms is thus strangely akin to Schinkel's fascination with classical forms, apparently in conflict with the new romantic vision that he was one of the first to express. In Schinkel one finds an oscillation between classical and picturesque principles, allowing us to see the basic eclecticism of his approach. Stirling's chosen conflict between classical and functionalist elements admits of a similar eclecticism, also based on nostalgia, but assuredly not on despair.

Both Stirling and Venturi have defined themselves publicly as modern architects; and, plainly, both produce a modern architecture that is far removed from the gigantism of hi-tech or the triteness of po-mo. They make architecture that is complex and often contradictory. In both we will find references and quotations, a sense of history and of the need to commemorate certain past events. Both honor the demands of the program. But whereas Venturi's practice derives ultimately from Aalto and a tradition of heterogeneity, Stirling's derives more squarely from Le Corbusier and a tradition of homogeneity. Venturi's theoretical position is influenced by literary sources and the semiological theory of communication to a mass audience, whereas Stirling's is more narrowly focussed on the dialectic in Le Corbusier and the possibilities of expressive contradiction which Colin Rowe demonstrated to exist within both modern and *seicento* designs. It is this theme from Rowe that provides the theoretical basis of Stirling's work. In avoiding a general polemic, Stirling concentrates attention on the power of contradiction, within a strict formal sequence, to renew an essence. In a Heideggerian sense, he leads us to the very point where essence has just been present. There is one important difference however. Venturi, bowing perhaps to the universal American system of construction by hanging the facade on a steel frame, allows his figures to be thin like banners, proclaiming a lost substance but not substituting for it. Thus the important figure in Venturi is often deliberately graphic and—as he insists—emblematic. With Stirling, features intended to be reminiscent are given weight and substance (such as the arcaded screen in the project for the Kaiserplatz in Aachen). Decoration in Venturi often leans towards graphic design, as in his treatment of the external walls in the Seattle Art Museum, whereas in Stirling, decoration applied to wall surfaces generally takes architectonic form, such as banding in different stone, as at Cornell Center for the Performing Arts or No. 1 Poultry, or color—often vibrant—applied to steel components to emphasize their metallic quality, as at Cornell or the Staatsgalerie. The "joke" ventilators at the Staatsgalerie, in the form of fallen masonry, are still sculptural in nature, and devoid of outright literary content, although with overtones of Piranesi.

It is not that Stirling is naive about the use of classical precedent, expecting it to survive into his work unchanged by modern conditions. At Cornell, the banded stonework is proposed as a veneer, not as structural masonry, and this fact is made clear—to the trained observer at least—by the insistence on open joints and the absence of mortar. But whereas Venturi's looser system of allusions is free to move about the surface in search of a communicating opportunity, Stirling enjoys the tight embrace of the constructional system, and voluntarily stays within it. This restraint is not accepted, as with so many modernists, in order that it may be proposed as determining the outcome, thus freeing the architect from artistic responsibility. For if the outcome is wholly determined by events extraneous to architecture, its status as a language of expression will be hideously deformed. To speak freely in the medium of cultural discourse, architecture must display elements that are, causally speaking, arbitrary, and are therefore determined only by the author within a total sensibility of architectonic forms, and within a system of rhetoric that refers to an architectural tradition. In this sense, while Stirling rightly insists that his projects are founded on site and program, he does not deny that he practices architecture as an art.

He has been led to admit this by observing in his own work certain sequences of buildings which conform to a stylistic limitation, such as the group of red brick and tile buildings at Leicester, Cambridge and Oxford Universities; or which employ the same motif in different circumstances: the Latina Library, the Performing Arts Center and the Compton Verney Opera House all incorporate a colonnaded loggia whose end bays are turned to display the sectional system to the front. This motif is clearly a preferred form, floating in the architect's imagination, seeking opportunities to be realized. It does not come out of a single set of circumstances, but out of a generalized sense of the possibilities inherent in architecture, the result of a lifetime of practice and premeditation. The turning of the end bays to display the section may be conceived as a modern idea, arising from the enjoyment of structure; but it also carries a suggestion of contingency, of incompleteness, as with a loggiaed courtyard from which the sides are missing, just as we find in the remnants of the Actors' Courtyard amid the ruins of Pompeii.

The development of an ideal form for the loggia is evidence of a curiosity and enjoyment of certain forms that can have a recurring validity: there were loggias, there will be other loggias. By re-interpreting the loggia in a way that exhibits both its integral nature and its incompleteness, Stirling shows his will to up-date the loggia for modern times, and thus to make an architecture that is both valid today yet is projected from the past. In this way he testifies to a constancy in human affairs. It is as if Stirling felt in competition with past achievement, wanting to equal it, or to go one better.

We find this dialectical urge still active in Stirling's latest work— the Braun Pharmaceutical Headquarters at Melsungen. The building is organized by two axes, at right angles: one lies across, the other parallel to the valley in which the complex is situated. The cross axis is established by a massive wall which screens the parking building and the more utilitarian functions beyond, and spans the valley side to side like a dam. The main circulation is carried across the front of this wall in a glazed corridor supported on a timber frame with the supports raked in one direction, imparting a dynamic quality, as if the building was in motion (Stirling said: "like a centipede"). Yet there is no doubt that this element is a re-statement of the ideal loggia, now far from its classical origin, but close to the point where architecture is in process of re-defining itself as an art of expressive potential.

The will to combine elements that define between them an area of tension and struggle I take to be a mark of the increasing maturity of Stirling's judgement, opening up for us an architecture of greater depth and richness. An opposition that we took at first to be a balance between classical and anti-classical elements can now perhaps be identified at a more general level as an opposition between progressive and perennial elements, involving a diachronic as well as a synchronic dimension. But it is also evident that this ability to encompass differences of intention permits him to adjust to differences of context. His interest in the ability of certain forms to communicate through their familiarity has allowed him to adapt to the climate of conservation in our cities, and to propose projects that can work with the existing urban environment and towards the completion of the city. But this has been possible without any scenes of renunciation or sudden changes in direction.

In the same way, as the shallowness of most postmodern architecture has led to a new longing for inwardness in modern design, with something of a reversion to the ideals of pre-war architecture, Stirling was well placed to lead that search for spatial poetry without compromising his discovery of the civic dimension. It is the loss of that vision that makes his death both premature and irreparable.

Originally published in *Casabella*, December 1992.

NOTES

The client refused to allow a visual connection at this point to puncture the experience of the paintings.

28   BRAUN PHARMACEUTICAL HEADQUARTERS: MELSUNGEN, GERMANY
James Stirling Michael Wilford & Associates with Walter Nägeli, 1992.

STIRLING AT MELSUNGEN

In the course of a long practice, Stirling made a number of large-scale designs for industrial clients, ranging from Dorman Long in 1965 to British Telecom in 1983—many of them for German firms. Finally one of these large projects has been built, in Germany, and the result is quite stunning. For this job, Stirling-Wilford worked in association with Walter Nägeli, who had formerly run the Stirling office in Berlin when it built the Wissenschaftszentrum. Nägeli's collaboration has undoubtedly contributed a fresh impetus, but the project has a boldness that testifies to the pressure of all those unbuilt projects, as well as being marked at many points by Stirling's unique sensibility. The client, Georg Braun, was determined to commission a work from Stirling, whose project was placed second in the competition, and was prepared to pay over the odds for a work of architecture. His percipience has paid off. He now has a building costing only 3% more than a utility version and that is certainly more memorable than many museums.

The mediaeval town of Melsungen is about two hours by car north-east of Frankfurt, and just to the east of it is the new Braun Pharmaceutical Headquarters, which makes plastic equipment for hospitals. The complex lies in a broad and shallow valley, not far from the point where it is crossed by a fine concrete railway viaduct. To this bridge the architects have answered with a dam—a high wall of concrete which crosses the valley and conceals from the visitor the parking building and most of the distribution plant. A parking building was proposed in order to avoid the banality of a building surrounded by a sea of cars. The area in front is landscaped in a deliberately parodic way, impressive for the casual visitor, unsettling for the critic. To the right is the production shed, an elaborate structure whose working floor is both column-free and germ-free, with two supporting floors below it for sterilization and packaging routines. To the left is the visitor's entrance with administration above and computer center below. The two sides of the building are united by a strange glazed corridor strapped to the "dam" wall and carried on raking timber legs, a corridor which dips and narrows slightly to the center of the valley, making one aware from within the building both of the dam wall behind and of the shape of the landscape out in front (fig. 28).

The terrain embraced by the glazed bridge is deliberately forced into a rhetoric where landscaping implies the aesthetization of life, artifice enclosing reality: for this reason the grass sward, the long straight terraces, the dense groups of trees, the bubbling lake were all self-consciously defined by Stirling, not as "corporate," but as "English;" and the sinuous canal is the summation of this artifice, because it also at the same time defines the car circulation, gathering up the approach roads into an ideal landscape form, and thus concealing them as utilities. These two roads are functionally differentiated, one being the route to the parking building, outside of the security system, while the other leading to the main entrance is strictly for important visitors and already under surveillance, and this fact, concealed to the casual visitor but evident to the frequent user, provides an additional twist of meaning within the suavity of the form. Artifice encloses a reality that is already marked with difference and discrepancy—an example of Stirling's frequent enjoyment of mannerist juxtaposition.

In the press conference at the opening events Stirling clearly took a keen pleasure in the outcome, speaking of the tree groups as "tree-henges," the glazed structure as "a centipede," the administration wing as the "head of the dinosaur," and the computer building sheathed in green copper tiles as "crouching" below in a "reptilian" way. Clearly, the building forms were imbued for him with metaphoric significance. It is not unreasonable then to see the glazed bridge with its concrete wall as a dam, holding back the processes of production behind it, and symbolizing the public realm of consumption in front of the wall. Along with the irony, there is a poetic enjoyment in placing the building metaphorically, as well as actually, in a setting of earth and sky.

Indeed, the building as a whole resonates with a metaphoric

aura, without being in any degree less effective as a functional answer to the building program. Its literal purposes perhaps even allow this added dimension to arise as an expression of an arcane industrial will. However this may be, the result is certainly more expressive, and more expressionistic, than we have been used to in Stirling's work. Thus, the glazed corridor on its multiform legs can be seen as a transformation of the usual Stirling colonnade, which at the Wissenschaftszentrum, at Cornell, and in the Public Library at Latium had a more obviously classical flavor; and the boldly outward-leaning upper face of the energy center as a transformation of the coved cornice which, in the Staatsgalerie, still testifies to a classical antecedent—almost certainly the open stair court in Lutyens's Viceregal Palace at New Delhi. The corridor that links the production building to the distribution center is carried on alternating wide and narrow bays, as if conforming to a classical canon, and in contradiction to the continuous *fenêtre en longueur* above. As for the strangely swollen conical capitals which support the administration wing along its center-line, because the bases, where visible, are sheathed in a dark Staffordshire brick, they become de-materialized to the point where the capitals seem to descend like funnels rather than provide support, raising possibilities of a distinctly mammalian nature. Seen in a certain light, the squat bases disappear and the arched form of the administration building looks like a reincarnation of the Roman wolf mother. This strange aspect gives the expressive language a mythic twist. At the far end of the complex, an elliptical loading shed covered in reptilian green copper "feeds" twenty-two trucks backed into separate bays—separated to ensure that nothing ever gets loaded on to the wrong truck—but thereby made expressive as orifices. Here too there is a sense of organic processes at work.

Many aspects of the building pay tribute to the achievements of the modern style. The administration building, for example, is a sort of homage to Le Corbusier's Swiss hostel, not only by its use of a single row of supports, but by the articulation of the stair and lift towers. Every part of this complex building has been designed in a way that, while fulfilling its immediate technical or functional requirements, goes beyond the rational satisfaction of needs, which characterizes the modern style, to revise the canon of modernity and to adumbrate a universe of metaphoric equivalences. The parts, dislodged from their ordinary meanings, become signs in an obscure and suggestive language. Those signs cohere, if indeed they do, by no patent rational narrative, but by another more mythic narrative whose import is as clouded as the forms that point to it are strong. Stirling thus positions himself far from Robert Venturi, who prefers to employ weak forms that, while suggestive, remain clearly fragile and emblematic. The paradox that is raised by the use of "strong" forms is that their strength, which appears to resist any attempt to dismiss them as "merely" decorative, at the same time invites the possibility that the whole material reality of the building is to take on the destiny of a work of art, and the quality of a dream.

One very clear example of this adumbration of a new language is in the principle facade of the production shed. This is intended to be, on completion, a long building, of the sort that the Italian rationalists liked to propose for universities on green-field sites. So far, only a sixth of it has been built. The structure is big, since the interior of the shed must be column-free to facilitate changes in layout, so we have a kind of impressive giant order. Yet many of the bays must harbor a cylindrical container for the plastic granules that are the raw materials of manufacture, held under pressure, and distributed to the work points by compressed air. These vats, where they occur, block the classical bays, "spoiling" the neoclassical reading of the ensemble. This rational and empirical disposition forces them, as it were unwillingly, to articulate the bays of the production shed, to be pressed into an architectural service that has the rhythm of a neoclassical museum. As well as spoiling the rhythm, they reinforce it.

It is also patent that the architects have not employed forms for purely recondite purposes. The relaxation areas, for example, are signalled by curvelinear forms, the accepted sign of *détente*. The social room has an undulating glass wall, and the undulating motif reappears in the gallery of the cafeteria. The cafeteria is a beautiful space, with its curved facade that points to the entrance landscape through a run of door-height glass all around, beyond which perfectly plain cylindrical columns impart a gentle rhythm. This horizontal glass wall is given value by the high volume above, a recess so thoroughly lined with sound absorbent that conversation even in crowded conditions is easy and relaxed. This makes a space that is practical yet filled with beauty in a way that anyone can enjoy.

Of course, happy workers are an essential aspect of enlightened capitalism. This building has not hesitated to accept its empirical job of serving the needs of the production process. The layout, extended to begin with, makes future additions economical in advance. The circulation between cafeteria, production and distribution is shared between humans and the robot carts that take the packed and sterilized material to distribution; if you encounter one of these robots, which is guided by magnetic strips in the floor, it stops until you go past: efficiency and politeness go together. It is impressive to see the giant robots operating in the production hall, and the robot towers that place and retrieve the packages in the high shelf storage. Everything is monitored and controlled by computer. Most impressive, perhaps, is the way in which the production rate of each item is commanded only when immediate demand is known—there is no redundant stock-piling of products. The factory is a perfect case of late-twentieth-century capitalism at work, governed in every particular by information flow. The architects have succeeded in serving that purpose and in revealing it to the visitor. But the client also wanted to acquire a building that would reflect cultural values, and this was the opportunity they needed to carry out an exemplary modern work.

It will already be evident that the design encompasses both practical and metaphoric aspects, making this factory both a direct response to the program of capitalist management and at the same time an attempt to transcend its own instrumentality and lay claim to an existence-mode appropriate to a work of art. In the excess of expression over utility, the architects have essayed to define a technically competent modern architecture that goes beyond utility to approach a world of allusions and metaphoric equivalences. There is a sense of hidden forces at work: the unknownability of a clouded future, and even, perhaps, the sense of a mythic past. In these terms, the industrial basis of the program does not produce a result weakened by practical constraints, but rather tested and strengthened by them. By passing this test the work becomes the more profoundly representative of modernity in architecture, and takes us to the edge of that modernity, where it must yield to the cultural limitations that place all rational efforts within an interpretative—that is, an hermeneutic—tradition. It thus places modernity under the sign of an enigma, so that it can no longer exult in its position of merely being ahead, but has to take stock of the nature of the landscape to which our obsession with technicity has brought us.

Originally published in *Architectural Review*, December 1992 as: "The Far Side of Modernity: Stirling's Braun H.Q. at Melsungen."

THE OLD IN THE NEW

29 A TOURIST IN ONE'S OWN CITY: THE QUIRINALE
Piranesi, *Veduta di Roma*, 1748.
From Jonathan Scott: *Piranesi*, Academy Editions, St. Martin's Press, 1975.

THE TROUBLE WITH ABSTRACTION

"... a living chain of tradition still links the art of our own days with that of the pyramid age."—Ernst Gombrich, *The Story of Art*

In the work of the Russian constructivists of the early twenties, architecture seems to have had an aura, at least for the artist working in abstract mode. This aura was, I believe, compounded of two things: first, a sense of the free proliferation of accumulating forms, the idea of "frozen music," such as we find in Malevich's Suprematist compositions; second, a sense of an inner necessity, in which the artist's freedom is somehow conflated with the spirit of the age: functional determinism doubles for inner necessity as though it were a kind of biological life-force. The invention of the artist was detached from any thought of artifice or convention: rather, it was to be a true uncovering.

So strong was this aura that artists imbued abstract spatial relations with a metaphysical power. This power strove to avoid definition by representational means, yet it was captured and made to vibrate within the confines of the work.

It is the mystery and privilege of artistic expression to transpose literal meanings into metaphoric ones. We would be quite wrong to take Malevich's Suprematist Architecture for a literal maquette of a projected city skyscraper; to take Wyndham Lewis's painting *Workshop* for a design for a workshop; to mistake Kurt Schwitters's construction *Merzbau* for a laboratory for an eccentric scientist. All these works refer to spaces originating in the real world only to transpose them into the metaphoric realm that rules within the constraints and freedoms of a concentrated work of art. The space of such a work is reconstituted in the mind. It is not the same space within which built architecture exists.

It is important to recognize that abstraction has a different impact within the kingdom of the artist's vision to what it may have within the space of use and habit to which architecture belongs. This is not to say that architecture is forbidden to enter the poetic, only that it must be circumspect if it attempts to do so. The author's intentions in architecture have to take issue with the intentions of users, whereas in fine art it is the users who have to look out for themselves, who are on the defensive. Anything can become artistically significant so long as an artistic intention can be imputed to it. A pile of bricks has a different meaning in the brickyard, on the building site, in the corner of a wheat field. Located within the gallery, it becomes doubly abstracted, doubly meaningful: as bricks, as not-bricks.

The crisis that arises between modern art and architecture has its roots in the failure of both artists and architects to understand the extent to which architecture is not free to dispense with real space and banal uses, and generally the smell of bodies. No building, however abstract its forms, is able to set up an ideal world without accounting for the penetration of its ideal space by real space. Conversely, children who dart through the interstices of a Henry Moore are unaware of the metaphysical dangers to which they expose themselves. However radical, the architect retains an instinct for the limits of decorum and propriety, even when stretching both. Whereas individual artists can feel free to attack settled convention, and trust to a handful of critics to follow them into the locker room for an intimate interview, architects cannot depend alone on the discerning critic. They have to have two stories ready: confidences for the critics, and a press release for the public, who in some sense is paying. The poetic impulse to make things strange is at odds with the public duty to make things familiar. Most architects are uneasy about admitting artistic intentions, in case they are accused of hypocrisy. It was not always thus, of course.

During the Renaissance, which is as far back as modern times can be stretched, we still find the ancient ideal of architecture as the mistress art, deprived of the privileged role of fine art to represent man's history and mythology, yet in another way representing the public realm within which worship of the gods and of the arts takes place. In this role it provides the proper setting for painting and sculpture. With Michaelangelo, it could be said that we have begun the era of angst. Mannerist tension and modern angst are both to different degrees the product of a restlessness about the rules. If we may review, very briefly, the story of the degeneration of public art, its removal from places of worship first to palaces, then to the galleries, then to the salons, then to the boudoirs, we cannot but feel that an uneasiness about the rules and a determination to bring them into question is essential to the spirit of modernity. Modernity can then be read as coeval with loss of faith, and loss of faith with growth in material knowledge.

With Piranesi, the simple wholeness of the public domain has already been lost (fig. 29). The present is no longer adequate: a dimension of historical nostalgia has entered. Insouciance of the presence gives way to an uneasiness about lost certainty. Modern man appears already as a tourist among the ruins of his own traditions. Like a Pandora's box, reason has opened fundamental questions about human destiny, about progress, about the limits of knowledge.

Once rules of thought have been liberated from propriety, no bounds can be put upon them. Whatever can be organized systematically imposes its own logic: it is a way of thinking that, within science, has been amazingly successful and that has justified in some sense the idea of progress. Helicopters have not been very long in the world. Yet these same logical systems, when considered as environment, approach the nightmare. It is an unfortunate fact that whereas Le Corbusier's individual buildings never fail to be works of art, his city plans, if they had been built, would have contributed to that nightmare as decisively as have the multiple imitations. The crisis of art and architecture is a symptom of the deep ambivalence of human mentality: committed to reason as a tool for dismantling nature and learning the secrets of her power; unable to offer to reason an unreason that does not smell of nightmare and death. The artist is sensitive to this dichotomy, and can deal with it independently in ways in which the architect cannot.

In architecture, the realization that modernity also evolves, that we are after all within history, that time does not have a stop, that pure rationality can be imagined but not built—all these realizations have produced a kind of schizophrenia: on the one hand, dementia

30 SOOTHSAYER'S RECOMPENSE
De Chirico, 1913.

about lost symbols; on the other hand, a game of equivalences (a game whose name finally is showbiz). Meantime in the real world—I mean the world of big business which already dominates the entire globe—those revolutionary gestures that were once the property of the avant-garde have been appropriated for material ends. Where once there was a making strange, there now is a making familiar. The Modern Movement, which originally paid attention to physical function as its first priority, has found itself servicing the simple calculations of real-estate vendors. Hannes Meyer's dictum—*architecture is function times economy*—has proved to be of inestimable value to businessmen.

Yet, I would suggest, most of the hysteria that we are at present suffering stems from unjustifiable expectations—the expectations of a utopian future that were raised by the sudden success of modern technology, enshrined within the Modern Movement. We have inherited a Hegelian sense of history which demands that we implant a purpose in human affairs. But to see each achievement of each time as only a step in a process is to empty meaning out of existence. Achievements of the heroic period of the modern movement are not denied by their failure to achieve a millennial order.

31 WOMAN IN THE SUN
Edward Hopper, 1961.

Alongside the nostalgia for a lost public domain, so beautifully expressed by De Chirico (fig. 30), I would place the stoical loneliness of the individual, so aptly expressed by Edward Hopper (fig. 31). They complement each other and set up a kind of dialectic between ancient and modern, between public sorrow and private angst. It is possible for the artist to attain a vision that accepts loss, but not with hysteria; that accepts ambiguity, not as a desperate loss of certainty, but as an inevitable consequence of the "play of the signifiers;" that represents the real-all-too-real world without being its servant; that is, finally, both abstract and concrete. Essential to that new vision is a loss of utopia, and a striving for the feeling buried within materiality rather than for simple material improvement. Important also is the sense of tradition, and of the uniqueness of each moment that defines and encloses perception.

Can architecture equal such a vision? Strangely, architecture, which lacks the autonomy of the fine artist's vision, is helped by its dependence on ordinary life. The very particularity and functionality that undermine the building as ideological statement accord it a unique position spatially, geographically and culturally. If we look, not at the Pompidou Center, but away from it, we gain a perspective that has the impact of a forgotten truth. Instead of the over-zealous modernity of the building we see the situation it takes up within Paris. We can see then that the architect has been guided, consciously or unconsciously, by a debt to history. It is a transformation of the Campo at Siena. Looked at from the year 2001 the Sainsbury Center already seems a building embedded in history—a late-modern shed which theoretically asserts the primacy of a geometrical order. Architecture too has its own special history, as specific as the history of painting and sculpture, and which is just as concerned to transmit a tradition while yet subverting it and converting it to pure spontaneity. Behind the Sainsbury Center lies the whole history of noble sheds, back through the Gallerie des Machines and the Crystal Palace as far as to King's College Chapel.

It has been fashionable for architects to reject such perspectives, to insist on the discontinuity with history. Functionalism was to represent the end of historical styles and the final emancipation of function and expression. But function, as the accommodation of human activity, as the acceptance of the generic physical needs of lying, sitting, standing, walking and running people, is quite insufficient in itself to determine space; and as soon as we add to function a psychological dimension, it must take on all the aspirations of an age, including the task of traducing and hence perpetuating a tradition. This task demands not only vision and sensibility, equal to that of the artist, but also intellectual work.

I began this piece with a quotation from Ernst Gombrich: I end with one from Mary Douglas, from her *Purity and Danger* of 1966:

> "There is only one kind of differentiation in thought that is relevant, and that provides a criterion that we can apply equally to different cultures and to the history of our own scientific ideas. That criterion is based on the Kantian principle that thought can only advance by freeing itself from the shackles of its own subjective conditions."

Paper presented at the Royal College of Art in a seminar on "The Modern Movement—A Death Dance of Principles," February 1982, and subsequently published in *Art Monthly, Art & Architecture Supplement*, April 1982.

32 PORTICO, SAINSBURY CENTER: UNIVERSITY OF EAST ANGLIA
Foster Associates, 1976–1978.

33 PORTICO, PALAZZO DEI CONGRESSI: E.U.R. ROME, ITALY
Adalberto Libera, 1942.

CONTINUITY IN ART AND ARCHITECTURE

I have tried to tell the story of art as the story of a continuous weaving and changing of traditions in which each work refers to the past and points to the future . . . a living chain of tradition still links the art of our own days with that of the pyramid age.

E.H. Gombrich: *The Story of Art*

When Ernst Gombrich wrote those words, in 1950, it also seemed to him that, in spite of threats to this continuity, the recent development of modern architecture had successfully re-established it:

". . . somehow and somewhere the final disaster was always averted. When old tasks disappeared new ones turned up which gave artists that sense of direction and sense of purpose without which they cannot create great works. In architecture, I believe, this miracle has happened once more. After the fumblings and hesitations of the nineteenth century modern architects have found their bearings. They know what they want to do and the public has begun to accept their work as a matter of course. For painting and sculpture the crisis has not yet passed the danger point."[1]

Forty years later, that distinction is not perhaps so evident. The architecture of conviction that Gombrich welcomed in 1950 produced considerable successes, but also widespread failures, and was due to be rejected in its turn some twenty-five years later, in favor of an architecture of surface nuances, in which links with past tradition were viewed as explicit signs to be manipulated. At the same time, forces of conservation have found themselves in collaboration with forces of consumption in order to protect the value of prime real estate—two elements of society in an uneasy coalition that broke across the normal political divisions of right and left. In compromises, many revampings of well-known buildings were carried out in the name of historical preservation. Equally, many new buildings were added in support of existing city centers which were as superficial architecturally as they were adroit commercially. Postmodernism in architecture often seemed indeed to emphasize continuity and historical allusion to the point of parody, but the sheer profitability of these ventures deprives them of the independence needed to express irony, and few of them would qualify as offering a critical view. The capability of claiming historical precedent along with functional efficiency was clearly a corporate advantage, and the continuities which Gombrich had seen only as the result of constant struggle and renewed vision were now adopted as the goals of corporate policy. The notion of dressing new buildings suitably to fit into existing contexts has brought with it a re-emergence of the ancient idea of propriety, as a social surface that has to be maintained. In the Renaissance, it was normal—and rational: churches were dressed on the front facing the square, and left naked on the sides. Today, "fitting in" is viewed suspiciously by conservationists who are worried that appearances dissemble some environmental disadvantage, and by purists who feel that dressing buildings is effete. It could only be a matter of time before younger architects would reject such continuities as illusory. The current wave of interest in constructivist architecture is no doubt the expression of that disillusion.

INNOVATION AND INVENTION

From the viewpoint of the engaged artist those grand continuities that link Western art to the pyramids may not be clear at all, and in the agony of incubation may constitute little by way of encouragement; or, if they are evident, are more likely to be perceived rather as commands to be disobeyed, a load to be shed. From the viewpoint of the consciously "modern" artist, there is a more intensive objection, since innovation has long been considered a modern duty, and the idea of working in a tradition has become suspect as never before. "In the arts an appetite for a new look is now a professional requirement, as in Russia to be accredited as a revolutionist is to qualify for privileges"—as Harold Rosenberg wrote in

1959 in the introduction to his book *The Tradition of the New.*[2] The paradox in his title very neatly encapsulates a central difficulty for all theories of art that lean on the concept of "modern." Can the new ever bow to tradition? Can the avant-garde stance be adopted as a posture, without automatically becoming imposture?

Since Duchamp, modern artists have taken it to be their prerogative to subvert convention, and it is usually taken for granted that this is an unambiguous stance. Yet there are clearly difficulties of a linguistic, if not a philosophical nature, in this assumption. The entirely new is not so distinct that it can be perceived along with the about-to-be-superseded. Any act of communication requires the preexistence of convention, or some equivalent element of continuity between originator and receiver, some structure that they share at least to the extent that it allows their differences to be revealed. Innovative work can only be identified by its differences from existing convention, and this implies that the innovative can only be a part of the new.

We may then define our problem by distinguishing broadly between innovation, which scrutinizes life for material with which to criticize art, and invention, which scrutinizes art for material with which to criticize life. Both activities seek renewal, which may be understood as change in the cultural framework. The job of the art critic, which in the 1920s was often that of introducing the new as "something completely different," has increasingly in recent years leaned towards the interpretation of the new as ultimately intelligible, if not exactly "more of the same."[3] On the one hand, the new has become a recognizable category—close to, if not synonymous with, the modern. On the other hand, newness is valued as the sign of originality, without which no artist is worthy of the name. Little space is left for those who seek a way forward by building on something already familiar, or who find a puzzle to elucidate in a known artist's work, or who simply feel drawn to a tradition. They risk being dismissed as mere craftsmen. In the general art market, the well-crafted portrait occupies a surprisingly small space, though there is plenty of well-crafted kitsch, from glass dolphins to diamond rings. In the field of serious art, which is undoubtedly self-conscious about its mission to revitalize culture, there is a general preference, I believe, for innovation over invention, precisely in order to escape the suspicion that what is offered may be not genuinely renewal, but only "more of the same."

In his epilogue to *War and Peace* Tolstoy made a primary distinction between the destiny of nations and the fate of individuals. What at the individual level may seem to be due to the incidence of luck or chance, at the historian's level has to be recognized as the result of inescapable tendencies, geo-political movements that shift with the inevitability of glaciers. But whether his luck is good or bad the individual retains a sense of his own freedom of action, along with his own need to struggle to achieve it. Clearly, the continuity in the eye of the historian is rarely evident to the individual caught up in the action. In Gombrich's view the play of chance which assured continuity for architecture seems strangely benign—perhaps influenced by some invisible cultural momentum: ". . . when old tasks disappeared, new ones turned up . . ." But for the revolutionary and the innovator nothing turns up without struggle and pain, even if the pain is savored for its conferment of a sense of being in life. One's ability to treat an oil spill as evidence of a tendency is in proportion to one's remoteness from its effects.

In the individual, the struggle for freedom is determined not only by the immediate impact of events, but by his own inner sense of purpose. At the group level, the search for a common point of view tends to externalize that purpose in terms of a political or social position, a position that is more or less fixed—and given form—by reference to the landscape of political or social action, and the established institutions, whether acknowledged or unacknowledged. The individual feels some combination of security or threat, opportunity or prospect. No one, it seems to me, has better formulated the tension between the individual and the group, the individual and society, than the sociologist Georg Simmel. In Simmel's view, the transition between individual and group perceptions is mediated by what he calls "the world of forms."

Forms are not only the forms of artifacts, whether utilitarian or artistic, but the forms of social institutions, rituals and observances, manners and behaviors, wherever those follow a recognizable pattern. In this sense hijackings and street barricades are "forms," along with parliamentary debates, TV shows, superbowls, hunting deer, church service and Sunday brunch.

Forms are characterized by a stability of outline that renders them independent of the individual perception. They have an invariance of form in spite of a variety of presentations, and in the

intellectual sense they hold an objective status analogous
forms of Euclidian geometry (a rose is a "rose," and a trian·
"triangle"). Forms, Simmel says, are an indispensable supr
life, but also a framework that eventually inhibits its growth:

"Life can express itself and realize its freedom only through forms; yet
forms must also necessarily suffocate life and obstruct freedom."[4]

"Life . . . can manifest itself only in particular forms; yet, owing to its essential restlessness, life constantly struggles against its own products, which
have become fixed, and do not move along with it. This process manifests
itself as the displacement of an old form by a new one."[5]

Applying this view of things to criticism of art and architecture
may provide a way of enabling us to see beyond stylistic barriers and
grasp something of the continuity that Ernst Gombrich can discern
in the story of art. Style itself becomes a form which, according to
the individual's point of view, can stand for freedom or for necessity.
Where, for example, one will condemn neoclassicism as mere bowing to tradition, another will see it as a way of reviewing contemporary flux. The architect Michael Graves makes use of neoclassicism
not only to establish certain continuities with the history of architecture and the shape of the city, but also to comment on the contemporary need for change. His buildings remain modern in conception
in spite of the use they make of recognizable features like columns
and pediments; and they will never be confused with the neoclassical
work of earlier periods, by comparison with which they appear to
break many rules of propriety. But the view from fifty years on may
easily accept them into the canon of neoclassical architecture, a style
that has already appeared in different periods. Before he adopted a
neoclassical style, Graves was recognized as a leader in the development of an American variant of the modern style, and while the
change of approach has changed the meaning of his work, it has not
thereby become less marked by the time of its inception, or less original. Style is thus one level of the hierarchy of forms by which we
relate to the flux of architectural evolution.

Whereas from a contemporary viewpoint there seems to be only
one legitimate style—the one that we see as conducting us into the
future—the retrospective view from a future viewpoint, where the
future has been achieved and found wanting, will no doubt reveal

many conflicting tendencies, part of the struggle with the forms that we have inherited. In the early nineteenth century, when architecture was seeking a new concentration after the impact of romanticism, we see the future being given very different forms in England and in France. Henri Labrouste, in his *envois* from Rome, proposed the Greek Doric style as the instrument of renewal in architecture; Pugin, in a different context, was advocating a return to Early English Gothic, for similar reasons. Within the different cultural contexts, these seemingly opposed proposals occupy a similar semantic space. Context, which confers so much of the meaning, is to be understood as situated within a cultural framework comprising many factors. In discussing the state of architecture today, we tend to remain blind to the complexity of the cultural context in which we are situated, and indeed a great deal of it is simply invisible to us. But it is there, ready (paradoxically) to become more visible to the historian who has to construct it from the available evidence than to us who are enveloped in it.

Following Simmel, we have to postulate a continuum containing a complexity of forms, which together constitute the norms of our society, and which at the same time are shifting and changing under the incidence of various social pressures. It is possible to put some order into this complexity by seeing it as made up of dialectically opposed tendencies, or qualities, one standing for the status quo, one for an innovative force.

Within architecture there are many examples that display the reflection of conservation and innovation. One very striking one is to be found in the comparison of two plates from Letarouilly, illustrations of rooms in the Museum of Pope Pio Clementino at the Vatican.

Here we see an uneasy balance between reason, as a classifying logic, and propriety, as a classical residue. In the Greek Cross Hall we find a mixture of motifs, each occupying its appointed place in a hierarchy of classical architecture. From the bas-reliefs that are a decorative element of the architecture, through the statues that are adornments and the busts that are part of the furnishings to the tombs that are the exhibits, each motif is appropriate to its setting. Next door, in the Gallery of the Animals, this hierarchy breaks down: the theme has become a specialized subject and all the animals are exhibits: a didactic exposition of the class: animal. Classification in the interest of advancing knowledge has taken over, and the rules of classical propriety have been broken.

In a broader version of this opposition, we may compare two aspects of the introduction of railways in England at the end of the nineteenth century: consider the difference between the Euston Arch —a fine Doric portico—and the Forth Bridge—a triumph of the new iron age. In the development of railway technology, bridges were crucial. Bigger and better bridges mark the advance of technology and its power to overcome the obstacles of nature and, in a sense, remove nature from its path. The benefits of technology are conferred through a scientific understanding of natural law, at the expense of substituting the rule of natural law for the rule of social decorum. The bridge is in one sense an achievement, in another a threat to society, bringing a change in social values, and proposing itself as necessary. By comparison the Euston Arch is anti-technological, retrograde and unnecessary: but it represents a re-investment in the rule of decorum, an attempt to make a gateway of honor to the paths of necessity, to redeem by its propriety the crudeness of commercial exploitation of the new technology. It became, in spite of its uselessness, a fetish of London, a cultural marker whose loss was mourned (and opposed by many modern architects) when it was swept away in a further access of commercialism.

The opposition of ideas of propriety and the uncultured impact of new technology is also evident in the comparison between the interior and exterior of Ferdinand Dutert's magnificent Palais des Machines in Paris (1886–1889, demolished 1910). Inside is simple engineering; outside, art as additive—sculptural groups either side of the entrance and Gothic encrustations to the windows above.

Here we have a weak attempt to reconcile technology and civilization. The sculptural groups give a human meaning to a building that in its indifference to decorum may seem intimidating. They edify the visit to the exhibition, uniting women and men as ladies and gentlemen of fashion, on their way to take in the latest thing. The interior, with its audacious steel bearings, is another world entirely, the world of necessity and natural law that was to form the backbone, at its inception, of the arguments for a modern architecture.

In the constant movement into the future, the innovation has to be brought into the polite world, but at its beginning it was conceived through an act of repudiation, rejecting social norms under the dictates of logic and reason. In architecture, the dictates of logic and reason are not so evident as in engineering, because there is always a substratum of social acceptance built in to the concept of functional necessity, when that function is the accommodation of bodies and minds. Dutert's gallery was a demonstration of the power of steel, but it followed an older form that was used down the centuries for barns and churches: the form of the shed. In the traditional shed a basic spanning device or frame is repeated as a succession in depth from the front, one behind the other, in order to create, by repetition, a vast space.

When the English architect Norman Foster was invited to insert an art museum into the ensemble of the University of East Anglia, he chose this form. The result here is a long structural envelope with huge glass walls at either end, channeling space like the barrel of a gun from one end to the other.

While this center was viewed as novel and disruptive when first opened, it has settled down into a degree of acceptance. This may be due at least in part to its position in the longer perspective, where it may be seen as the latest in a long line of "noble" sheds. In the recent history of the Modern Movement it is of a type seen in Gropius's famous turbine shed for A.E.G. in Berlin. But before that there is the succession of such sheds produced in the hey-day of steel during the nineteenth century—the Palais des Machines, the Crystal Palace, and so on. And finally, is it so different in method and form from that most venerable shed, King's College, Cambridge, which in the time of the Gothic Revival was viewed as simplistic and lacking in finish? Each end is special, with a large window centering the space; the sides are but a succession of identical bays. The parallel even holds true on the inside, where in both cases an intricately modeled roof passes from one end to the other in identical bays confused by the accumulation of details into one long movement. The space follows the roof, jumping over the obstructions at ground level (the rood screen at Cambridge, the enclosure for offices at U.E.A.) to define a total volume of majestic proportions. That one is a horizontal, the other a vertical space, is as much a technological as a cultural evolution. One may be forgiven for discerning here a cultural continuity within English architecture, that consists in the appeal of pragmatic space, constructed with economy and rigor.

It is even possible to see, in the Sainsbury Center, a further perspective, for the space that rushes so headlong from one end to the other is tamed, at Sainsbury, by two porches, or porticos (only one affords entrance), which terminate the volume by means of a recessed bay rather than a flush surface. With this portico establishing the axis of the internal space at either end of the volume, the Center takes on the aspect of an ancient temple, dominating the landscape, enclosing a mystery—the power of the goddess, the power of the machine—and directing this power outward to the horizon.

One further comparison may be of interest here. Let us compare the Sainsbury Center with the Palazzo dei Congressi at the E.U.R. outside Rome. Adalberto Libera is an interesting architect of the Modern Movement in Italy, interesting particularly because he is perilously balanced between the modern and the classical: his Palazzo also has solid sides, and a recessed portico at either end with a glass wall, and, in this case, actual doors. Both buildings share not only the classical notion of the portico, but the celebration of steel construction by the use of light lattice work. At E.U.R. this takes the form of latticed mullions supporting the glass wall; at U.E.A. it takes the form of exposing the last bay of the main structural supports in the latitudinal walls (figs. 22, 23). The connection is not a causal one, with Foster imitating Libera. It results rather from the ideology of modernism, which values the idea of steel lattice and inserts it into its semantic space at certain focal points. It is a value originating in the ideology of functionalism, and borne up in the tide of culture as a recurring motif. Thus it is possible to insert Foster's building in a cultural history of 50, 100, 500, or 2000 years' span. While its allegiance is clearly to the goddess of technology, it is not void of references that tie it into a cultural tradition.

CONCLUSION

Modern architecture has been explained and justified by linking it to the technological revolution, itself an outcome of the application of scientific method to human affairs. The project of science—to uncover the laws of nature—is supplemented by the project of technology—to control nature for material benefit—and the advances that have resulted are not to be denied. But the opposition between innovation and established convention is not a purely material matter, in which material progress is seen as primary and due finally to triumph. To be acceptable, modern architecture has to be humanized, that is, rendered into a human tradition and subjected to human values. Traditions and values cannot be stated in advance without being reduced to ideology, but they remain a powerful force —in Simmel's terms the only force that is capable of renewing forms through its dialectical action upon them. It is not possible to take sides, to be "for" form and "against" life, or "for" reason and "against" feeling, since the outcome requires an accommodation that is outside the individual's control. The dialectical play of life forces and the forms that make them visible is thus a cultural struggle that is both necessary and unavoidable, and has no end.

The impact of deconstruction on poststructuralist thought would suggest a similar resolution. Truth is not embedded in language or in any other form but can only be glimpsed, like an elusive quarry. Certainly there is an endless relativity, but the inertia of the psyche ensures that from a certain distance (perhaps the interval that separates the writing of commentary from the writing of history) it becomes possible to discern the continuities that link the present to the past. Deconstruction may be seen as a denial of the over-emphatic discoveries of structuralism, as temporary in its effect as the form it supersedes. Yet neither can be dispensed with by the historian or the critic who has to continue, in a constantly shifting landscape, to make sense of the forms thrown up by the passage of time. Only one thing has to be abandoned: the idea of a timeless resolution, of categorical truth.

In a sense, the certainty that we can identify within a purely logical system takes on the allure of the traditional notion of truth— truth "discovered" rather than "revealed." Scientific certainty becomes a substitute—of mythic dimension—for the appeal of the traditional notion of salvation and eternal life. The very notions of moral identity and personal responsibility become something not fixed, but endlessly to be renewed. Technology is not to be worshiped, but scrutinized for its unwanted consequences, bringing perhaps a gain in terms of our ability to absorb and civilize it.

In art and architecture, the new will still be necessary, although we may have to renounce something of that spirit of "eureka!" that clings to the latest in fashion; the temporary euphoria that signals to its devotees the absolute end of the line. The new will continue to be endlessly sought, and we will know in advance, as with science, that it will soon become part of the old, due to be superseded and replaced by another form. In this respect, the method of science and the model of language become paradigms by which our place in life may be structured, replacing or modifying older paradigms of redemption and eternal life.

The difference in our viewpoint stems from the recognition that we exist in an endless flux of change which we can structure and bring into order only by means of forms. Forms are a means of perceiving relations, and as such they are essential for orientation and action. But no forms are final. Although each is due to be superseded it embodies a moment of discovery, of truth even, certainly of achievement, within the tide of the future. So, as part of the objective repertoire of forms we have to admit also the usefulness of those forms that we have to seek to reject because they now appear to us as "mere" forms—the forms of rhetoric. Thus the new is at the same time new and "new." Even the new has to be introduced in opposition to an existing quality. The utterly new is no longer possible, within the individual's compass, although it will take shape ineluctable over time in a social setting, just as De Saussure insisted that the individual alone has no power to change the language—only the community of speakers possesses that power.

Similarly, in Derrida, criticism as a scientific project is reduced through the linguistic uncertainties he insists upon, but this reduction does not appear to inhibit him in his exploitation of the very rhetorical devices he has pointed to as a source of insecurity. Thus the discoveries of deconstruction do not terminate the game of language, but rather reinforce it as a game. It is within the field of rhetoric that the "new" will be identified and take shape. Indeed, it could be argued that the very existence of this ambiguity in many writers (and clearly in metaphysical artists like de Chirico) is a mark of the impossibility of resolving the conflict between art and life.[6] Both are of necessity in a dialectical relationship, and can never at any moment in time be summarized, or reduced to definitive statements, but can only be intuitively sensed as forces. This in no way prevents the artist from drawing at will from one side or the other in his struggle to find a point of application. If this is so, it follows that both invention and innovation are essential for renewal and both, as well as either, may become the source of inspiration for work which will eventually be recognized as new.

Originally published in *The Structurist*, No. 29/30, December 1990.

NOTES

1   E.H. Gombrich: *The Story of Art*, (c) 1950, Phaidon 1972.
2   Harold Rosenberg: *The Tradition of the New*, Chicago, 1959, 1960.
3   Compare for example the writings of Adrian Stokes with those of Rosalind Krauss.
4   Georg Simmel: *On Individuality and Social Forms*, Chicago, 1971, p. 391.
5   Ibid., p. 376.
6   I refer to art and life as defined in the work of Georg Simmel (*On Individuality and Social Forms*) and Ernst Cassirer (*The Philosophy of Symbolic Forms*).

34 SCHRÖDER HOUSE: UTRECHT, THE NETHERLANDS
Gerrit Rietveld, 1924.

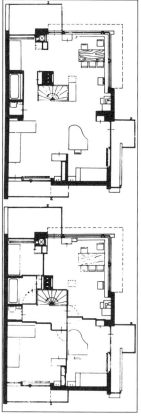

35 SCHRÖDER HOUSE (FLOOR PLANS)
Gerrit Rietveld, 1924.

ABSTRACTION AND REPRESENTATION IN MODERN ARCHITECTURE

"No person who is not a great sculptor or painter can be an architect. If he is not a sculptor or painter, he can only be a builder . . ."

Ruskin: Lectures on Architecture and Painting, #61, Addenda

ARCHITECTURE'S RESISTANCE TO THEORY

Kenneth Frampton, in a recent lecture, discussed the history of the International Style, a label affixed to modern architecture through the success of the book of that title by Philip Johnson and Henry- Russell Hitchcock.[1]

By describing the salient characteristics of functionalism in terms of a "style" those writers created a vast excitement for a new form of architecture that was both effective in practical terms, yet admitted of the nuances appropriate to artistic production. Frampton pointed to the characteristics of the "international style"—evidently an attempt to narrow down and specify the defining marks of modernity—compared with the very much wider range of characters illustrated in Albert Sartoris's book—*Functional Architecture*, of 1929—and the still wider range of expression that came later with postwar development. The white, purist style identified by Johnson and Hitchcock, of which the frontispiece illustrating the Villa Savoie of Le Corbusier may be taken as emblematic, has been replaced by a motley collection of buildings, so varied that they have become representative not of a style but of social and economic conditions generally; and, as such, they lose the attribution of singularity. It would seem then either that a functional architecture is independent of style, or that there are an infinite number of ways in which function can be expressed in stylistic terms.

This was not the outcome that was anticipated with the advent of functionalism: rather, it was thought of as ending the arbitrariness associated with nineteenth-century eclecticism, inaugurating an era when truth and beauty would be identical. Architecture would not be art, exactly, but it would reveal the truth, as all great art must do.

Yet this variety in built form can also be taken as testimony to the success of the functional idea as a unique ground of architecture. The undertaking to give more attention to functional requirements and economic limitations was perhaps inevitable, in order to adjust the pretensions of architecture to a utilitarian age; for how much longer should schools and clinics be expected to provide Corinthian columns across their facades? The idea that a functional building could be at the same time spare, practical and, in some sense, beautiful, has been at the root of the modern idea.

Practicality was always a concomitant of architecture; it is only in the twentieth century that the idea of uncovering the roots of utility has been raised to the level of an imperative, no longer a matter of common sense but of moral fervor. Utility now contains the seeds of right thinking and becomes a source of form, of new feeling, of artistic expression. The transition may be clarified by comparing the Vitruvian trinity of Commodity, Firmness, Delight, which held sway over eighteen centuries of architectural practice, with Hannes Meyer's equation, introduced in 1928: *like all things in the world, Architecture is Function times Economy*.[2] a shift, we may note, from the form of a religious axiom to that of a scientific one. In this way an architecture justified by function could claim to be the result of a privileged insight, and join in the modern desire to shatter convention and go directly to the sources of innovation. It could be part of the avant-garde.

The discovery, then, that functionalism could after all be identified as a style, that it was presumably part of a historical sequence of styles that included "baroque" or "art nouveau," was bound to raise controversy. For some, this condemned it, for others it authenticated it, made it available. In particular, we may note that, largely through the influence of the work produced by the office of Mies van der Rohe in Chicago, the tag of "the international style" was subsequently applied in America to the glass box office building, a form so successful in practical terms that it has become in turn the mark of the successful city: no American downtown of any size is now without its quota of glass office towers. The very multiplication of glass towers confirms their effectiveness as an economical way of enclosing rentable office space—their popularity confirms their functionality. Is this not strong evidence to vindicate the more general claims of functionalism?

Within the circle of the protagonists of the Modern Movement in architecture, form and function were claimed to be indissoluble. In the office building, as a type that truly represents our commercial civilization, the adoption of a utilitarian "style" is both appropriate and efficacious. Architectural design takes on the role of a powerful instrument. Thus the ability to appeal to function is an appeal to an underlying necessity, and so to power. Where the architect's authority had traditionally depended upon his standing with his patron, it now could depend on his own insights into the facts of the matter. Moreover, if we consider the contribution made not only by "modern architecture," but by the office of Mies van der Rohe, we glimpse the power that now attaches to the individual architect: surely it was largely due to the personal influence of Mies, to the prestige of the Seagram Building, that this proliferation came about.

Faced with the task of catching up with the authority of the old universities of England and France, the German university of the nineteenth century based itself on a superior knowledge of nature. In some similar way, it seems, the power that knowledge of function would confer on the architect now outweighed the freedom of expression that attended the use of abstract forms. The new architect of a scientific age claimed to base his designs on an insight into the program, not to express his own desires.

Yet if we consider Mies's visionary project for the Friedrichstrasse in Berlin, of 1921, the Seagram Building in New York City of 1958, and almost any downtown glass tower of the sixties and seventies, we have a series of three which adumbrates a progressive loss of visionary power. This absorption of a unique architectural vision into the familiarities of a built practice prompts some unavoidable questions about architecture's status as art. Is it not inevitably exposed to forces that the individual artist is able to keep at bay? Since it is both art and utility, it evidently cannot avoid putting itself at the service of society. How then can it achieve that special insight which, since the

Renaissance, the artist alone claimed to confer. Or, in terms of the view of art as an avant-garde phenomenon, how does an architect escape from the normal, how does he achieve that strangeness, which is the mark of a unique expression, without which a true product of art must be assimilated to social norms or popular taste?

Of course, it would be equally possible to consider together a series of oil paintings starting with, say, Picasso's *Les Trois Danseuses* of 1925, Franz Kline's *Crosstown* of 1955,[3] and almost any abstract canvas from an exhibition of local artists in Santa Fe, New Mexico, last year, and find a similar story of dissipation and decline. This series illustrates just as clearly the assimilation into society of the ideas of the progressive avant-garde. The use of abstract forms appears in the early years of the twentieth century as a force of liberation, and has become, by the declining years of the century, a convention for doing art spontaneously without having to learn a discipline.

Some would claim that Kline's canvas, far from showing decline as a corollary of assimilation, speaks of the increased power of the New York school of abstract expressionism. The artist is able to present his gesture in its authentic spontaneity; he is no longer forced by convention to represent mimetically the forms of the visible world—a duty which was still evident in the experiments of both analytic and synthetic cubism through the role played in them by distortion. In that reading, Kline would stand for the attainment of a goal of modernity: the total liberation of inner feeling. Abstraction as a principle empowers the easel painter to find an expressive truth in his own gesture on the plane of the canvas; it frees him from the necessity of measuring anything in the world before him. The notion of abstraction, once demonstrated, proves to have endless possibilities for expression, much as the "abstract" glass tower, once embodied, proves to have endless possibilities for the property developer. These possibilities are inherent in the new field, independent of the individual statements that can be made within it. However, expression comes from within, while program comes from without. artist and architect are in that sense diametrically opposed.

Loose though this comparison may be, it does allow us to reconsider the uses of abstraction in the visual arts and in architecture. The comparison prompts the question: if abstraction in art liberates the artist from the duty of representing natural forms, in what sense may we apply the same idea to architecture? What duty, within architecture, corresponds to the duty to mimic the real world?

It might seem that the overriding duty in architecture is now and always has been, to function, which comes directly out of the real world.[4] But I think it will be obvious, on reflection, that the effect of abstraction on architecture was not to liberate it from function, but from traditional form. The cause of function itself was advanced by the adoption of abstract forms, precisely because they owed no duty to propriety. Traditional form, in painting, was based upon the principle of mimesis, that is, the duty to represent the world. Indeed, this duty had produced a whole tradition of art, a virtual language of art. In architecture there was a similar duty to the inherited language by which the conventions of propriety were transmitted. Since propriety was inevitably tied to the system of power and patronage, this was also a duty to the principle of representation. It was not embodied in a singular style, it existed in Renaissance as in Gothic, in Classical as in Revival. It required simply that a surface of representation be raised to the observer, that an act of building be therein presented as an extension of a well understood set of meanings, and thus placed into society.

That the architectural tradition was borne upon social as well as natural influences had been recognized since Perrault revised the Orders. It is this purely architectural tradition which is finally placed under question by Ledoux, who first advanced the possibility of constructing meaning directly through the action of symbols, and in the parallel explorations of Durand, who proposed that spaces could be aggregated on an abstract modular basis according to need, instead of according to the organic requirements of a composition. These architects, in questioning the traditional language of architecture by introducing alternative analyses through expression and abstraction, became the precursors of modernism.[5] It is expression and abstraction which are to become the dominant elements of the modern style in art, but it is also evident that, in Hannes Meyer's appeal to functionalism as the only basis of architecture, abstraction's role in permitting a new freedom of expression is denied. Forms are now free to move around under the law of functional necessity, but not in the interests of personal expression.

We are faced thus with a paradox in the history of modern architecture. Insofar as functionalism was truly able to free architects from convention and from Corinthian columns, it was in practical terms a great success: glass office towers became an accepted aspect of modern development. Modern architecture was assimilated into society; architecture no longer had to conform to inherited rules of propriety, and what had at first been only a futurist vision soon became a fact of commercial life. On the other hand, the very success of these new forms soon removed them from the realm of the strange. They could no longer present a vision of another state of being. If the true test of avant-garde art was to point to an ideal state of being not yet realized, and in so doing offer a resistance to current norms of behavior, and above all to the excesses of bourgeois consumption, functional architecture through its very success had gone over to the other side: it now promoted consumption. Rational analysis of the program turned out to be a report beneficial first of all to the capitalist developer. Modern architecture had either been wrongly theorized, or it was resistant to theory.

FUNCTIONALISM FILLS A VACUUM

Throughout the history of the Bauhaus, where architectural theory was thought to reside in the years up to the second world war, this paradox was continually felt not as a theoretical weakness, but as a strange debility of architects, in terms of their susceptibility to form. The theory was that abstract forms freed architecture from the duty of propriety and placed it at the service of mankind. If these forms came to be valued for themselves, whether as part of a search for beauty or as a means of expression, they became suspect, no longer a means, but an end. In this way they obscured the true end, which was to reveal the truth. They were a distraction, and they were against the theory. Formalism became the sin against which architects were continually warned.

These tensions reflected a wider ambiguity in architectural circles. As the most influential architect to operate under the sign of modernism, Le Corbusier was quick to adopt abstraction as a principle of his practice. Having learnt to work in it through his association with the artist Ozenfant, he applied it ruthlessly, both in his rationale and in his play with architectural forms. Purism in his painting became functionalism in his architecture. His famous Domino diagram (of 1914) had already proclaimed the freedoms of the new, rational architecture, by way of an abstract analysis of construction. It thus provided the theoretical basis of those compositions in which he later discovered the elements of a new abstract style. The Villa Savoie illustrates the qualities of the new style, as well as conforming to a theoretical basis. He thus gave the theory of a practice yet to be realized, defining theory before practice—an impressive and unusual achievement. He never had doubts that architecture, practiced with insight, could aspire to be art, and that this was revealed through the manipulation of form.

The opposition to form as a weakness in applying theory has been most vividly revealed through the criticisms made by Kanel Tiege of Le Corbusier's Mundaneum Project, when Tiege condemned it for employing the traditional form of the pyramid, thereby succumbing to formalism; together with the latter's careful and reasoned response in his essay titled: "In Defense of Architecture."[6] Le Corbusier, while holding to the belief that technology was a source of new form, had no hesitation in claiming the architect's right, as artist, to go beyond the engineer, to choose by intuition the forms that would "speak to the heart."[7] He believed in certain human "constants," which allowed the modern man to feel himself the brother of the cave man, and which implicitly recognized the recurring power of certain forms as archetypes.[8] Against him Hannes Meyer, the champion of the Sachlichkeit, insisted that architecture was engineering, that it proceeded from, and was directed towards, a rational process of organization; that to consider it as art was derisory. In this claim he seems to assert the appeal to power as primary. Architecture becomes only an instrument for organizing life, but a powerful instrument. Of course, this had a direct political meaning, the Sachlich standing above all for the dissolution of personal expression in favor of a group responsibility, a priority that placed it firmly in the socialist camp. The architect's job was to serve the state. Insofar as the Sachlich allowed an aesthetic at all, it was to be an anti-art aesthetic, imbued with rationality, accepting only the unfolding of possibilities of form already immanent in the premises. In the outcome, this form of aesthetic was to be displaced by the new proprieties of social realism imposed by Stalin, when art, accepted as "art," was again placed at the service of the system in power and given the task of representing it.

In the postwar years, when the Hochschule at Ulm aspired to be the successor to the Bauhaus, the same search for an authority higher than the merely political was resumed, the same anti-theoretical weakness had to be fought. Form, good form, was continually in danger of becoming an end in itself; it interposed itself between the program and its realization, emerging as an arbitrary act of the architect, preventing the ideal situation where form would be transparent to the program, would be the program, in all its authenticity, made real.

In painting, on the other hand, no one claimed that the work of the New York school was undermined by its formalism. The artist's gesture was in principle authentic. No one claimed that Jackson Pollock's method of dribbling paint on to the canvas was an obstacle to the way the paint really wanted to be dribbled: on the whole, he was thought to be doing a good job on behalf of the paint. His dribblings were sufficiently accidental, in principle, to be effective. If he quietly cheated, arranging the dribbles artistically, that was his prerogative. Tinged or not with personal preferences, his paintings were still effective as a protest against academic conventions. When, as a result of the normal processes of assimilation, they became accepted, no one retrospectively accused him of formalism. On the contrary, their acceptance was proof that he was right all along.[9] In searching for the expressive gesture, the absolutely right form, the artist may consult nothing but his own inner feeling, a source of which he himself may not be fully aware, but within which, if he can do it at all, his mind works with his intuition in perfect companionship.

In searching for the right building form, the functional architect has no such right of privacy. He must make a rational case for his approach: the basis of what he will later put before his clients—who will pay for the building. Thus the architect is involved from the beginning in a sort of propaganda. He must always look to see how his idea will be received, even as he produces it. Moreover, his ability to consult his own inner feelings is anyway reduced by his need first to carry out a rational analysis—an analysis that, being rational, will command assent, and give him the power to assert his preferences. In theory, the appeal to function accorded power only to the degree that it was not compromised by the expression of aesthetic preferences. The insertion of a purely aesthetic judgement seemed to rob the proposition of its authenticity in reason, substituting an authenticity of voice. It appears, then, that it is the social role attributed to artist and architect in capitalist society that determines the degree of freedom that they can assume in carrying out their mission. Seen in these terms, the resistance to theory within architecture was a product of the persistence of social norms in the conditions of practice. It may be thought also to testify to the degree to which theory, in seeking its logical form, in seeking purity of form, itself becomes a form: achieving its destiny only by becoming detached from life.

To see in the clearest way this conflict between feeling and reason, we have to return to the moment before the Sachlichkeit theorists had forced the issue, to a time when functionalist architecture, hardly yet discovered, still held the promise of a new dawn, along with the complete aesthetisization of life. This was the aim of the De Stijl movement, which originally included artists and architects. In Rietveld's Schröder House we find the most heroic attempt yet made to hold together feeling and reason, form and function, in the symbiosis that was to express the aspirations of the new era at the end of "the war to end all wars."

The Schröder House, attached inconsequentially to the brick gable of a five-story apartment building, stands out even today as an expressive gesture of the artist, proclaiming its refusal of norms and conventions (fig. 34). Instead of standard bourgeois apartments humped together, an isolated individual object that emerges from a colorful play of abstract forms: clearly an "artistic" statement. As with the famous chair, the form of a conventional object (a machine for sitting, a machine for living) is visible only after its elements have been recomposed by the viewer. The first effect is to present a broken up, deconstructed version of the functional premise. It is a surprise to find that you can sit in the chair, and generations of people, in thus being forced to recompose the very act of sitting, are heard to pronounce it surprisingly comfortable. In the same way, when we consider how soon the Villa Savoie was abandoned by its owners, it is a surprise to find that Mrs. Schröder lived out almost her entire life in this house, that it served her well.

In the case of the house we note how the deconstruction of the traditional idea of "house" is achieved through the play of varied abstract forms. Planes are defined and juxtaposed independently of their function as walls, as roof. Looking at the main facade, we see two upper windows, one on the left, one on the right. Bedroom windows? They do not take up the traditional duty of expressing the volume of the house as a social unit. One is associated with a balcony, one with a hovering roof; their different treatment speaks to a different set of imperatives, a play of abstract forces in a delicate equilibrium. We notice particularly how the vertical plane, that divides the ground and second floor windows on the left also ignores the horizontal plane of the balcony, in front of which it passes. The total height of the house is at this point divided into three elements, not two. In this way, a variant that denies the simple division into two stories of habitable space is introduced, and the composition's right to depart from functional divisions is asserted. Every detail follows the same path of dissociation, like the steel joists which support the balcony, and the upper roof plane. These elements are detached from the traditional language of architecture, detached even from a technological analysis of architecture, completely abstracted from their origins, and then recomposed, now as part of an independent artistic composition, not of a "house."

If we turn now to the interior, we find another refusal to repeat the traditional divisions, with their firm distinctions of proper social meaning (fig. 35). The whole interior, at the upper level, is conceived as a single space—a "free" space—that revolves around a single obstruction—the fireplace. The free space releases one in principle into the whole realm of the composition as defined by its interiority. Then, by an amazing technical virtuosity, partitions can be drawn out from all sides to subdivide the total space, and allow a measure of privacy for eating, sleeping, bathing the body, playing the piano. The house becomes equal to its specific functional tasks, it responds to functional needs. It is, more clearly than Le Corbusier's Villa Savoie, a "machine for living."

But what is there left of the aesthetic of the exterior? This remains, perhaps, as an echo, in the form of the fireplace, in some details. In no sense, however, are we inhabiting the "composition" which the exterior projects. If we are not returned exactly to the traditional domestic realm of living room, dining room, bathroom, we are at least invited to identify spaces where one can live, dine or bathe. The power of the house lies in its transformational capability, its agility. As intended to be used, it is not a work of De Stijl art, but a functional miracle. As we enter the work of art, literal divisions supplant abstract divisions, and the interior of the De Stijl composition presented on the outside proves to be a vacuum. A vacuum that is filled with function.

THE ART THAT CANNOT SPEAK ITS NAME

In Rietveld's Schröder House ideal form adheres to the outside, ideal living occupies the inside. Taken together, these two aspects provide in one building a synthesis of form and function, the ideal of the new architecture. As an experiment in search of an architecture of De Stijl, the work is both intelligent and moving. Does this mean that we can take it as a symbiosis of art and architecture?

Considered as architecture, we cannot say that the outside is truly transparent to the functions within, rather that it interposes a new entity—an artistic composition—to the observer. This is "not yet" the true Sachlich architecture in which form and function are one. At the same time the interior, obsessed as it is with dimension and transformation, does not present an aesthetic that synthesizes interior space, decor and furniture, in the way that was attempted by architects as diverse as Wright, Hoffmann, Mackintosh, or van der Velde,[10] all of whom depend on decorative forms as a means of presenting a single sensibility. Specifically, it excludes the idea of decoration. In the search for an aesthetic of abstract forms, decoration perhaps returns us too quickly to a realm of representation, or at least to a world of relative scales, which may include stained glass windows, floral fabrics, liberty silk dresses, striped shirts, the whole paraphernalia of bourgeois living. We may note that Adolf Loos had no problem with oriental carpets placed in his interiors; nor did Le Corbusier, though he would have limited wall art to products of the abstract school. In the project of aestheticizing life, however, there is evidently a difficulty in defining an all embracing aesthetic that does not exclude in advance all art not of the same kind.

Insofar as life is institutionalized, it is conventionalized. It needs boundaries, limits, distinctions, and partial solutions. Abstraction, on the other hand, speaks of the universal, the limitless, the scaleless, so even works of abstract sculpture, when placed in the city, raise problems in which limits are applied to the limitless, as was revealed by the debacle of Richard Serra's *Tilted Arc* when installed in a New York plaza. If architecture is defined as a machine for living, the life that is literally lived in it must be hostile to the realm of art.

A few steps beyond the Schröder House, on the other side of an elevated roadway, as if in different world, we come upon another work of Gerrit Rietveld—a block of row houses constructed only a few years later (fig. 36). There is now no remnant of a De Stijl composition to be seen. The white walls, large windows, and cantilevered balconies with ship's rails place the building squarely within the International Style: indeed a canonical work of it. Now the exterior speaks, in a muted voice, only of the functional reality within. At the gable ends, there is a certain plastic interest which comes from the disposition of the section reading through to the outside.

So the composition, if indeed there is one at all, is concerned to "express" only the reality of the organization. This is architecture, not expressly art. We may continue to pursue the question as to whether this building can be taken as representative of a new functionalist art, an art of functionalist architecture, an art perhaps only so defined through it's possessing certain identifying traits or associations, an art that dare not speak its name? In any case, it exhibits a complete rejection of the synthesis attempted by Rietveld in the Schröder House. Why did Rietveld give up in this attempt? Did he experience a loss of vision? Did he come to see the disparity between the languages of inside and outside? As far as I know, these questions remain unanswered. It may simply be that there are inevitably limits to the aesthetisization of life, limits that arise not only from the objection to a total unity—the difficulty of defining limits without denying aspirations—but indeed from the very fact of habitation. In architecture, the body is always awaited. It remains a constant element. It establishes a scale, a pattern of use, and a series of expectations which are dominated by the "norm" of human intercourse, which, as I have suggested, is organized culturally not by a single principle, but by a whole series of institutions. The body has no difficulty with art when it is present as decoration, because decoration reinforces, or can reinforce, the sense of human scale. It is the boundlessness of abstract art that raises problems for the body.

In another De Stijl experiment, Theo van Doesburg's scheme of decoration for L'Aubette café-cinema, in which he expands his motif of diagonal rectangles into a total environment, we read the chairs and tables, even the projecting balcony with its simple ship's rail handrail, as intrusions. The human scale and the associations of use implied by these elements destroy the scaleless, timeless realm of the diagonal pattern applied to walls and ceiling. A realm of art which should be nowhere, is suddenly all too clearly placed somewhere, subjected to normal values, reduced to "decoration." It becomes apparent that a succession of canvases, hung in a museum, allow the spectator as he pauses before each one, to enter a "nowhere" realm. In L'Aubette the spectator is also the user of the building, and as user he imposes the sense of being there. This has nothing to do with the diversity of human tastes, everything to do with the singularity of human dimensions, and with the difficulty of peopling paradise with anything other than resurrected bodies.

36 ROW HOUSES: UTRECHT, THE NETHERLANDS
Gerrit Rietveld, 1931.

This is not to say that van Doesburg's scheme is trite. On the contrary, it is very powerful, and by its large scale and diagonal movement it anticipates the kind of dynamics now considered proper for dance halls.[11] To speak of what is proper for dance halls is to admit the return of conventional limits. Part of the appeal of both L'Aubette and Schröder to us today comes from our recognition of their boldness then, together with our perception now that the world of conventions is somehow indestructible. They therefore speak of a pathos of the human condition.

We must look to a similar explanation for the failure of van Doesburg's collaboration with Cornelius van Eesteren. By using the medium of the axonometric projection, the schematic design for a villa presents a pattern of hovering planes that approximates the appearance of an abstract work of art. Unlike the perspective, the axonometric does not imply a real viewpoint: it depicts space entirely as concept, not as scenery. If it suggests appearance, it is the distant view presented to an all-powerful deity. The artist working in two dimensions does not have to think of any viewpoint other than his own interior eye. So long as we are looking at a drawing, we remain in the realm of nowhere, where the artist's will is sovereign. If the drawing is treated as a construction document, it enters a different realm, a realm of future real possibilities. If it is constructed, it becomes a "place," unique on the surface of the earth, subjected to all the limitations of that placement. This collaboration did not lead to a symbiosis of art and architecture, but it undoubtedly influenced the development of a more abstract style of architecture.

In another case of great interest, we may cite El Lissitsky's Proun Room, of 1923. Here the artist has extended a work of abstract art to cover three adjacent walls, with specific motifs linking them, so defining a metaphysical space into which we can walk. When it was reconstructed, it was possible to insert oneself tentatively into the artist's ideal space and note no change to oxygen supply, pulse rate, vision, but an embarrassing sense of being an intruder. It is as if real space destroys metaphysical space. The same sense of incongruity occurs when the children climb through the hole in the Henry Moore sculpture. Neither the children nor the sculpture are the worse for wear, but a breach of etiquette has occurred.

These examples suggest that what prevents the symbiosis of art and architecture is the difference between space as metaphysical and as purely physical realm. Sculpture may employ suggestions of architectural space without penalty, but architecture, which somewhere just out of sight contains bathrooms, is inhibited by its particular reality. When we enter Chartres Cathedral, we give no thought to our need for a bathroom. We are firmly ensconced in a cultural perspective, and responding to an architecture which is everywhere representative of the cultural reality. The need for a bathroom is irrelevant. In the Modern Movement, just as thoughts of religious motivation were rejected for a materialist view of life, thoughts of the bathroom attained a peculiar schematic importance.[12] In the search for functional necessity, Le Corbusier found bathrooms—and staircases—were particularly useful incidents by which to press the idea of the "machine à habiter." In the Villa Savoie, we perhaps approach nearest to this ideal. The bathroom contains a tiled slab shaped to the body, and the curved shapes on the roof shield the body from the wind. The similarity between the roof curves and certain curved motifs in Le Corbusier's purist paintings is evident, yet there is no confusion as to the entity in which each curve occurs. If the Villa Savoie is a work of art in a cubist mode, it is not a cubist painting. It never denies the reality of inhabited space, it remains in a space measured by the act of inhabitation.

THE DECONSTRUCTION OF WHOLES: ARCHITECTURE AS OPERA

In spite of architecture's subjection to the body, it has never completely given up the dream of sharing in the basic enterprise of creative art: that is, to uncover new regions of the spirit. In spite of its subjection to the banal, it has not lost the hope of making things strange. The whole story of postmodernism in architecture is tied in to the completion of this process.

First, comes the unmasking of functionalism. This did not happen explicitly until Robert Venturi advocated that architecture should return to the space of representation, that fronts could be decorated and backs remain plain. His Guild House, a home for old people, had a decorated front, and was plain everywhere else. He compared it with Paul Rudolph's Crawford Manor, a building with a broadly similar program.[13] By emphasizing certain "functional" elements—stairs, elevator wells, kitchens, stacked one above the other in a tower—Rudolph was able to corrugate his exterior surface into a sculptural play of verticals that carried a charge of expressive intent. It was equally active on all sides, thereby avoiding any sense of front or back, and hence avoiding any sense of erecting a representational image. In the name of the Sachlichkeit, if not in its spirit, all sides must equally "express" the way space was internally organized. Venturi is able to say, with justice, that, instead of spending money sparingly where decorum requires, the whole building is convoluted in plan in order to achieve the desired effect, at great expense. The program itself is pressed into the service of an ideological position: functional form becomes the source of plastic richness. The building, refusing a representational duty, ends by representing its own status as an artistic product.

Where the glass box presents a bland and unified exterior, the brutalist structure presents a composition of many elements. This is no natural process, but the fabrication of an image. Since the architect controls the plan formation, he controls expression. The extreme to which this leads is exhibited in the high-tech fabrications of Richard Rogers, where the exterior is created entirely by the service elements—elevators, ducts, structure, none placed there except in the intent of creating an expressive surface of sculptural richness, justified in the name of creating "free" interior space. Everything that appears is apparently due to the severest necessity, never to the expressive intent of the architect as artist. This is truly the art that cannot speak its name.[14]

If this insistently sculptural architecture is self consciously manipulated to present an image, so also is the architecture of representation advocated by Robert Venturi. His facades, raised to reclaim a public realm, are paper thin. He glories in this thinness, calling the motifs depicted on them mere "emblems," sufficient to recall a past cultural richness, not sufficient to reconstitute the social reality which first brought them into existence. In this way, architecture is given a kind of afterlife, made into a sort of stage set for life. Life is viewed as a species of operatic production, which will need attention to be given to decor as to libretto, music, choreography, lighting. It is no doubt true that works of a representational nature here and there raise their facades among the crumbling frontages of our beleaguered cities. However dangerous, the streets of our cities are still a public realm, in which the individual must look out for himself. While in the shopping malls, a different view of life, as needing to be produced all over again, holds sway, a view that eliminates all elements not considered favorable to the laws of production and consumption.[15] Music, lighting, the choreography of display, the ear-piercing pavilion, the sweepstake for a luxury car, everything works together to lull the shopper into a sort of Dynasty fantasy, while isolated stalls selling sweetmeats or costume jewelry reconstitute the image of the old urban market. Thus, life as a whole is orchestrated into an artistic symbiosis, a remembrance of things past, at a level of excruciating banality.

Whether this orchestrated experience is the only reality of our times, as Frederic Jamieson claims, I doubt. However, without unduly emphasizing the apocalyptical dimension in late capitalist society, we can be fairly sure that we are in the grips of a general malaise which the recession only serves further to cloak. The malaise is visible in the increasing extent to which the poor are disenfranchised, and thus sacrificed to the general wish for everything to be harmonious and whole. Life not so much imitates art as seeks an artistic perfection in all things. In a way, the wish to have life orchestrated is only a trivial by-product of market organization, as if the market forces, like the brutalist architects, must needs manipulate the entire program in order to come up with a satisfactory image of harmony and richness. We note the invitation implicit in Ralph Lauren ads to have everything in our lives harmonious, without necessarily ourselves owning only designer jeans. The extent and the blatancy of the influence is nevertheless sobering, to the extent that it indicates how much we are swayed by surface and glitter. What seems to be the over-riding sentiment today is nostalgia. It is the very basis of Ralph Lauren's appeal. It is nostalgia for real Cape Cod houses that drives the vernacular of the tract housing and condominiums. It is nostalgia too that underlies the return, among a younger generation of architects, to the pre-Sachlich moment when abstract forms liberated art, but not architecture, from the thrall of convention. Since function has proved ineffectual as a basis for new form, and since rational analysis has once again led into an impasse, why not go back to expression, to the intuitive search that was suppressed by the search for functional truth? Why not "come out" as artists, why not be as free as the easel artist to express an individual vision?

In the early days of Russian Constructivism, architecture appeared to be an element of art; not as built form, but as graphic invention. Now, under the rubric of deconstruction, graphic and architectural forms are again turning in to each other. If the result is totally decorative, should this be taken as condemnation? Can not the building be, as a whole, an expression of a single artistic vision, an expressive work of sculpture? Can not the spaces of habitation also be invaded, and reconstituted, as art? This is the intention, I believe, behind the new expressionism of the fin-de-siècle, an expressionism no longer inhibited by the duty to function, nor afraid of the accusation of being "merely" decorative. It is too early to say whether this further attempt at the symbiosis of art and architecture will in turn succumb to the demands of the body. Without excluding architecture entirely from the realm of the expressive, we may do well to pay heed to Adolf Loos's warning, that only a very small part of architecture belongs to art: the tomb and the monument.[16]

Originally published in *The Structurist*. Special issue on "Symbiosis in Art and Architecture," December 1992–January 1993.

NOTES

Titled "The International Style," at the Museum of Modern Art, New York, on February 10, 1992, to mark the fiftieth anniversary of the publication of the book in 1932. Reported in *Building Design*, London, March 6, 1992.

2   "All things in the world are a product of the formula: (function times economy) . . . architecture as an 'embodiment of the artist's emotions' has no justification:" from "Building," an essay first published in 1928, in *Hannes Meyer—Buildings, Projects and Writings*, ed. and tr. Claude Schnaidt, Niggli, 1965.

3   Illustrated in Vincent Scully's *American Architecture and Urbanism* of 1969, and cited by him as an example of the aleatory process in Abstract Expressionism, to be compared with an aerial view of Minneapolis-St.Paul at night, where the random patterns of the colliding street grids appear as cosmic gestures.

4   The regular reversion to functionality as the prime moral corrective in architecture has been very fully chronicled by E.R. de Zurko: *The Origins of Functionalist Theory*, New York City: Columbia University Press, 1957.

5   As with Emil Kaufmann: *Von Ledoux bis Le Corbusier*, 1933, and many other texts.

6   Originally published in *Stavba 2*, Prague, 1929; reprinted in French in *L'Architecture d'Aujourd'hui*, No. 10, 1933, p. 38.

7   "You employ stone, wood and concrete, and with these materials you build houses and palaces. That is construction. Ingenuity is at work. But suddenly you touch my heart, you do me good, I am happy and I say: This is beautiful. That is architecture. Art enters in." Le Corbusier: preamble to "Pure Creation of the Mind" in *Towards a New Architecture*, p. 197, tr. Etchells, 1927.

8   "Avec joie . . . (l'homme) . . . a vu que la géométrie l'a fait progresser; il prend un goût très vif à tout ce qui la manifeste; il a pris conscience que, loin de s'éloigner des constantes physiologiques, intellectuelles et sentimentales, loin de s'aventurer dans les artifices échappant à sa loi, il a, par la pratique intensive de la géométrie, retrouvé ce qui, au tréfond de lui, est le plus spécifiquement humain!": Le Corbusier in "Formation de l'Optique Moderne," *L'esprit Nouveau* No. 21.

9   When the Museum of Modern Art celebrated its fiftieth anniversary, the leading donors and officers were photographed for *The New York Times* against a Jackson Pollock, now as background reduced to an emblem of "with-it-ness," a perfect decorative surface, as if it were a new fabric from Dior.

10 Or even Gropius and Meyer's Sommerfeld House (of 1921), which followed a Wrightian-Hoffmannian line in integrating inside and outside through a unified sensibility of decorated forms.

11 Isozaki's renovation of the Palladium music hall as a dance hall is another more recent case where a huge abstract pattern of lights and video screens declares a scaleless, roboticized universe, only to be overcome by the strict rituals of rock video presentation, and by body-sized dancers.

12 In the *Oeuvre Complète*, when he comes to Ronchamp, Le Corbusier feels it necessary to explain why it is all right for the architect to design a church: he had earlier believed that it was wrong to attempt such a culturally loaded thing in the modern style.

13 With the section: "Heroic and Original, or Ugly and Ordinary" in his book: *Learning from Las Vegas*, Cambridge, M.I.T. Press, 1972, reprinted 1986, pp. 93–100.

14 As at Lloyds of London, the Pompidou Center in Paris, and Foster's Bank in Hong Kong, this kind of imagery comes out very expensive, contradicting the Sachlichkeit equation of Function times Economy.

5   A few years ago, a judge ruled that Hari Khrishna groups could not solicit in shopping malls, without the express permission of the mall's owners. Contrary to appearances, shopping malls are not in the public realm.

6   ". . . The work of art is the artist's private affair. A house is not . . . The work of art aims at shattering man's comfortable complacency. A house must serve one's comfort. The work of art is revolutionary, the house conservative . . . Only a very small part of architecture belongs to art: the tomb and the monument." Adolf Loos: "Architecture, 1910," tr. Benton et al in *Form and Function*, ed. Tim and Charlotte Benton, Open University Press, Granada, 1975.

37 LIBRARY
Boullée, 1780.

MYTHS OF MODERNISM

For someone like myself who was born in the twenties, the doctrine
of functionalism is as old as oneself. At one level, its message seems
obvious; at another, it now seems altogether too ideological. It postulat-
ed not merely a common-sense accommodation to the program of a
building, but an expectation that to follow the program closely would
enable the architect to reveal an underlying source of new-ness, a
strange-ness parallel to that produced in high art. The functionalist
architect who could free himself from convention was an iconoclast,
and a bona fide member of the avant-garde. To follow function was
then to approach the eloquence of high style. Functionalism was not
just a method, it was a way of doing things differently and with insight,
and therefore distinctively. Buildings designed in the functionalist way
took on a new look, and functionalism became a style.

The coming of functionalism thus became closely identified with
the Modern Movement in architecture, a revolution that changed
both the method and the look of architecture and established a new
style. Yet strictly speaking, the idea of making the function primary,
if taken seriously, would abolish architecture entirely, by removing
its autonomy. For if architecture should be nothing more than the
meeting of functional requirements by rational means, the only
point of interest would be, in any particular case, did it meet those
goals? Architecture would then be judged by criteria which were outside of it and independent from it. Building would serve human
needs, and nothing more. It would be purely instrumental; but in
compensation for this, it would also follow necessity, and by doing
this it would exhibit truth, and its results would be unavoidable.

The appeal to function as a form of truth owes as much to the image of science as a discipline as to that of high art. Even if architecture itself were to be nothing but the application of technical knowledge to problems of inhabitation, it would still reveal something fundamental about human life. There was an underlying biological necessity in life, in relation to which cultural concerns seemed to amount to a useless accretion, to be a drag on progress, an obstacle to the new, in short what Reyner Banham termed "baggage." The idea of new-ness in science was thus conflated with the idea of new-ness in art, and the prestige of scientific discovery was added to the appeal of iconoclasm. Architecture in the traditional sense was abolished, but it was quickly replaced by an architecture that, however contingent, was always identifiable by its appearance. It had the appeal of efficiency, but also the appeal of revolutionary art. This was the meaning of architecture which began to have such enormous appeal —and to architects—in the early years of this century.

It never quite worked out like that: somehow, there was always something in there which had to do with other things than accommodating the function. Within the heroic period of the Modern Movement, the most celebrated buildings have appealed to something other than efficiency; can we think of any case where such a building is valued and remains valid only because it perfectly met its program at the time of its inception? It is certainly not the suitability for its clients' needs that has ensured the canonic quality of the Villa Savoie; and there is a great deal of beauty in Frank Lloyd Wright's Unity Chapel that is not called for in his description of a church as a simple utility. Equally, Fuller's Dymaxion House remains an unfulfilled promise, and Hugo Häring's farm buildings at Gut Garkau seem now to be primarily works of German Expressionism, not the last word in animal husbandry. Even if there was indeed a real attempt in these works to avoid the simply conventional, exploit new situations and express new aspirations, they derive their form from something other than the physical limitations that defined their programs. Indeed, all our models from the heroic period give evidence of an enthusiasm, and in some cases a passion, that goes beyond simple physical function. It is not just the obvious fact that the conditions that impose a functional solution are transitory, and soon disappear out of sight, leaving the form that answered to them as a mute witness, a *corpus delicti*. The object, in its very strangeness, attracts a gaze that looks beyond its immediate use for something more like a meaning. Yet the idea of function, and the idea of shedding superfluous concerns and baring the pure function as a source of form, has been a major myth in the shaping of modern architecture, and continues to exert its appeal today.

To understand the enormous attraction of the functional idea, and hence its ideological appeal, we have to show how it relates to concepts of nature, and to the power of science as the means of baring nature itself and exposing the functional necessity within it.

While the idea of Function is a unitary one, one that brooks no confusion, its status in practice has never been so secure. It has tended to break into two, one part corresponding to void and one to solid: first, the shape of the space that reflects human activities and use; second, the bare bones of construction, the physical structure, that encloses it. Both have turned out to be more complicated, and less obviously meaningful in themselves, than first was supposed. In 1957, a student called De Zurko wrote a book *The Origins of Functionalist Theory*, based on his doctoral thesis, which traced the history of functionalist thought back all the way to Aristotle. Baring the function, in De Zurko's story, is tied up with a search for the naked truth, something like an absolute value, and, as the recent history of philosophy has shown, the more naked truth is, the more it is elusive. To recognize the truth, when one is presented with it, requires that it has a recognizable face, and so its recognizability becomes crucial. The naked truth, to be visible, must already be represented within culture. Here is the source of the confusion that has dogged the doctrine of functionalism since its inception: to expose the "real" function is impossible without at the same time projecting it, that is, presenting it. Thus made visible, it does not offer a sure escape from culture, but takes up its role as a motif that can only point to that escape. It projects a strangeness that hopes to be seen as the recognition of a state of nature.

Modernity, it is agreed, is the result of a new relationship between rational discourse and empirical proof that was established during the Enlightenment. Consider again the opening towards nature that was ushered in by the discoveries of the Enlightenment: principally through Newton's mechanical universe and Descartes's rational encyclopedia of the world. In science, these discoveries brought a genuine power over nature: it was Newtonian physics that guided the Apollo rocket to the moon and back. This power of intervention is real. It exists for us today in the form of a question:

do we wish to destroy the biosphere by the use of the nuclear bomb? This is a real power that we possess. How does this immense power appear within architecture?

Perhaps Boullée best expressed the sense of this power, at a time when its full extent was not yet known. He does this through images that speak of the immensity of space and the insignificance of man within it (fig. 37). Architecture appears to mediate this relationship, conforming to the laws of geometry, obeying a law greater that man, yet leaving a place for man if he will but accept his reduced role, no longer as the generator of myth and nature, but as a part—a rational part—of that nature, which is assumed to exist independently of him. Reason becomes the key to power, and its workings are independent of human society and its conventions, and hold good at any scale.

But not everything is mere representation. The power of rational thought may be applied to architectural construction and may have a real effect on it. So what we see, in architecture, is a constant struggle between that part that comes from science and represents the discoveries of rational thought, and that part that comes from a tradition of architecture as representation, in which the rational is presented within a larger and more humanistic stream of thought.

This struggle, which follows the course of a dialectical opposition, is particularly clear in the work of the nineteenth-century French architect Henri Labrouste. While studying architecture in Italy, as the winner of the Prix de Rome, he was intrigued by the early Greek temples at Paestum, and particularly by the unexpected form of the Temple of Hera I, which was susceptible to interpretation as a double temple divided down the center by a row of columns, or as a single building of unusual form. Labrouste favored an interpretation which saw the central row of columns as allowing a circulation throughout a single space—a space which he maintained was rather that of a meeting place or forum than a temple of worship, accessible only to the priests. Labrouste's rational, but unhistorical, interpretation earned him the reprimand of the establishment, but this did not prevent him from making a further interpretation of the single space divided, and united, by a central row of columns, in a new construction of his own. It forms the basis of his masterly design for the Library of Ste. Geniève in Paris. This design makes the central row of columns important as structure, using their permeability as spatial articulation to permit the doubling of a structural span. The result is a double shed, using iron and masonry construction in a new partnership that combines the structural principle of Gothic with the representational power of Classical architecture. But the presence within this building of two quite different ideas, reconciled within an artistic principle, brings a result quite different from the unqualified observance of a single technological principle, as in a simple train shed.

Train sheds start appearing from around 1850: an uninhibited new space, inhabited by a new form of grumbling beast, whose articulation works through rail tracks, where nothing moves for a cultural purpose, but only to service the beasts. After the original thought of making a single enormous space, there is nothing left for architecture to do. Or the Crystal Palace, which first presented the vast possibilities of glass and iron construction, but still following the form of a latter-day palace, with pavilions and cross-axes. In neither of these examples do we find the peculiar pleasures proper to architecture considered as an art, where the new and the old can be brought into a meaningful tension, that extends the cultural envelop.

Perhaps Ferdinand Dutert's Galerie des Machines affords the most obvious example of the opposition between technology and culture. This is an advanced structure of steel portal construction, employing roller joints at the apex of the span and at the bases of the girders. It is articulated on purely structural principles, there is no attempt to bring it into culture. In contrast, the glass membrane that closes out the ends is decorated with vaguely Gothic encrustations; and at the entrance are placed two massive pieces of statuary, classical nudes to bring high tone, an attempt to make the visits of ladies and gentlemen into something more exciting, into more of a cultural event. Culture and technology, however, remain opposing principles, and the result is quaint, not powerful.

In many buildings of the turn of the century, such as Berlage's Stock Exchange of 1879 and Perret's Clothing Factory of 1913, we see more successful attempts to integrate the new forms of steel and reinforced-concrete construction into an architectural whole: but these examples are still hybrids, not landmarks in the evolution of architecture. The unsatisfactory nature of such hybrids may perhaps account for the search among twentieth-century architects for a new principle that would obviate compromise, and have the directness and clarity of certain forms found in the natural world.

For the generation of young architects that were taking part in this search after the first world war there was one source that seemed utterly convincing: the book by D'Arcy Thompson, *On Growth and Form* of 1917. Leslie Martin, former Head of the Architecture School of Cambridge University, told me that this book was viewed as gospel in his group—the group that went on to publish *Circle* in 1937. D'Arcy's illustrations were as compelling as his text. Not only are the skeletons of massive dinosaurs seen to follow engineering principles, but the patterns of growth in hard-shell mollusks are seen to observe strict mathematical rules, using logarithmic series to preserve a constant proportion as they grow. Nature thus seems to be the equal of a professional engineer, and the professional engineer in turn must follow Nature's Laws. So why not the architect, too? The forms of nature follow laws, and yet they have a clarity that approaches something we call beauty.

Thompson shows us a photograph taken by the scientist Egerton at Massachusetts Institute of Technology, of a splash in milk, invisible to the naked eye but caught by a high-speed exposure—the result is strangely like a crown. Thompson compares this with the form of a hydroid polyp—Nature is full of beautiful ideas. From structure we slide imperceptibly into analogy, and hence into the shadowy domain of dreams.

With Amédée Ozenfant's marvelous book *The Foundations of Modern Art*, published in 1928, analogies become the source of new possibilities. He touches on some material similar to Thompson, but he also ranges far afield into artifacts of primitive cultures and aspects of machine technology. The fascination with machines is no longer limited to what they do, what they accomplish as instruments, but extends to their mystery, their inwardness as objects. Duchamp and Picabia exploited this aspect most directly in high art, but the fascination of the machine penetrated artistic culture widely. One of his most telling examples is the illustration of the 1928 Jaeger speedometer: a mysterious object not only in itself, but through the engineer's dead-pan method of presentation. It is instructive to set it against Boccioni's *Bottiglia, Tavola, Cassaggiata* (of 1912), to show how the enigmatic forms of machines had already fed into the vision of cubist and futurist artists.

Architects, as professionals, might have been thought to be less "romantic" in their response to mechanical and engineering forms, but they were just as much under the spell of their strangeness as the artists. Le Corbusier not only led the way here, but he supplied a whole rationale to justify the imitation of industrial forms, particularly clean white cubes and cylinders. But Moholy-Nagy, in his

1929 book *The New Vision*, gives us more obviously mechanical forms in his illustration of the Ford factory, and this more expressionist aspect of industrial installations has remained of obsessional interest to architects. It is these enigmatic machine forms that are also celebrated in Becher's 1979 book *Anonyme Sculpturen*—sculpture without sculptors—which has recently been reprinted. So we find that the idea of functionality is validated by the example of the machine, and functionalism as a style becomes conflated with the machine aesthetic.

In a certain sense, Le Corbusier's influence, and his preference for clear-cut prismatic forms, gave a new life to a sort of latter-day classicism, and it is evident that in the so-called International Style, as defined by Johnson and Hitchcock, the machine aesthetic is transformed into a new set of conventions. But the machine as the emblem of purity, untainted by culture, remains present as a reproach, and when modern architecture becomes in turn the new orthodoxy, after the second world war, it reappears in a more brutalist and expressionistic guise. Stirling's History Faculty Building at Cambridge has a certain classical suavity as space, but if you look directly up, the machine looms over you, like a hugh moth attracted by the lights of learning (figs. 38, 39).

In the work of Louis Kahn, who went on to redefine Roman architecture in contemporary terms, it is evident that for a time he too succumbed to the romantic attraction of buildings-as-machines. I remember how important here was the opinion of Arthur Korn, a refugee from Hitler who taught at the Architectural Association after the war, and used to make us look at the frontispiece of Albert Sartoris's canonic book on functional architecture, which was a picture of a petroleum-splitting plant. "That is how our cities should look!" he said. Small wonder that the next generation—including the architects of the Archigram group—should return to that vision of machine-cities. Ron Herron, of Archigram fame, once gave me two slides he made during a trip to California of a petroleum-splitting plant in Los Angeles. Therein we can see the shape of the Archigram city.

The biggest influence among the post-war generation in London was that of the Smithsons—Peter and Alison—who may be thought of as prototypes for Robert Venturi and Denise Scott Brown, because they combined a moral imperative about the importance of everyday forms and pop culture with a determination to do buildings that would shock the bourgeoisie. There is a real attempt in the

38 HISTORY FACULTY: CAMBRIDGE, ENGLAND
James Stirling, 1964–1967.

Smithsons' architecture to bring industrial forms into culture, stretching the cultural envelope by the effort of its assimilation. One can only wonder why this attempt to foster a genuine dialect of culture and technology was not more successful in their case. It fell to the Archigram group to carry the banner of functionalism squarely into what Reyner Banham called the "second machine age."

The Pompidou Center may be thought of as their first built project, if only because so many of their group were employed by Piano and Rogers in the team set up to do the design development and working drawings. For me this building is interesting not purely as an example of machine architecture, but to the extent that it seems to place itself within a tradition of functionalist architecture. Ramps and staircases, like chimneys, vents and pipes, are the humble parts of architecture that can most easily be read as mechanically effective. See then the importance of the escalator that ascends the face of the Pompidou Center in one continuous sequence, prompting a comparison with the escape staircase in Hannes Meyer's Peterschule, of 1926. The abstract diagram takes on the mantle of reality. The uncompromising form of the escalator reduces the face of the build-

**39 THE MOTH AT THE WINDOW (AIR-CONDITIONING MECHANISM),
HISTORY FACULTY: CAMBRIDGE, ENGLAND**
James Stirling, 1964–1967.

ing to a rational diagram of accessibility, privileging the mechanical movement system, which in itself is treated as an empirical fact, not as a symbolic statement. The same literalness is true of the pipework, exposed throughout the building, and which dominates the elevation on the other side to the Rue de Renard.

Yet the privileged place given overall to the mechanical systems is exactly what gives the building its ideological content. In my view, the Pompidou Center is too purely ideological to be able to incorporate within itself a consciousness of the irony that attaches today to the attempt to place man within nature. It does not admit of the tragic view. More successful in achieving this status as a work of architecture is Aldo van Eyck's Home for Unmarried Mothers in Amsterdam. Here there is a similar idea of privileging the staircase, not here thought of as just a physical thing, but as a place outside of social programming, an uncertain place where shy people might be able to find words to greet each other and make friends. The function of the staircase is seen as both a physical and a social fact, and this endows it with a greater importance as part of the architectural composition. The way in which the staircase is exposed to the street,

40 STADIUM
Boullée, c. 1785.

41 POMPIDOU CENTER: PARIS, FRANCE
Piano & Rogers Architects, 1977.

and the street facade is ambiguously cut into for this purpose, achieves a formal balance which does, in my view, lift the building out of simple literalness and allow it to speak within culture.

John Johanson used to make a polemic for his brand of brutalist architecture by claiming that there should be no facades, as such, that all exposed faces should be, as it were, working sections. This was an attempt to eliminate the whole notion of representation, and exhibit architecture as nothing but brute fact—one way that the modern movement, conceived as an avant-garde movement, tried to place itself outside of culture, by displaying motifs that were to remain, as it were, uncooked. In that sense, we can take Boullée's section to his stadium, another immense structure that presages the giant stadia of our own times, and see it as the precursor of a modern architecture that wants to refuse its cultural role (figs. 40, 41). The escape stairs are there out of pure necessity, they make no attempt to acclimatize themselves to human use. In the modern stadium the administrative rules that limit the number of steps that may be employed between landings return a small measure of humanity to such "vomitaria," where deaths may still occur without

42   LA SALINE DE CHAUX (SOURCE): CHAUX, FRANCE
Claude-Nicholas Ledoux, 1773–1779.

43   PIERRE BOULEZ MUSIC CENTER (VENTILATOR): PARIS, FRANCE, 1976

any register of the tragic nature of death.

We must interrogate ourselves continuously about this, the deliberately inhuman, aspect of functionalism. Which speaks more eloquently: the bare functional ventilator, or the decorated motif? The ventilator at street level above the Boulez Music Center, adjacent to the Pompidou Center, is truly functional, although since it takes the form of a ship's ventilator, and is placed raw against the urban wall, like a condemned man, it is not without pathos (figs. 42, 43). Does it still carry an awareness of its symbolic role within culture? The sculpted "origin" on the wall at Ledoux's Saline de Chaux is purely representational, there is no actual water nor salt crystallizing; does it still carry a political statement about the French King's right to impose a tax on salt? In neither case is the artifact perceived independently from its cultural context. Culture is a complex web of associations that primarily exist in and through the language, and even the raw fact becomes entangled in this web in due course. Here is an area where de Saussure's concept of a science of meaning may still serve as the means to elucidate our cultural situation, and where our artifacts may serve as the clearest reflection of cultural reality.

Let us take a breath at this point, and recapitulate. Compared to traditional architecture, modern architecture offered an entirely new set of values. The idea that function should be privileged in place of propriety was not only effective as a brand of iconoclasm, overturning convention, but it also appeared to offer a new source of form, a source of new forms. It conveyed an excitement, analogous to the excitement of scientific discoveries, and turned attention away from the past, where everything was bound by convention, towards the future, where convention hadn't yet taken hold. The infinite possibilities of science and technology would ensure that everything would continue to change and become new. This was the sentiment that Aldous Huxley enshrined in his title "Brave New World," itself lifted from *The Tempest*, where Shakespeare discusses the advantage to the philosopher of the concept of withdrawal and return, the polemics of the "fresh start."

A very similar excitement reigned in the world of art, in the first decade of the twentieth century. In Paris, at that time the art center of the world, this excitement converged in the discoveries of cubism, and here we are talking about the impact of abstraction and its importance for modern art. Abstraction is, of course, the very basis of the scientific method. You abstract only those factors that are susceptible to measurement; you look for a causal relation between abstracted parameters. Abstraction in art is different, because the elements that are abstracted depend entirely on the subjectivity of the artist, and are not causally related to anything outside that subjectivity.

Abstraction in art was not entirely new: at the outset of the twentieth century, it is already evident in the work of artists like Paul Cézanne and the Russian Expressionist Vrubel, and others. But with few exceptions, western art up to the end of the nineteenth century had been dominated by the ancient concept of mimesis: art is given the task of imitating the real world, even if the imitation allows great freedom to create ideal appearances. Now it seemed as if art could be freed of the duty of representing appearances, and thereby become free to represent the artist's feelings directly. But before that freedom could be grasped, there was still a debt to be paid to the art of representation. It could be done more profoundly, not stopping at the surface of appearance, but penetrating into the essential nature of things. In cubism, the artist claimed the freedom to do this by representing different views of the object simultaneously, not necessarily as the camera would register them, but at a conceptual level. Thus the mind of the artist was felt to be a superior kind of lens, improving the photographic image with an added psychological dimension. This dimension took concrete form, as it were, through the concept of the fourth dimension. Was it a dimension of space? Or was it time? Or was it metaphysical—purely of the mind? No one was quite certain. What was important, however, was the sense that not only was the world changing functionally, through the power of science, but the conditions of perceiving the world were changing also. Science spoke of a world of atoms held apart and held together by unimaginable forces. Artists somehow felt that they, too, could glimpse new depths in things that had up to now been solid and impenetrable. The thing-in-itself was different, but different also was the space the thing contained, as well as the space in which it was perceived.[1]

How does this sense of a new spatial reality, underlying human perception but invisible to it, appear in art? We find it in many forms, but probably nowhere so succinctly presented as in the work of Marcel Duchamp. While rejecting the world of appearances, Duchamp is still fascinated by the way that certain techniques like mechanical perspective allow appearance to be reconstituted as a part of abstract thought processes. Mechanical perspective, and, later, axonometric projection as used by Theo van Doesburg and Cornelius van Eesteren, allow the three dimensions of ordinary perception to be dealt with as abstractions and then re-combined by an effort of thought. Why then should thought not be capable of extending this reconstituted reality to take account of four dimensions?

In works like *Glider Containing a Waterfall in Neighboring Metals* and *Virtuality as a Fourth Dimension*, Duchamp made a new connection between drawing and conceiving, that takes evenly from both abstraction and representation, and that also absorbs from the title itself a narrative potential. In a way, Duchamp anticipated the universe of cyber-space that we confront today: there, reality is exhibited on a two-dimensional screen that simulates not only the third dimension and time, but suggests the dimensionless realm of space. Space is, however, circumscribed by gravity in ways that even Einstein's equations have not yet fully revealed. But if reality is conceived of as entirely mental, as it is when transmuted into computer language, it need not be so circumscribed within the domain of art. Here artists are clearly looking towards the world of science, and the mysteries that the new physics of relativity and quantum mechanics were in course of revealing. In mathematical thought, gravity does not impede the handling of abstract space, even space of more than three dimensions. N-dimensional geometry, for instance, is just as conducive to rules of calculation as Euclidean geometry. Artists were particularly influenced by certain geometers of a mystical caste, such as Denys Hinton, an expert in the concepts of multi-dimensional geometry, who, as early as 1880, had published an article entitled "What is the Fourth Dimension?" and who brought out his book *The Fourth Dimension* in 1904.[2] Diagrams such as the *Intersection of plane and spiral 60*, perfectly simple from a mathematical point of view, become potent mysteries when looked on with the eye of the artist.

Duchamp's *Handler of Gravity 61* is all of thirty years later than that diagram from Hinton's book, but I would interpret this as the delay that necessarily attends the assimilation of scientific facts into the cultural consciousness. Where Hinton's diagram is elementary, Duchamp's figure, with its portentous title, is deliberately enigmatic. The artists were not interested in the limited meaning of the diagram as a step in mathematical logic—an entirely rational process—but in the strangeness of such diagrams when torn out of their scientific context and presented as part of the enigma of life.

In this sense the concepts of surrealism are not limited to the works of the surrealists as such, but are more widespread as a response to the impact of modern science on culture, because scientific causality is no longer linked to ordinary causality, and common sense no longer works within the abstractions of science. A scientist working in n-dimensional geometry stays within rules that work, he does not have to visualize an existence in n-dimensional space. The artist, confined within the three-dimensional world of the living body, beats against this limitation as if it contained the secret of the universe. Boccioni's *Muscular Dynamism 62* should not be looked upon simply as a sculpture of a football player, which is what it probably is, but as a meditation on the mysterious impact of living reality within the static world of the artifact. In a sense, artists are trying to penetrate behind the representational surface of life, in a way analogous to what they perceive the scientists as doing. But the method they use is created by the very limitations of the medium.

But the futurists, with their yearning for speed and political change, broke out of this fixation. In Boccioni's *Bottle Evolving in*

Space, the bottle is evolving in conceptual space, not in real time, and we are still within the mysteries of time and place; in Balla's *Speed 63*, the fourth dimension has become concrete as time, and movement is represented simply as multiple image. Time considered as the fourth dimension is still capable of paradoxical interpretation—as in H.G. Wells's thriller *The Time Machine*—but it is no longer the source of a metaphysical puzzle.

Cubism came to terms with the mysteries of science by inventing a new painterly style that put the artist firmly back in control of the one thing that truly limited his scope—the plane of the canvas. In the earlier phase of cubism—analytical cubism—the use of multiple image is partly due to the idea of different viewpoints, partly due to the sense of the canvas as a medium in its own right. Within the diffracted *Portrait of Ambrose Vollard* we may still glimpse the single Ambrose Vollard who "sat" for Picasso. The effect is not too far from multiple image, produced by inadvertence by our camera. But cubism quickly evolved into a second phase—synthetic cubism—where the artist's right to organize the plane of the canvas according to his own sensibility becomes dominant. The extent to which cubism owed its success to the acceptance of the limitations of the plane of the canvas is shown when we turn to the attempt to invent a "cubist" architecture. Raymond Duchamp-Villon's Maison Cubiste at the 1912 Salon d'Automne is another hybrid form, quaint rather than powerful.

Naum Gabo is one of the artists whose work is featured in the book *Circle*, edited by Leslie Martin, which I have already mentioned. His polemic on the nature of art—the nature of constructive art—emphasizes the dominion of the artist by stressing the thingness of the art object. It no longer owes any allegiance to the duty of mimesis—of representing the visible world—but exists in its own right as a thing-in-itself, with its own inner logic transposed into a three-dimensional world. The power of the object may be thought of as "warping" the space of everyday existence, but only to the extent that you honor the sensibility of the artist and follow him into his subjectivity. With Moholy-Nagy's *Light and Space Modulator* of 1924, a clear distinction is made between constructed reality and projected image. A strong beam of light falls on a construction whose parts are in movement. So long as we stand in front of the machine we are in the world of cause and effect, we can see what's happening. But if we move around and see only the shadows cast on the screen from behind, we are transported into a magic cinematic world where cause and effect become irrelevant, and the only reality is the mysterious changing pattern evolving on the two-dimensional screen. It's now time to ask, where did architecture fit in to these discoveries of the autonomy of the artist? How does the concept of the fourth dimension influence the architect? In a sense, the evolution of architecture was hijacked by Le Corbusier, whose particular rationale fell naturally into the realm of engineering and scientific discovery. During the period of the first world war, following his spell in the office of Peter Behrens, his ideas on architecture were dominated by the craft tradition he had received from his teacher L'Eplatanier, with structural analogies taken from nature. It is from this period that we get his famous Domino diagram, illustrating the rationale of framed construction. He also hoped to invent a neat way of handling pre-cast concrete that he could patent and get rich on. So his first really interesting work, with double height space—the Villa Schwob at La Chaux de Fonds—is still a hybrid work. It's not until after his collaboration with Ozenfant that he finds his own manner in architecture—no longer a cubist architecture as such but one in which the idea of function is already crystallized into a style. This emerges already complete in the little villa on Lake Leman for his parents, of 1924. For the really poignant attempt to apply the spatial discoveries of the new abstract art to architecture, we have to turn to Theo van Doesberg, who around 1920 experimented in art and architecture simultaneously.

If we compare his *Rhythms of a Russian Dance* (1918) with his *Relation of Horizontal and Vertical Planes* (1920–1922) we are seeing a similar abstract pattern of discrete units: lines versus planes. Both results are complete, can be taken as artistic statements, but in one we have an element of representation not present in the other. One looks like the plan of an exhibition layout, perhaps, but this is not what the work necessarily implies. The other could be a scheme for a three dimensional construction in space, but, again, this is not necessarily what the work implies. We are still within the domain of the artist, not perhaps the cultural space of the painter's canvas and the implication of high art, but at least the medium of the graphic artist, working outwards to explore the space around an object, but not effectively bounded by the edge of the canvas.

Van Doesberg did try to go on to adumbrate a new kind of architecture that could be represented in a similar way in what we call "axonometric projection." In his work done in collaboration with the architect Cornelius van Eesteren in 1923 he arrives at the limit that marks the change between an abstraction that exists in two dimensions and represents three, and one that exists in three dimensions, no longer as representation, but as reality. On the canvasses there is a frequent overlap between the separate lines that make up the pattern. In the axonometric compositions, there is a similar overlap or mutual penetration of the volumes. With modern steel construction, the axonometric could be turned into an actual three-dimensional object without too much loss of abstract precision. But with the technology available at the time, this translation would have been hard to achieve. But that may not be the only reason why Van Doesburg stopped at that point. The abstract composition which so much resembles the photo of the model exists within a different mode of perception, and this difference would be greater still were the model to become a livable construction with bathrooms and running water. We have passed from the realm of the artist, who may control his presentation within the four edges of his paper, to the realm of inhabitation, where it requires an effort to view the environment surrounding us as art at all.

This transition was, in a way, effected by Gerrit Rietveld, in the Schröder House of 1924. The object is undoubtedly a habitation, and was inhabited by Mrs Schröder until she reached a ripe old age, so it must have been pretty habitable. On the outside it achieves an astonishing degree of autonomy as an art object. It can stand for a de Stijl object, as clearly as the famous Rietveld chair. On the inside, the nature of its forms change from those of an art object to those of a habitable house. If the space suggested on the exterior is the unlimited space of abstraction, that of the interior is the strictly limited space of use and habit.

Although he thus successfully makes the transition from axonometric composition to constructed reality, the loss of the artist's ideal realm was clearly a problem for Rietveld. Some degree of freedom, analogous to the imagined freedom of the artist, had to be restored. This is accomplished by the use of sliding partitions, which allow a practical alternation between something approaching the free plan, and the use of separate rooms with definable roles like sleeping, eating and washing. But this very flexibility, admirable in itself, and due

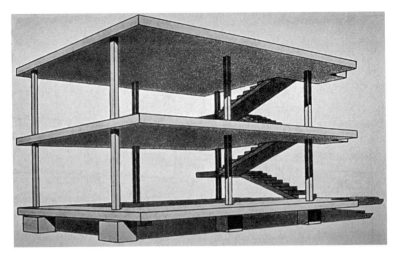

44A DOMINO DIAGRAM
Le Corbusier, 1914.

to be adopted as a hallmark of functional design, only underlines the limitations of real space compared with imaginary space. Space becomes a question of use, not of metaphysical definition, and the fourth dimension settles down as time—time that allows different conditions to pertain at different times. In this transformation of the interior of the Schröder House back to three dimensional reality, we see the final limitation, perhaps, of the avant-garde goal of removing architecture into the superior ideal space of the art object.

If Duchamp was able to infect simple diagrams with a mysterious inner life by appending an enigmatic title, we may play a similar trick with Le Corbusier by transposing to the Domino Diagram the title from Duchamp's famous *objet trouvé* "With Hidden Noise," made by inserting a ball of twine into an old brass clock frame (figs. 44a, 44b). Look back now at the Domino diagram and it is possible to see it as pregnant with hidden noise. The staircase resounds to the patter of feet, as life unwinds within the pristine abstract object. The technological diagram now fulfills the role of a work of conceptual art. However, this transfer is only a conceit, it exists only on this printed page. In lived time, it is more difficult, perhaps too difficult, to impose an abstract frame that will allow the mental to dominate the physical. This appears to be the problem that has been adopted by our deconstructionists, but it is the equivalent of asking for a

44B OBJECT WITH HIDDEN NOISE
Marcel Duchamp, 1916.

work of architecture the status of a museum object, and we may doubt if this is possible except as an exceptional circumstance.

Architecture is undoubtedly capable of arousing strong emotions, as strong and as strange as those aroused by art. But in doing this it must not attempt to usurp the events of fine art, which take place, not in real time, but within the timeless subjectivity of the observer. In its attempt to cross this barrier, modernism created its own myths of space and function.

This chapter is based on two lectures from the lecture course "Architecture as Cultural Expression" given at Princeton University between 1983 and 1992.

NOTES

Alan Colquhoun points out that the use of the concept "space" in the modern, abstract sense, (as in *Space, Time and Architecture*) dates only from 1905 (in Schmerdow). It is truly a twentieth-century idea.

See Linda Henderson: *The Fourth Dimension and Non-Euclidean Geometry in Modern Art*, Princeton, 1983. The similarity of Hinton's diagram and Duchamp's *Handler of Gravity* is just one of the striking comparisons she makes.

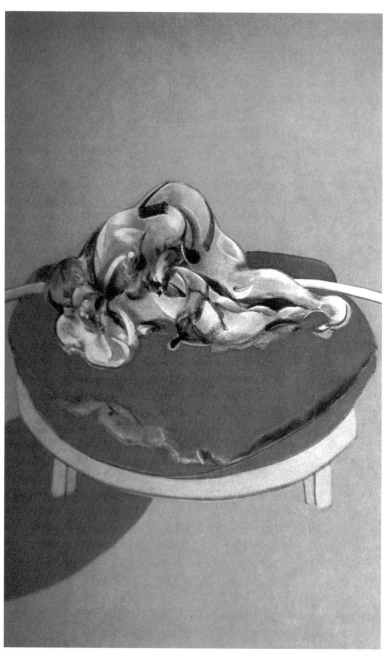

45 THREE STUDIES FROM THE HUMAN BODY (CENTRAL PANEL)
Francis Bacon, 1970.

THEORY AND ARCHITECTURE

No ideological position is possible without premises: these provide an axiomatic base that corresponds to belief, and that allows the construction of a more or less logically precise superstructure. Derrida's work in exposing the cracks and elisions that permeate the superstructure, resulting from the limitations of verbal logic when applied to the phenomena of existence, must not lead to the work of construction being abandoned. Equally, the contingency of the underlying beliefs has to be accepted. The kind of operation to which one is committed is all too clearly analogous to the play of children on the beach: proud and precise structures are erected whose fate is to be levelled by the next tide. As play, they bring an immediate reward. As history, they testify to the importance of hope.

Starting then from the skeptical position induced by a Presbyterian upbringing, I have long assumed "the abandonment of the sacred vision of existence, and the affirmation of the realm of profane value instead, that is, of secularization." From that follows the need for a dynamic in human affairs, a goal within history rather than as after-life, some explanation also of the progressive changes in philosophy that came in with the Enlightenment and the application of science to human affairs. In something like three centuries of exploitation of the scientific method, there has been evident progress in understanding natural phenomena, in molesting nature, and in changing the conditions of material life. There is no evidence in history to suggest that helicopters were ever in use before the twentieth century, or that a previous race of men discovered and renounced the power of the atom bomb. Yet though material progress seems to be a given condition of modernity, it does not lead, as yet, to an approaching state of saturation, when everything is just about to be explained. "Progress is just that process which leads toward a state of things in which further progress is possible, and nothing else." This dynamic, which uncomfortably resembles the situation of the donkey following a self-propelled carrot, results in a perennial interest in the latest thing, in ". . . affirming the new as the fundamental value."[1]

At the same time, this general framework, while it rationalizes the conviction that eternal life is not the same as living for ever, and that the joy of life is a value inscribed in the certainty of death, does not altogether satisfy one's sense of the importance of building sand castles. While history in the larger sense is contained in a material framework, governed by the law of entropy and the apparent recession of the matter in the universe, there is a second scale of values that relates to that part of history that belongs to human life, for which other explanations have to be sought. Here it becomes imperative to oppose the rule of entropy and allow the construction of a humanist measure. We may as well call this value the renewal of hope, and seek its confirmation within the history of human affairs.

To summarize the premises, then, we have two opposing principles: one is the knowledge we have of the material evolution of the universe, which includes everything that science can discover about its laws, without ever assuming any human content whatsoever; the other is what we know of the historical development of mankind, which, while it exists within the other and does not escape natural law, is not adequately explained by that law. To explain those things about which natural law has nothing to say, we have to invent a concept that will contain and delimit human affairs. That concept is what we mean by culture. It is a medium in which human values may be propagated, rather as nineteenth-century physicists were initially forced to posit the existence of the ether, the medium they thought necessary for the propagation of electro-magnetic waves. If culture proves to be an unnecessary concept, it will surely be discarded, but for the moment, it seems to be unavoidable.

The behavior that corresponds to the recognition of culture is the study of language; and the impasse with which we are faced in studying language is that it appears to be entirely cultural, and deals with the natural world only through the use of conventions, and not through any direct causality, a fact that is amply demonstrated by the difficulty of translating between natural languages. This limitation of language is also its grace, for while it allows the lecturer to show the relation between saying "I drop the chalk" and doing so, it also spares him the necessity of eating the chalk, in order to produce that sensation in the audience. Within science, this limitation has not prevented the growth of the power to interfere with nature, through the discipline of the working hypothesis and "the empirical test:" but scientists understand that the scientific truths expressed in language, including the language of mathematics, are provisional, and never final, however immaculate the logic may be.[2] In the dynamic progress of science whereby abstract models of behavior are constantly being compared with empirical observation, new truths overcome and extinguish old truths, and there is no end in sight. In human affairs in general, this relativistic approach is still found struggling with the archaic belief in the pre-existence of truth (as witnessed in the Greek tradition of "essence"), with the belief in absolutes as the only guarantee of a moral order, and with belief in origins as the only guarantee of identity. All these areas of belief are opposed to materialism. While from the materialist point of view they seem to be made of illusion, it is not clear that human existence could continue without some regular expression of the underlying desire that they betray, which is that of hope.[3] And certainly no account can be given of human history without allowing the importance of belief as a sustaining force, even if it is reduced to the force of a metaphor.

In one sense, the materialist point of view is oriented towards the future, and is opposed by a point of view that cannot ignore, and constantly clings to, the past. It looks like progressive forces arrayed against reactionary ones, but that would be a gross simplification. While material progress is the main source of change, and brings to bear a constant pressure on belief, it does not contain any statute of limitations, any impedance to the clarity of logic, any restraint on logical but murderous projects—in short does not offer a system of values for human conduct. There is ample scope for irony here, for it appears that most of the world's troubles stem from the over-zealous insistence on belief, as with religious fundamentalists, racial purists, tribal warriors. Yet the knowledge we absorb in earliest childhood, steeped in belief though it is, is our only means of personal orientation and practical organization.[4] We cannot abandon belief, although we must struggle to adapt belief to the conditions of life revealed through the value-less eye of the scientist, who follows only those conventions that can be shown to engage causally with the laws of nature.

So much for the general premises: but already we have set up a system that involves a dialectical struggle between past and future, between reason and custom—or, in the terms that Le Corbusier made relevant to architects—between brain and heart. Neither of the two opposing aspects described in these different ways are self-sustaining, each needs the other. No complete and consistent account of human history can be constructed within one of them alone, yet by dealing with the accounts it can give of each severally and together, language only exhibits the more its limitations as a form. It is not only that language is a circular self-defining system, all the words in the dictionary being needed to provide meanings for all the words in the dictionary. It is also a moving yardstick, a shifting scale of values. A clear indication of the inadequacy of language as a repository of truth is the fact that is itself is in a state of constant evolution; new words are invented to describe new concepts, old words are given a new meaning. At any one time, language is stable enough to be of use; but already we need special knowledge to understand the English of Chaucer, the French of Molière. Culture, of which language is the closest indicator, must also be conceived of as in a state of evolution.

There are only two conditions where the limitations of language can be transcended: when, by the rigor of the scientific method, logical relations can be paralleled by causal ones, and a conditional, but effective, grip on a single parameter of nature made real. The other is that implied by Roland Barthes when he said: "Only poetry escapes rhetoric."[5] For the language in which we are culturally immersed and which we use for our every-day purposes does not create truth, but only that which is credible. Credibility is the counterpart of Wordsworth's "pathetic fallacy," it is a strictly human attribute that serves to personify the universe, to give indifference a human face. Thus we find incredible the account of a middle-aged man who constructed a dungeon for a little girl, although it happened; and the Russian people found incredible the economic promises of a political system that could not admit the contradictions wrought in it by the conditions of life. Although it is logically inconsistent, and creates factual errors, the rhetoric that articulates human relations is neither despicable nor ineffectual. But we do well to recognize its existence, and beware of proclaiming eternal truth when what we have in hand is a contingent value. If poetry allows of a momentary escape from rhetoric, it is only by disturbing credibility.

In the very act of disturbance, we glimpse the possibility of an opening towards a more fundamental certainty, a certainty that never stays within our grasp; in Heidegger's terms, the trace of Being.

In place of the certainty that belief brought when it could obliterate the operations of incipient science, belief today is at the mercy of new scientific formulations. After three hundred years, the Roman Catholic Church has belatedly accepted the Copernican Revolution, which once seemed to threaten its existence. The Christian concept of eternal life was a vivid truth for the European people of the Middle Ages: with the advent of comparative religion during the enlightenment, it lost certainty; it remains, for those who cling to it, rather an aspect of hope. The erosion of belief from one point of view represents an escape from illusion; from another it exhibits the absence of a measure, the subsistence of a lack. This lack is, however, partly filled by allowing the existence of the aesthetic as a substitute for eternal values. Aesthetics, and the desire to aestheticize life, seem to be inseparable from the idea of secularization, and are probably the principal means by which contingent values are substituted for transcendental ones, and some sense of value preserved. The growth of the aesthetic category, since it was invented in 1787,[6] has paralleled the growth of technology, and it is hardly surprising, then, that art has become the other area of university study, and that science and art have become the poles of contemporary culture.

The extent to which art has invaded secular life is evident from the extraordinary growth of the entertainment and recreation industries, and from the growth of tourism. The work ethic, insofar as it holds good, is no longer a moral imperative, but a means of gaining credit for time to be spent in play. Everyday life struggles out of penury, wherever it can, in order to dispose of enjoyment; and enclaves devoted to enjoyment—theme parks, golf courses, retirement villages—are increasing in number. The domain of the modern shopping mall, and its extraordinary popular appeal, can only be explained as an attempt to exclude the disturbing, and substitute a realm of the carefully careless for that of sweet disorder.

Although many people would wish to deny that the category of the aesthetic has any relevance for architecture, I maintain on the contrary that the aesthetic touches every aspect of contemporary life, a scope that easily includes architecture. It is not necessary to be a classical revivalist to accept that western architecture originated in the form of the temple, and that the change by which temple fronts were in turn applied to churches, palaces, villas and banks, exactly parallels the historical process of secularization that we have ascribed to the evolution of culture in general. The supreme value of the temple as the unique situation of myth and identity is "borrowed" to validate an entire range of cultural needs. This perspective is also useful in attempting to understand the myths of modernism (when it seemed for a moment that history might release its grip) and today it makes sense of the on-going development whereby abstract forms continually attempt to substitute for representational forms, in order to free life from tradition. I see it as more or less inevitable that in this continuing conflict, some will identify with the future, some with the past, and some will attempt to take account of both perspectives, to adopt a position suspended between past and future.

Architectural culture reflects the ambiguity of society by developing two "easy" positions, where the conflict is seen not as inescapable, but as a matter of choice, of taking sides—something in itself congenial, like adopting a favorite football team, and rooting for it against all others. So (in England especially) architecture is like a baby with a traditional mother and a hi-tech father, and the argument is about custody. The popular English take on postmodernism, which views it as an error in promoting "false" representational forms at the expense of the "true" forms of technology, is however clearly tendentious. While it seems to have to do only with temperament and preference, it is essentially escapist. It is really an attempt to avoid the impasse of language, and remain in the illusion, so comforting to those who crave certainty, that form can be transparent towards function, and that truth is every day within our grasp.

Only within architectural culture is this illusion cherished. In the wider area of cultural studies, postmodernism is not an aberration of fancy architects, but a pervasive condition of life that follows from the recognition that modernity has not removed us from history or conferred the certainty of logic on the choices of life; an inescapable condition that follows more specifically from the evolution of cultural consciousness, the collapse of the Enlightenment belief in progress and perfectibility, the discovery of the subconscious and its dependence on symbols, and in a more general sense, a perspective that accepts the process of secularization and the Nietzschean proclamation of the death of God.

The criticism that I have attempted to practice in these pages is undoubtedly based upon the recognition of an unresolvable conflict between rational discourse and the rhetoric of belief. The contemplation of this tension may be a facility that some will enjoy exercising more than others; and this critic's preference for it may be part of his psychological bias, affecting the judgments made. The argument, as opposed to the judgements, depends on that tension being present in the first place. If it is not, then the criticism itself is addled. Of course, this tension is not equally displayed in all the activities of a society. The enjoyment that arises naturally from good health occupies most of our waking sensations, if we are lucky. In many areas of life, besides shopping malls, there must be an attempt to push aside the sense of irreconcilable conflict, if only in order to get on with the business of living. Still, there are other moments of life, and for the individual, bitter moments, when that recognition returns with some violence and forces upon us a sense of doom, of the need to resume the struggle. The ability to hear this voice is probably the residue of proper religious feeling. I hear it the more strongly when it emerges from within the sweetness of sensual fulfillment, as with lyric poetry or Mozart's Requiem or late watercolor apples on a plate by Cézanne. For those of us who feel the suspense of the abyss in which the human condition is placed, there is a need to return to this recognition, and for many of us, it is great art which alone can make it visible, and bearable.

No artist of our times, it seems to me, has done this more succinctly, and more clearly, than Francis Bacon, and the advantage of Bacon's work to the present argument must be apparent. All his work seems suffused with a recognition of suffering, of the thin membrane that separates physical enjoyment from pain, and that separates the sentient body from the corpse. In the center of his pictures, a human being is displayed in mortal captivity, sometimes screaming, sometimes writhing in agony, sometimes amputated like butcher's meat, sometimes smeared with dirt, sometimes contorted in struggle, sometimes abandoned in unspeakable loneliness, sometimes mad. These violences are done to the subject by the artist, not out of sadism, but in an attempt to seize more violently the sensation of the sitter's presence, of his having been there. This fleeting presence is nothing but an image executed in pigment, and it arises in part through the accidents that can occur in working the pigment. Because the medium is thus incorporated in the message, the results are clearly works of art, not propaganda, the violence is metaphysical, not literal, and contemplation is possible. The violence of the image is calmed, and indeed made accessible, by the way it is framed. The elements of this framing are a strict formality, strong and sweeping contours, colors of a sometimes lyrical sweetness, and certain abstract figures—a disembodied cube, an ellipse, an applied arrow—that have the effect of distancing the observer further from the agony depicted within. The result is an art that faces the postmodern condition, an art of first and last things that places together the heat of sensation and the cold of abstraction.

Bacon himself insists on the function of the artist as a witness to life; yet this process of bearing witness cannot be at the level of illustration, or the passive recording of appearances, however accurate: the life of the sitter has to be brought back, resurrected, by an act of violence that breaks the mold of simple mimesis.

> "What I want to do is to distort the thing far beyond the appearance, but in the distortion to bring it back to a recording of the appearance…Why is it possible to make the reality of an appearance more violently in this way than by doing it rationally? Perhaps it's that, if the making is more instinctive, the image is more immediate … where you are reporting fact not as simple fact but on many levels, where you unlock the areas of feeling which lead to a deeper sense of the reality of the image, where you attempt to make the construction by which this thing will be caught raw and alive…"[7]

What strikes us here is the importance of the work as a witness to the having-been. Bacon explicitly rejects abstract art as, in general, lacking the human and reserving itself to the purely aesthetic. It is clear enough that an abstract artist like Rothko does not renounce all feeling when he renounces the human figure: indeed, in most abstract art that is not wholly decorative, the absence of presence is still a weight within the weightlessness of the work. What Bacon enjoys, however, is clearly concerned with the consciousness of life, the imminence of death and suffering, and his art is thereby an attempt to return us to the sense of a tragic destiny and the quest for meaning. This is both an obsession and a torture, a pain and a deliverance. Enjoyment is not exactly the word to describe his state of mind; his own word for it is "exhilarated despair."[8]

"Sylvester: [I come back to] your desire that the form should be at once very precise and very ambiguous . . . a hard bright ground, a *maleusch* handling of the form, with the paint getting more and more scrubbed—with a hard flat ground so that you violently juxtapose two opposite conventions.

Bacon: Well, I've increasingly wanted to make the image simpler or more complicated. And, for this to work, it can work more starkly if the background is very united and clear. I think that probably is why I have used a very clear background against which the image can articulate itself . . . I want to isolate the image and take it away from the interior and the home."[9] (fig. 45)

An art removed from the interior and the home is an art of the public realm, and there are probably few, if any, homes with Bacons on the walls. The interior and the home have become the target of the recreation industry, they are now the subject of Ralph Lauren's ministrations, with his carefully careless choice of nostalgically charged clichés, they are no longer the site of eschatological thinking. Even in the museum, art has become part of the recreation industry. But museums are still operated as charities, not for profit, and they seem to have taken on a good deal of the role formerly played by churches, allowing of spiritual refreshment in a ritualized setting for a secular audience. Bacon, with his liking for triptychs, is clearly aware of the general change by which art has become the religion of our times.

It is this concept of art that in some sense purges and renews that seems to govern the subject-matter and method of Bacon. It conveys a tragic view of man's condition, not the bland elimination of the tragic as too disturbing for sales, which is the result of the commercialization of values. In Bacon, then, we sense both the past and the future as poles of feeling, the figurative and the abstract taken together constitute a mechanism by which he hopes to "unlock the valves of feeling and . . . return the onlooker to life more violently."[10] The two are not blended, but left in dialectical opposition as unreconcilable, yet equally present. Each modifies the other, and out of their opposition a glimpse is afforded of a different scale of values.

> "Reading him [Bacon], we are brought back again and again to the thought that the friction between opposites is essential to him and that unless an issue can be felt to be grinding between those *either-ors* it has no vitality for him. Everything must be either loved or loathed. The last thing he is looking for is remission from this tension. 'Friction' is too weak, it is the incompatibility of opposites that counts. Resolution goes with comfort."[11]

Not all art demonstrates so clearly the process by which values put in danger by the advances of technology are recuperated by an effort of the will. I would call Bacon a great artist. His effort is parallel to the great minimalist, Samuel Becket, who also seeks the last remnant of human dignity in the face of a remorseless fate. Such high points of our cultural effort, while giving nothing away to false sentiment, are not either given over to despair: in Bacon's own phrase, exhilaration enters in. If this kind of art represents the best that we can hope for, is it an effort beyond the scope of architecture?

Not many architects would even think of placing themselves in that company. As Aristotle was keen to point out, architecture is a useful art, not a fine art—absolved therefore from taking on the burden of fine art, which is to trace the destiny of mankind through its myths. I believe that one architect of our times has approached this level of achievement, even if his conversation never gave the faintest recognition of any conscious purpose in that direction. I refer to the late James Stirling.

I have tried to show, in my discussion of Stirling's work, that it also is structured by a series of polar oppositions, that it resembles the work of Le Corbusier in that respect. Sometimes the opposition is between classical and anti-classical elements, sometimes between representational forms and abstract ones, sometimes between the rule of form and the accident of contingency.

What is constant is the desire to set up an opposition between two principles that allows of a simultaneous feeling of fulfillment and transgression. It is in this respect that his chosen method is through a structure that produces contrariness:

> "Our work has oscillated between the most 'abstract' modern (even High-Tech), such as the Olivetti training school, and the obviously 'representa-

46   BRAUN HEADQUARTERS (DETAIL OF CONICAL SUPPORTS TO ADMINISTRATION BUILDING): MELSUNGEN, GERMANY
James Stirling Michael Wilford & Associates with Walter Nägeli, 1992.

47 THE PHILOSOPHER
De Chirico, 1925.

tional,' even traditional, for instance Rice University School of
Architecture. These extremes have characterized our work since we began,
but significantly, in recent designs (particularly the Staatsgalerie) the
extremes are being counterbalanced and expressed in the same building ...
We hope that the Staatsgalerie is monumental, because that is the tradition
for public buildings, particularly museums. We also hope that it is informal
and populist—hence the anti-monumentalism of the meandering footpath,
the voided center, the coloring and much else."[12]

For someone who on the whole preferred not to talk about his art,
but simply about his buildings (and not so much of that, either) this
comment suggests that Stirling was becoming increasingly conscious
of the method in his own madness, of the underlying juxtapositions
that made possible the pleasures of tension so evident in his work.
The words that he himself uses stress the juxtaposition of contrasting
characters, and speak of an oscillation between extremes. This use of
juxtaposition was evidently preferred to any idea of reconciliation: as

48 THE GIANT
Goya, 1826.

we find in the work of Francis Bacon, the opposites have to show, and have to produce a tension:

"... Both extremes have always existed in our vocabulary; so if we have a future, I see us going forward oscillating, as I did as a student—between the formal and the informal, between the restrained and the exuberant."[13]

This comment also recognizes that the Stirling method is of long standing, dating from his time 'as a student,' and this I believe puts it beyond doubt that the source of his method derived from the enthusiastic interest in mannerist juxtaposition that was promoted by Colin Rowe, his tutor for Thesis at Liverpool University. It is noteworthy that while Stirling objected to Charles Jencks's suggestion that the porthole windows used in the St. Andrew University Dormitories were part of a "marine metaphor," he never objected to Peter Eisenman's analysis of the Leicester Engineering Building, where he proposed it as a work of modern mannerism.[14]

That there is a process of maturation and increasing inwardness is also suggested by the appearance in his later work of a deliberate strangeness, a kind of *terribilità*, apparent in parts of the Staatsgalerie, in the later Music Academy tower at Stuttgart, in the Mansion House project, and culminating in the highly expressive forms of the Braun Headquarters at Melsungen (fig. 46). This is an architecture that goes beyond the bounds of functionality and touches a source of strong feeling. Elements that originated, no doubt, in a functionalist vocabulary, now reappear in exaggerated or distorted form, fluctuating between parody and precision, populism and an elite exclusiveness, setting up echoes of the past along with the vibrations of the machine. By these means it becomes an architecture structured by the use of antitheses, that addresses both nature and culture, that proposes a view of man that is inclusive rather than exclusive. It is an architecture that does not deny a tragic view of man's destiny, and that may prove to have deliberately approached that idea.

The tendency today to see architecture in strictly exclusive terms as either a sentimental return to the past or a futurist fantasy in the service of the 'latest thing' must result, either way, in an architecture of propaganda that looks to win by attracting adherents, that looks to take over and simplify the scene, that reduces architecture to the complacency of a *fait accompli*. One side clings to belief and excludes reason; the other concentrates on material betterment and believes only that things will go on getting better. Both seem to me to deny hope. Neither provides in itself an adequate philosophy of life.

Yet both are present, not as exclusive realms, but as mere aspects of our culture. Both are mediated within that culture. At one extreme, the high-tech does not exactly follow the laws of nature and the rules of science: it projects an image that wants to do that. At the other, classical revivalism does not exactly restore the wholeness of belief: it projects an image that wants to do that. Both are impregnated with ideology, and both are partial in nature. The existence of each one calls out for the other to restore a balance in the field. This is the reason why at a lower level, conducts such as those evoked by ideas of sweet disorder and the carefully careless have a merit: they are positions taken on the tightrope and are aware of operating between extremes. It is also the reason why, at a higher level of the spirit, we can feel both the doom and the attraction of an art that does not reconcile the extremes so much as exhibit them, an art that disturbs as it consoles. Is it too much to look for an architecture that could measure up to the tragic dimension?

In our rather hollow position, we cannot abandon belief, yet we must use reason. We are suspended between them: they are antitheses that never find their synthesis, but only a provisional resolution, that must be endlessly lost and recuperated. Both reason and belief have their dark side. The dark side of reason is the unfeeling of abstraction: I choose de Chirico's *The Philosopher* (1925) as emblem of this side (fig. 47). The dark side of belief is the frenzy of killing that attempts to wipe out doubt: I choose Goya's *The Giant* (1826) as the emblem of that side (fig. 48). Our culture exists within the space of these emblems. While architecture is too much a part of daily life to be the main source of ideas in society, its failure to reflect the ideas that are present in the best productions of the other arts can only impoverish life. An architecture is needed that will recognize the dilemma of modern man, suspended as he is between terrible beliefs and a dangerous future. Then architecture can hope to be itself reflected in the most moving images of our times, as we see it reflected in the wonderful lines of Eliot:

"O city city, I can sometimes hear
Beside a public bar in Lower Thames Street,
The pleasant whining of a mandoline
And a clatter and a chatter from within
Where fishmen lounge at noon, where the walls
Of Magnus Martyr hold
Inexplicable splendour of Corinthian white and gold."[15]

NOTES

1   These quotations are all taken from Gianni Vattimo: *The End of Modernity*, tr. Snyder, Johns Hopkins, 1988, in "The Truth of Art," p. 101.

2   This incompleteness of formal language was most dramatically demonstrated by Gödel: see Nagel and Newman: *Gödel's Proof*, New York University Press, 1958.

3   Pointing in a similar direction, Bernard Tschumi asserts the anti-entropic power of the erotic, which seems to me to be a younger and more restricted word for what I call hope.

4   Gayatri Spivak: Lecture: "The Staging of Origins," Princeton University, December 5, 1990.

5   See Roland Barthes: *Mythologies*, Editions du Seuil, 1957; tr. Annette Lavers, Jonathan Cape, 1972.

6   Kant's category of the "transcendental aesthetic" was included in *The Critique of Pure Reason*, 1787. According to the Oxford English dictionary the term "aesthetic" was first generally used in 1798, restricted to the meaning of "things perceptible to the senses." It goes on to state that it was "misapplied by Baumgarten to 'criticism of taste,' and so used in England since 1830."

7   David Sylvester: *Interviews with Francis Bacon*, Thames & Hudson, 1975, p. 66.

8   Ibid., p. 83.

9   Ibid., p. 118.

10 Ibid., p. 17.

11 Andrew Forge, in *Francis Bacon*, edited by Dawn Ades and Andrew Forge, Thames & Hudson, 1985.

12 James Stirling: 'Design Philosophy and Recent Work' in *Architectural Design*, Special Issue, Academy Editions, 1990, pp. 7, 8.

13 The concluding sentence of Stirling's speech in acceptance of the R.I.B.A. Gold Medal, reported in *Architectural Design Profile*, 1982.

14 Published in *Oppositions*, No. 4, October 1974.

15 From T.S.Eliot: *The Waste Land*.

SOURCES OF ILLUSTRATIONS

INDEX OF PROPER NAMES